Be a Confident Driver

John Henderson

For UK order enquiries: please contact Bookpoint Ltd,
130 Milton Park, Abingdon, Oxon OX14 4SB.
Telephone: +44 (0) 1235 827720. Fax: +44 (0) 1235 400454.
Lines are open 09.00–17.00, Monday to Saturday, with a 24-hour
message answering service. Details about our titles and how to
order are available at www.teachyourself.com

For USA order enquiries: please contact McGraw-Hill Customer
Services, PO Box 545, Blacklick, OH 43004-0545, USA.
Telephone: 1-800-722-4726. Fax: 1-614-755-5645.

For Canada order enquiries: please contact McGraw-Hill
Ryerson Ltd, 300 Water St, Whitby, Ontario L1N 9B6, Canada.
Telephone: 905 430 5000. Fax: 905 430 5020.

Long renowned as the authoritative source for self-guided
learning – with more than 50 million copies sold worldwide –
the Teach Yourself series includes over 500 titles in the fields of
languages, crafts, hobbies, business, computing and education.

British Library Cataloguing in Publication Data: a catalogue record
for this title is available from the British Library.

Library of Congress Catalog Card Number: on file.

First published in UK 2007 by Hodder Education, part of
Hachette UK, 338 Euston Road, London NW1 3BH.

First published in US 2007 by The McGraw-Hill Companies, Inc.

This edition published 2010.

Previously published as *Teach Yourself Better Driving*

The **Teach Yourself** name is a registered trade mark of
Hodder Headline.

Typeset by MPS Limited, a Macmillan Company.

Printed in Great Britain for Hodder Education, an Hachette UK
Company, 338 Euston Road, London NW1 3BH, by CPI Cox &
Wyman, Reading, Berkshire RG1 8EX.

The publisher has used its best endeavours to ensure that the URLs
for external websites referred to in this book are correct and active
at the time of going to press. However, the publisher and the
author have no responsibility for the websites and can make no
guarantee that a site will remain live or that the content will remain
relevant, decent or appropriate.

Hachette UK's policy is to use papers that are natural, renewable
and recyclable products and made from wood grown in sustainable
forests. The logging and manufacturing processes are expected to
conform to the environmental regulations of the country of origin.

Impression number	10 9 8 7 6 5 4 3 2 1
Year	2014 2013 2012 2011 2010

Contents

Image credits

Front cover: © Stockbyte/Getty Images

Back cover: © Jakub Semeniuk/iStockphoto.com, © Royalty-Free/Corbis, © agencyby/iStockphoto.com, © Andy Cook/iStockphoto.com, © Christopher Ewing/iStockphoto.com, © zebicho – Fotolia.com, © Geoffrey Holman/iStockphoto.com, © Photodisc/Getty Images, © James C. Pruitt/iStockphoto.com, © Mohamed Saber – Fotolia.com

Meet the author

Driving is a life skill and you must approach it with the attitude that you are learning something to serve you for the rest of your life. I soon realized that the more experienced I became as a driver, the more I enjoyed driving and the less tiring I found journeys, so I strove to learn more about it. If you are reading this book, I expect you have the same attitude. If only everyone felt that way!

This book is written for the UK market and your legal responsibilities as a car owner and driver vary greatly around the world, so should be checked locally. While this book will be updated from time to time, please be aware that legislation changes – so even in the UK there may be differences over time. If you have any doubt, seek professional advice from a government agency or motoring organization.

This book is also intended for people who have passed their test and gained a little experience. If you are learning to drive you will find useful information here, but there are many books aimed at learners which concentrate on the things you need to know for your country's driving test.

Where it is unavoidable we have used masculine terms to refer to drivers purely for simplicity's sake. Naturally, not all drivers are male but this avoids littering the text with the clumsy 'his/her'.

You will find a glossary at the back of the book and all the words in it are printed in bold when they first appear in the text.

Keeping your car in good working order is important to your safety and if you want to know more about that see this book's sister publication *Car Buying and Ownership* in the same series.

John Henderson, 2010

Only got a minute?

The route to better driving begins with examining your attitude. You must try to think of driving as a skill, and one which you want to improve.

The key to good driving is, without doubt, observation. If you are not aware of what is going on around you, you cannot possibly react to it.

Good observation comes with experience. You will learn, not only what is relevant to your progress on the road, but also what other people do. Most experienced drivers have had those 'sixth sense' moments when they have known that something was not right. Perhaps it was feeling someone was not going to turn off as they were indicating or was not going to stop at a red light. They probably could not tell you what rang the alarm bells because they have observed, not one thing, but several small clues they would have to think hard about to analyse. As we shall see, anyone can train themselves to be more observant.

But it is also important we ensure others can observe us, are more aware of our intentions and that we don't do anything they may not expect.

Read the Code

Since 1931, *The Highway Code* has been the official UK drivers' 'bible'. Now produced by the Government's Driving Standards Agency, it sets out the rules of the road on which the country's driving test is based. If you passed your test some years ago and haven't read it since, you should: it is regularly updated so its advice changes with our laws, roads and cars. If you are visiting the UK, the Code is a useful, and cheap, way of finding out the rules of the road. Surprisingly, not all countries have an equivalent.

5 Only got five minutes?

A good driver is an adaptable one because someone who does not adjust their driving style to suit their speed or the road conditions is a danger to themselves and anyone unfortunate enough to be on the road around them.

If you are cruising down a dry motorway early on a summer morning with little traffic, the demands on you as a driver, and the way you drive, are entirely different to driving through a city centre on a dark, wet night.

The first step for any driver wanting to improve is to train themselves to recognize when the situation around them is changing, by observation and interpretation of what they see. Even when it should be obvious, like the motorway in front getting crowded or a bank of fog drifting across the road ahead, it is surprising how many drivers do not even slow down. An adaptable and observant driver would recognize that they were gaining on the slower, heavier traffic ahead and adjust speed earlier instead of hammering on the brakes at the last minute, which gives little chance of escape if something unexpected happens. The adaptable driver has their lights on and has slowed down before entering the fog, not 100 metres into it.

With good observation you can often anticipate problems, instead of reacting to them. For example, if you are leaving a well used main road, or urban area, to head into rural minor roads on a cold winter's evening, a glance at your car's outside thermometer lets you know if there might be ice. If you see a lorry coming towards you on a wet road you know it will spray you with water, so turn your wipers on before it gets to you.

As we shall see, being in the right gear puts less strain on the car and saves fuel. Observation can help you to be in the right gear for the situation. For example, if you notice the road climbing you can change down and maintain a steady pace rather than waiting until the engine is struggling with the slope, then changing down and having to pick up speed again.

Adjusting your driving to the conditions has nothing to do with observing speed limits. Naturally, noticing and observing speed limits is part of good observation, but a limit is simply a maximum and just because a sign says '40' it does not necessarily mean that is a safe speed. If the nearby school has just turned out, the fog is thick or the snow on the road is starting to freeze, 40 mph would be much too fast, especially if all three events coincide.

This is the most important aspect of driving to suit the conditions: if your speed is appropriate, everything else becomes easier. You give yourself more time to see and assess what is happening and react to it. If anything goes wrong, you also reduce the potential damage, including improving the survival chances of any pedestrians you hit.

That is not to say a fast driver is not a good driver. Knowing when to use speed is also part of being adaptable. But a good driver only uses it when it is safe and appropriate and recognizes the danger signs that mean he must slow down. If you find yourself coming up on things too quickly, having to brake harder than you expected or the car starting to feel unstable, you must recognize that you are starting to push the boundaries of what you and the car are capable of. That also means you are starting to reduce your safety margins unacceptably because if you and the car are on the limits, you have little or nothing in reserve if anything goes wrong, be it a patch of oil on the road or a child running out.

By developing the right attitude to driving, improving your skills and recognizing you limitations, you help expand your driving safety margins. It is almost as if you create greater space around your car, because you are much more aware of what is happening around you and you are putting yourself in a better position to deal with it. To a novice or unobservant driver riding with you it will often look as if you have perceived a hazard by super human powers, when you have done nothing more than observe, assess and react in plenty of time.

1

....

What makes a better driver?

In this chapter you will learn:
- *the right attitude*
- *the importance of observation*
- *sharing the road.*

Most people would define a good driver as someone they feel safe with as a passenger. It does not necessarily mean someone who drives slowly: many quick drivers are safe, knowing when and how to use speed, but there are plenty of bad slow drivers with little knowledge of, or care for, what they are doing.

The essential characteristics of a good driver are:

▸ *the right attitude to driving as a skill not a chore*
▸ *good observation*
▸ *quick at adapting their driving to the road conditions*
▸ *consideration for passengers and other road users*
▸ *mechanical sympathy.*

The right stuff

Better driving is largely a question of the right attitude. The school-run mum might not deliberately do anything dangerous but sees driving as a chore to be done while her mind 'multitasks' on the rest of the day's diary, so she gives little attention to the changing road conditions around her. That makes her at least as dangerous as the teenage boy-racer who likes taking risks and has an over-inflated opinion of his ability to cope with the results.

The aim is to treat driving as a skill, which deserves thought and judgement, both in regard to what is happening around you and to the way you are dealing with it. If you have near misses, analyse *why*, asking yourself what you could have done to avoid it. It is not enough to dismiss it as someone else's fault: *they* may have been doing something wrong, but should *you* have noticed it earlier? Did someone 'stop suddenly' in front of you or were you driving too close to give yourself time to react to their signals?

The fact that you are reading this book suggests you have the right attitude because you have been honest enough with yourself to recognize that you need to know more. If you can apply that honesty on the road to assessing what you have done in a given situation and whether you could have done it better, you will improve and learn.

Consideration

If you are a good driver your presence on the road should have little impact on other road users, so consideration for others should be part of attaining the right attitude.

This means giving others space to do what they need to do, so:

- *don't get into the turning space a lorry driver has allowed himself*
- *give cyclists and motorcyclists plenty of room*
- *don't block side turnings or pedestrian crossings when you're in a jam*
- *in slow traffic, let people out of drives and side turnings*
- *on dual-carriageways and motorways move to the next lane, if you can, to create space for those joining from sliproads*

- *pass horse-riders very slow and wide*
- *if you must drive slowly where you can't be overtaken, pull over to let others pass.*

Most people repay courtesy with courtesy, and anger with anger. If you do something stupid, wave your acknowledgement to the offended driver, and at least mouth your apologies but try to keep your temper if someone does something stupid in front of you. Never retaliate to such things.

It is also surprising what a smile and eye contact can achieve. This human contact, even when made remote by being in a car, can diffuse situations or make another driver show you the courtesy of letting you out or letting you go first.

This does not mean allowing everyone to walk over you or that you treat every other road user as an angel. There are times when positive driving is required or you will have to wait until the rush hour ends to get round the roundabout.

Insight

If I get irritated with others' behaviour, or road conditions, I find it helps to think about how I am holding my body. If you are physically tensing your body, that increases the feeling of psychological tension, because the two are linked. So, drop your shoulders, stop setting your jaw, ease your grip on the wheel and relax your muscles and you break the cycle, which should help you return to a more relaxed state of mind.

CYNICISM

In addition, other people make mistakes so you must not assume other drivers will always do what you expect. There will be people who forget their indicator is on or enter a roundabout in the left-hand lane when they are turning right. So, don't pull out in front of a car indicating a turn until you are sure that is their intention, and keep a mirror eye on others on the roundabout to see if they are doing what you expect.

This is another of those things that comes with experience. The new driver may take someone's actions at face value but the more experienced person develops a sixth sense (largely good observation) for the 'not quite right' and backs off to see what happens.

Top tip

You are not in a race so you don't have to be in front. If you are trying to join or leave a road and are not sure what someone else intends, you can always slow down or wait and make your entry or exit behind them.

Observation

Observation is the key to good safe driving. If you are not aware of what is happening around you, you can't react to it. If you see the bend well ahead you can be in the right gear and at the right speed early enough to take it safely and smoothly. If you see the interior light come on in a parked car, you can be ready for someone to open the door.

Eyesight

You can't expect to develop good observation or drive safely if you have problems with your eyesight, and in most countries the sight test associated with the ordinary driving test is basic. The UK's number plate reading exercise, for example, does not show if you have tunnel vision, night myopia, distance vision problems or poor depth perception.

Any new driver would be well advised to take a proper eye test when they apply for their licence, even if it is not legally required. Many safety experts want compulsory sight testing for all drivers, as lorry and bus drivers must be tested biannually, and it is certainly wise for anyone aged over 40 to also be tested this regularly. If you find you can't read direction signs until the last minute or have trouble reading things you used to be able to see, get an eye test.

Some eyesight problems are easy for the sufferer to diagnose: if you can't read this page, you know you need glasses. But if you have had certain defects since birth you may have no idea anything is wrong. The person with tunnel vision thinks everyone has the same field of view and people who suffer night myopia (short sight in poor light) often believe the world looks fuzzy in the dark to everyone.

Insight

When I discovered I needed glasses it was quite sudden and worrying because I realized one morning that I couldn't read a book I had been able to read the night before. An optician showed me a test that proved the brain had been ignoring the poor signal from one eye and said that because I had been looking into the distance outside immediately before coming in to read, I had made the brain accept the signal from that eye so the page was blurred. He pointed out that I was probably getting headaches on long drives or from working at the computer and could not read direction signs from as far off as I once did. All of that was true, but I hadn't put it all together. If I had been honest with myself, I would have taken an eye test much earlier.

DEVELOPING OBSERVATION

The problem for new drivers is learning what to ignore among the considerable visual inputs a driver has to cope with. This comes with experience and is one reason why the first year after their test is the most dangerous time for a driver.

Trainee police drivers are often asked to give a running commentary of everything they see around them as they drive, to help develop observation and so their instructor, or examiner, can hear what they have noticed. Some drivers find that doing this, even mentally, helps sharpen their observation skills and concentration, but others just find it distracting. It is worth trying it to see if it works for you.

CENTRED AND SOFT

By observing something we do not mean that you are actually looking at it. When you go for a country walk you don't look at every daisy, but you do notice they are there. In the same way, a driver with good observation has noticed things around them while watching what is happening on the road ahead. Such a driver might be able to tell you what a woman on the pavement was wearing while still reacting to a car pulling out in front of them.

The technique can be thought of as centred and soft vision. The centre part is the part of your field of view that you are truly looking at. This varies with the circumstances: at 120 **mph** on an autobahn it might be quarter of a mile ahead because you will be there in seven seconds; in a crowded city street it might be only 50 yards ahead because that is as far as you can easily see and when driving slowly across rough terrain it might just be the ground a few yards in front of the car because that is where the obstacles lay that may damage it. It always centres on the route ahead of you.

The soft part is everything else that you are aware of. On the autobahn it ranges from the vehicles in the lanes around you to what is happening as far down the road as you can see. In the city street it is the movement of pedestrians you are passing, the parked cars around you, road signs and even the reflections in the shop windows that might let you see what cars ahead are doing. The off-road driver is aware of where the track goes but also of what obstructions are sticking out of the trees and banks beside them.

WHAT ARE YOU LOOKING FOR?

You are looking for anything that might affect you. In the road ahead, the hard part of your view, that is pretty obvious: you need

6

to know where your route goes and if there is anything in the way. In the soft part of the view there are no rules. It might be something as obvious as a traffic light or it might be a pair of feet moving behind a parked car. This is where experience comes in: it is experience that enables us to separate the visual wheat from the chaff.

With experience you develop a way of taking in the view around you so that what you notice is that something is not as it should be. If there is a general flow of pedestrians along the pavement, you filter them out as normal movement so that you, hopefully, notice the one moving across that flow towards the kerb. Returning to the country walk analogy, the newcomer to bird-watching goes out looking for bird shapes and so walks past the well camouflaged nightjar, but the nature reserve warden's eye is tuned to what is normal for the undergrowth so the blackness of the nightjar's eye stands out, drawing his attention to the bird.

Mirrors

The mirrors are part of observation and the driving test mantra of 'mirror, signal, manoeuvre' means they are often under-used. Yes, you must use them before any manoeuvre, but they should also be part of your observation process. You don't just look through the windows, you glance in the mirrors too, even if you do not intend to carry out a manoeuvre. In fact, it even pays to keep an eye on them when you are waiting at the traffic lights or trying to get out of a junction, just so you know if anyone has pulled up close alongside.

Using mirrors regularly keeps you in touch with what is happening on the road behind and alongside you, which also means you have more idea of what the safe options are if anything untoward happens. If you know there is nobody close behind or overtaking, you know you can brake hard or swerve to avoid something without making the situation worse. You also know what should be there if you look in the mirror prior to signalling for a manoeuvre. If there was a motorbike behind you and you can't see it now, you know it could be in your blind spot and so must react accordingly.

ADJUSTING MIRRORS

Adjust your mirrors so you can see as much as possible around the car without having to move your head too much. Your driving instructor may have told you to set mirrors so you had to move your head, but you no longer need to ensure an examiner sees you use them so set them to be comfortable and effective.

The interior mirror should show as much of the view through the rear window as possible. If there is nobody in the back, lower or remove the rear **head restraints** to maximize the view, but make sure they are correctly set when you have passengers (see Chapter 3).

Door mirrors should show the view behind and to the side of the car. This, combined with the interior mirror, should give you a view of behind and of the lanes alongside you on a dual-carriageway.

Insight

Your view of the mirrors and out of the car depends a lot on your build, so what suits me at a long limbed 6 ft 2 in may not work for a short and stocky person sitting much closer to the mirrors. However, I find in most cars, the driver's side mirror is best set so the side of the car is just out of view. The passenger door mirror on most cars gives the best view if a small part of the side of the car is just visible in the corner of the mirror. If I set it so none of the car is visible I generally find that, with my angle of view, I am seeing too far to the side of the car and creating a blind spot between the interior mirror and that door mirror.

Always check the view in the mirrors when you return to the car. Not only may they have been knocked while you were away, but you may have shrunk. During the day, especially if you have been on your feet a lot, your backbone may be compressed by as much as a centimetre, which, in some cars, significantly changes the view in the interior mirror.

Top tip

Get someone to walk around the car and if the mirrors are correctly set you should be able to see them for most of the way round.

How far away?

Though the interior mirror is flat glass, the door mirrors may be convex to give a wider field of view but that makes vehicles behind appear further away than they are.

In some cars this may be limited to one mirror but many cars have convex glass in both and the degree of curvature varies considerably from car to car. American and Korean cars often have a warning etched in the glass, but most do not, so check the view.

When you are new to a car, park it where you can see down the road in the mirrors and take time to compare how far away things appear in the mirrors with what you see when you look behind.

Blind spots

It is important to understand the things that restrict your observation. All cars have blind spots, though some are worse than others. Make yourself aware of where they are on your car and what you need to do to compensate for them.

IN MIRRORS

There is a point on most cars where anything overtaking you gets between the interior and driver's door mirrors and isn't yet far enough forwards for you to see them out of the corner of your eye. This is the most dangerous blind spot because anything in it is alongside you, so get in the habit of glancing over your shoulder before pulling out.

Many cars now have a curved outer edge to at least the driver's door mirror to combat this blind spot (see Plate 1). There is usually a line to show where the increased curvature starts. You can also buy stick-on blind spot mirrors to do this, but make sure you place them so they do not interfere with the main view behind. Though a welcome aid, these features are not infallible and it is still possible for small things, like cyclists and motorcyclists, to find a blind spot.

PILLARS

Windscreen pillars have got thicker in recent years, to protect occupants, so they can create a significant blind spot when emerging from a junction. In some cars it can be big enough to hide a fair sized vehicle, and in all cars the pillars are big enough to hide a motorbike. You must be aware of this and make sure that when emerging from junctions you move your head to see round the pillar.

In an unfamiliar car, check the affect of this blind spot. Cars with steeply sloping windscreens often have worse pillar blind spots than cars with more upright screens because the angle of the pillar has the effect of widening the cross section in your line of view. So, you would get a bigger blind spot on a Ferrari than the same pillar diameter would create on a Range Rover. In cars whose windscreen pillars are like an inverted Y, housing a small triangular window, the fork creates a huge blind spot for people of a certain height.

MAKING YOUR OWN

Don't create extra blind spots. If you stick anything on the windows, be it stickers supporting your favourite charity or a

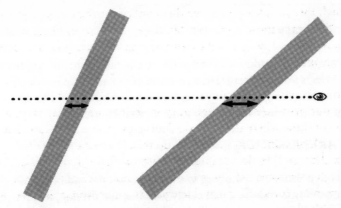

Figure 1.1 Pillars of the same thickness create bigger blind spots if angled more steeply.

portable **satellite navigation** screen, make sure you position them where they will never affect your view of the road.

Avoid hanging things from the interior mirror because it not only creates a blind spot but you may become accustomed to ignoring movement in that portion of the screen. Some experts say dangling objects can also trigger car sickness in children, which is a distraction drivers don't need.

Keep the glass clean so you are not trying to see through a lacework of muddy spots. A spattering of mud you barely notice becomes an opaque glare when the sun gets behind it. If that happens at a junction, open the window so you can see out and, as soon as you can, stop to clean the glass.

Insight

Carry a cloth and a combined squeegee and scraper so you can clean glass and lights if you need to. In summer, a 'bug sponge', which has a mildly abrasive surface (not a pot scourer), can be kept damp in a Ziploc bag for removing splattered insects the screen washers can't shift. Debugging also gives you something to do when you stop for a break.

Concentration

Driving well demands concentration on the task in hand. Anything that affects your concentration must be eliminated if possible: if that means telling a passenger to shut up, don't be afraid to do so. Point out that their safety is at stake as well as yours.

CARELESS TALK

If a conversation, or listening to something on the radio, needs more attention than you can safely give it while driving, it is much safer to pull over.

Certainly, never turn round to talk to someone while driving: if they don't understand that you can't, that's their problem. This is particularly important at speed because of the distance you travel in a short time. At 60 mph, glancing at someone for half a second means you travel almost 15 yards blind: that's the length of four small cars. At speed, an unconscious movement of the steering wheel could send you veering into the oncoming traffic or off the road.

CHILDREN AND PETS

Try to train your children and pets never to distract a driver and to understand if the driver can't give them the attention they crave. If children become insistent, or there is something wrong, stop as soon as you can even if there is another adult in the car to attend to them, because it is not safe to be distracted by them.

Make sure children are safely strapped in (see Chapter 3) and that child locks are on, so you do not have to worry about that. A pet that can't be trusted to sit quietly in the back should be in a travelling cage or behind a dog guard.

Insight

A travelling cage is probably the best way of transporting a dog. Apart from the fact it stops them messing up the interior, it is also safer because, as long as the cage is strapped down, it stops the dog becoming a lethal missile in an accident. Our springer spaniel sleeps in his at home, which seems to help settle him down more quickly in the car.

STRESS

Stress can seriously affect your concentration and observation. Do all you can to reduce stress while driving, leaving plenty of time for your journey and planning ahead so you know where you are going.

If you find yourself becoming stressed or upset on the road, stop for a while and rest.

Be particularly careful when driving while coping with life's extremely stressful times, like bereavement, marriage, divorce and moving house. Your concentration suffers badly at these times and your brain can be so overloaded that it can't cope with all the signals being directed at it when driving.

Top tip

Take special care at junctions when under such stress. If your head is swinging from side to side as you look, your brain has to cope with the affect on the view of both the movement of your head and the movement of oncoming vehicles. Sometimes this becomes too much and the brain simply does not register the moving vehicle, even if it is close to you. Take time to turn your head, hold it still while you look and then repeat the process the other way.

AUDIO SYSTEMS

We all enjoy music while we drive and the radio can give us useful travel and weather information, but it must not become a distraction.

Think carefully before adjusting the system on the move or trying to manhandle a CD in or out of the system. If you are a serious music fan, consider installing a CD autochanger, which holds a magazine of CDs, or an MP3 player connection so you can change music at the press of a button. Even better, some cars and audio systems now have USB sockets so you can put many MP3 tracks on a cheap memory stick, which is easy to tuck away when you leave the car.

When a lot of concentration is needed, it is better to turn audio off, like when driving in fog or if you are lost in a busy city and trying to cope with lots of traffic while reading road signs at the same time.

SATELLITE NAVIGATION

Satellite navigation, or 'sat nav', is gaining in popularity and can help to make you a safer driver by allowing you to concentrate on the road while the machine tells you where to go. Sat nav was shown to be safer than a map by the same study that proved using a mobile phone while driving is dangerous. When we take on peripheral tasks while driving we either do it while looking at a limited part of the view ahead or glancing away from the road for short periods. Researchers found that if we perceive something as connected with driving, we do that for longer. So we might glance quickly at a CD case to see what the song is called, because we know we shouldn't be doing that, but we take our eyes off the road much longer to check a map or directions. Sat nav reduces the risk of doing that.

However, it can also be a distraction, especially if you try to adjust it on the move. Always set up the route when you are parked because typing in addresses and checking that the route is sensible takes time and attention. If you do not need guidance for the whole route, pre-enter the destination so you only have to press 'start navigation' at, say, a set of lights or while stopped at a junction.

If your sat nav has the option of a 'safety setting' to limit what can be done on the move, use it to help avoid temptation. Also make sure you know how to cancel the navigation so you are not irritated by it when you decide you know where you are or want to follow your own route.

With portable systems, position the screen where it does not interfere with your view of the road and will not obstruct **airbags** if there is an accident.

MOBILE PHONES

It is illegal to use a hand-held mobile phone on the move in most developed countries, though the degree of enforcement varies. It is also very unwise to use one and some research suggests that even drivers using hands-free phones are unsafe.

If you are holding the phone, you can't be in full control of the car. Even with hands-free, if the conversation gets so involved that your concentration suffers, either pull over or call them back later. No conversation is worth an accident.

Do not accept incoming calls unless you are sure dealing with them will not unduly affect your driving. All phones and hands-free systems have a button you can press that, if it is set up correctly, transfers the caller to voicemail.

OUTSIDE DISTRACTIONS

One of the pleasures of driving is seeing the passing scenery, but it must never become enough of a distraction to affect your concentration. If the view is good, stop to admire it.

Never let your hobby take precedence over driving. Anyone who has driven past an airfield or bird reserve when something has attracted those passionate about planes and birds knows how little regard spotters have for road safety when adding a tick to their list is at stake.

Most of us have been distracted by members of the opposite sex. One survey suggested 60 per cent of women drivers had been distracted by a good-looking passer-by and with men the percentage was far higher. We are all hard-wired to look at people we find attractive, but resist it when driving, especially in city traffic that may stop suddenly.

Indeed, the problem with external distractions is that you can do nothing to stop them and it is likely you are not the only driver being distracted by them.

Drink, drugs and illness

Concentration, your ability to react to what happens around you and your car control, are all affected by drink, drugs and illness.

DRINK

All countries have drink-driving laws and some in northern Europe are so strict that they effectively mean you can't drink at all when driving. Drink lengthens your reaction times and reduces your ability to concentrate. Eventually it affects eyesight and your ability to use your limbs effectively. In addition, it ruins perception so you do not realize how badly you are driving (you may even think you drive better) and do not perceive danger. As a result you may take risks that would be unacceptable to you when sober.

In the UK the driving alcohol limit is 35 microgrammes of alcohol per 100 ml of breath or 80 milligrammes of alcohol per 100 ml of blood. Above that limit you can be fined up to £5,000, jailed for six months and face a driving ban. If you are convicted of drink-driving twice in ten years or are more than 2.5 times the limit you must convince the **Driver and Vehicle Licensing Agency** (DVLA) that you don't have a drink problem. (For information on the UK's drink-drive laws visit www.drinkdrivinglaw.co.uk.)

It is important that you remember the following:

▶ *Treat advice on a 'safe' number of glasses with caution because there are too many variables. Alcoholic strength varies even in a given type of drink and its effect varies according to your body weight, how much you have eaten, your health and your emotional state.*

- ▶ *Drinks served in someone's home tend to be more generous than those in pubs, clubs and restaurants.*
- ▶ *If you have drunk a lot, or carried on drinking until the early hours, you may still be over the limit when it's time for work the next morning. This is particularly so in countries where the limit is lower than the UK's.*
- ▶ *You can absorb alcohol by inhalation, so take care when using products in which alcohol is the solvent, like adhesives, resins and paints.*

DRUGS

Driving under the influence of drugs is as dangerous as drink-driving and in the UK carries the same penalties.

However, while most people realize it would be dangerous to drive while using illegal recreational drugs or strong prescription medicines, few realize that many over-the-counter and herbal remedies affect driving ability. Always ask your doctor if it is safe to drive while taking prescription medicines and always read the instructions on over-the-counter preparations to see if they warn of drowsiness or problems with concentration.

Even then, take care with drugs you are not familiar with because you may react to them differently to most people – a 'non-drowsy' antihistamine, for example, may make you sleepy or affect concentration. Indeed, it pays to start a course of drugs on a day when you are not driving.

Never misuse drugs. If you are told not to drink with a drug it may be because it exaggerates the effects of alcohol, so a small amount affects your driving as if you have drunk much more. There have even been cases of people going to sleep at the wheel after using the common cold remedy *Night Nurse* during the day, in spite of its name and clear warnings that it makes you sleepy.

Herbal and alternative remedies can also be risky, not least because many have not been medically tested. It has been shown that some herbal sleeping preparations stay in the body longer than prescription sleeping pills.

ILLNESS

Suffering instead of taking tablets may not be the answer, either. Even minor illnesses like colds and flu affect your driving, with some research suggesting a bad cold can have as much impact on your skills as drink. Any complaint that makes you feel sleepy turns you into a risk behind the wheel.

Conditions that affect your ability to move your arms, legs or head, seriously inhibit your driving and even something that merely makes you uncomfortable is bound to reduce your concentration and patience.

Any illness that may result in loss of vision or consciousness, including diabetes and heart conditions, affects your ability to drive. Driver licensing authorities publish long lists of complaints and conditions that prevent you from driving and your doctor should tell you if you have one. However, in the UK your doctor is not legally responsible for telling the DVLA if you are unfit to drive: *you* are responsible and can be prosecuted and banned from driving if you do not inform them.

Top tip

If you believe someone is unfit to drive due to illness or age you should tell the DVLA who will treat the information in confidence and investigate. This may seem unkind, but it could prevent a loved one killing themselves or others on the road. The UK list of conditions that stop you driving can be found at www.direct.gov.uk

10 THINGS TO REMEMBER

1 Treat driving as a skill, not a chore.

2 Show consideration for other road users, giving them space to do what they need to do.

3 Get your eyes tested every two years, especially if you are over 40.

4 Make yourself aware of what is happening around the car as well as ahead.

5 Adjust mirrors properly and use them often.

6 Be aware of your car's blind spots and move your head to see into them.

7 Keep windows clean and avoid stickers that might block your view.

8 Nothing must be allowed to interfere with the driver's concentration on driving.

9 Using mobile phones on the move is proven to be dangerous.

10 Never drive under the influence of drink or drugs, including over-the-counter remedies.

2

Know your car

In this chapter you will learn:
- *how the car's systems work*
- *how to make the best use of them*
- *what electronic driving aids do.*

Manufacturers have made cars easier and safer to drive, incorporating many features to protect us from our own mistakes and electronic driving aids that react far more quickly to potential problems than any driver could. But you can only get the best from these systems if you know how to use them.

We can only talk in general terms here so you must read your car's handbook which explains all the systems your car has and how to use and maintain them. In many cases it also explains how to recognize when things have gone wrong and what to do if that happens.

Why we need gears

Changing gear gives most learners problems and many experienced drivers know how to do it but not why. Put simply, gears enable us to match the engine's performance to the demands being placed upon it and to the car's road speed. Most cars have five-speed gearboxes but six is becoming increasingly common and there are now automatics with seven and eight. Some off-roaders have an additional high and low dual-ratio gearbox, effectively doubling the ratios available from the main box for off-road work.

If you look at a car's specification sheet in a brochure or handbook you will see that the engine's peak power and **torque** (twisting or pulling power) are shown with an engine speed in revolutions per minute (**rpm** or **revs**). In everyday driving terms, torque is the more important because it is what gives the car its flexibility, puts punch in acceleration and hauls you up hills. The engine has a usable band of torque either side of its peak point, though how much of the rev range that band covers varies considerably from engine to engine.

Gears enable the driver to keep the engine in that usable torque band regardless of road speed. First gear is a short ratio so it enables high revs at low speeds, letting you bring the revs up high enough to provide enough torque for pulling away. Top gear is a tall ratio so the engine revs slowly for the speed at which the wheels go round to give relaxed, efficient cruising. In most cars, top is geared to put the car close to its peak torque output at between 60 and 80 mph for high speed flexibility. The intermediate gears allow you to meet the demands on the engine at a range of speeds and in a variety of circumstances.

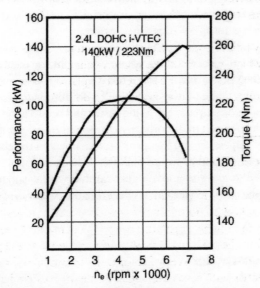

Figure 2.1 This graph for a Honda 2.4 litre petrol engine shows how power (steep line) and torque are delivered across the rev range.

Control

Using the gears can also give you more control either by granting a wider rev range to work in (as when driving a twisting road) or by helping to slow the car down.

Drivers used to be told to use 'engine braking' to help the brakes slow the car down. If you change down without raising the revs with the throttle, the car slows because it needs higher revs to maintain the same speed in a lower gear. These days brakes are more efficient so this is largely unnecessary and you are advised to use the brakes to slow down, only changing down to match the engine and road speeds so you are in the right gear to accelerate away again (an automatic does this for you).

But there are still circumstances where you might use engine braking. When going down a steep hill it pays to change down or hold an automatic in a lower gear (see 'Using automatics' later) because this helps stop the car going faster and reduces the need to use the brakes, which might otherwise overheat on a long descent. On slippery slopes, using a low gear may enable you to retain control where the brakes would make the wheels lock up, though you still need to move to a lower gear carefully or the sudden change may make the car skid (see Chapter 9 on bad weather driving).

Manual gearboxes

In Europe, manual gearboxes are still more common than automatics. Many people feel they give more control to the driver, but it is up to the driver to make sure the car is always in the optimum gear for the situation.

There is a common assumption that a high gear is always the most economical, but this is not always so and if your car has a trip computer with a current consumption readout, as well as an average one, you can often demonstrate this. The car may pull in top right down to 30 mph but if that puts it at the lower end of its usable torque, it will be working harder to manage that speed as the road goes up and down and you take bends. Changing down increases the revs and, therefore, the available torque so the engine is working more efficiently and using less fuel.

This is also why you change down when climbing a hill: the engine needs more torque to pull the car up the slope, so changing down provides that without increasing the road speed.

Insight

Many who learned to drive in a manual recall the bafflement of how you could tell when to change gear, and we have all been driven by people who seem to have passed a test without ever working it out. There is no magic recipe to it: you can't say change up at 40 mph or 2,000 rpm because it varies according to the car, its load, altitude and whether the road is flat. Most cars today have rev counters and if you change in a way that keeps revs around the peak torque point (check the specification) you generally make good, efficient progress.

However, if you listen, the car tells you. As a motoring writer driving many different cars I find you start with a brief 'getting to know you' period where you learn the car's characteristics, like how flexible the engine is. When you are accelerating you note when the performance drops off as the revs climb and change up before reaching that point (this is very noticeable in diesels). At steady speeds, ask yourself whether the engine sounds busy for your speed and see if you

(Contd)

can change up without loss of pace. As speed drops listen for the engine starting to sound strained or juddery and change down if it does. Many cars seem fine at steady low speeds in a high gear but judder and complain when asked to accelerate. If that happens you are better off in the lower gear because it grants more control, better response and, almost certainly, better economy.

ACCELERATION

Fuel-saving advice used to be to select as high a gear as possible and gradually bring the car up to speed. But with modern cars, with very tall top gears, that is no longer so. Indeed, acceleration uses more fuel than anything else so if you reduce the period of acceleration, you improve overall fuel consumption. So, the leisurely haul from 30 to 60 mph in sixth may use more fuel than changing down to fourth or fifth to attain a higher cruising speed more quickly.

But while the advice now is to accelerate briskly up to speed in a lower gear before selecting a higher one, this doesn't mean dropping from fifth to third and flooring the throttle like a rally driver – such hard acceleration uses more fuel. That technique should only be used for brisk overtaking when economy must be abandoned for the safety of spending as little time as possible on the wrong side of the road.

SMOOTH OPERATION

Smooth gear changes are a sign of a good driver. A gear change should only be obvious to your passengers from the change in engine speed, not because it jolted them awake. Smoothness partly comes from the progressive way you lower and raise the **clutch** pedal and anticipate the point at which things start to happen, which varies from car to car. But it also comes from helping the engine through the change.

As we've seen, changing gear changes the engine's revs so if we can help match the revs to the new gear, it will happen more smoothly.

When you change down, the engine revs climb, so by making sure your throttle foot starts going down before the clutch is fully engaged (pedal up) you can lift the revs towards that higher range and smooth the change. When you change up, the revs drop so your throttle foot should not go back down until the clutch has fully engaged.

Top tip

If you have trouble making smooth gear changes consider taking a few driving lessons because an instructor should be able to see what you are doing wrong and help you improve. This is worthwhile not only because it makes driving more pleasant for you and your passengers but because every jolt you feel is a shock running through the **transmission,** so smoother changes put less stress on the car.

SKIPPING

You don't have to move through the gears in sequence. You are often taught to do this as a learner because you are less likely to make mistakes this way, say, shifting from fifth to first at speed. In some cars certain gear ratios may be too widely spaced to skip gears, resulting in too big a jump in revs, but in many it is possible to skip at least some of the gears when shifting up or down. High performance cars with very close ratioed gearboxes make this very easy because there is only a modest step up or down the revs when you change gear.

A fairly common skip change is with a six-speed gearbox where fourth provides good acceleration to a cruising speed high enough for sixth, so you shift directly from fourth to sixth.

But only skip changes if you are confident in your gear changing and know the box.

Insight

The gear change mistake I worry about is when changing from a six-speed manual to a five-speed because sixth is where
(Contd)

reverse often lives on a five-speeder, opposite fifth. Slipping into reverse at motorway speeds would be an expensive mistake, so take care if your family has cars with five- and six-speed boxes.

Automatic gearboxes

Automatics have long been the norm in America and are gaining popularity in Europe. This is because they have improved greatly and therefore cope better with the more demanding, twisty roads of Europe.

Many modern automatics give as precise control as a well used manual and where there were once performance and economy penalties to pay for the ease of driving, those are now greatly reduced. Indeed, there are some cars where the automatic's acceleration and economy are better than the manual's because they change gear so efficiently and adapt to changing conditions so well. Modern electronics mean automatics can recognize different demands, like going up and down hills or whether the car is towing a trailer, and change their shift patterns accordingly. Some even 'learn' from what the driver is asking of them.

Insight

Automatic gearboxes were once the choice of people who didn't like driving. No keen driver would have wanted one, but they have become so efficient that you now lose little by having one. In fact, I have gone from tolerating them to owning a car with one.

TYPES

Once, all automatics were three-speed with a hydraulic device called a **torque converter** taking the place of the clutch, but now there are many different types, though the torque converter is still used on most.

On modern cars, most automatics are four- and five-speed, though up to eight are available on a few luxury models. Some boxes are true automatics while others are effectively manuals with an automatic clutch taking care of the shifts.

The Volkswagen Group's dynamic shift gearbox is a six-speed box with two electronically controlled clutches. One clutch looks after even number gears and one handles the odds, so when one gear is engaged the next is selected and ready to go, allowing quick smooth changes. It is so efficient that cars fitted with it are quicker and more economical than the equivalent car with a manual gearbox.

Some boxes don't even have real gears. Continuously variable transmissions (**CVT**) have electronically controlled pulleys and steel belts, which, as the name suggests, continuously vary the ratios so they should always be in the optimum for the demands being made. They usually require a slightly different driving style to a conventional ratioed gearbox, as we shall explain later.

MODES

Most automatics now have a mode switch. This usually allows you to switch between a normal or 'comfort' setting and a sport mode, though increasingly they also have a manual mode (see Plate 2).

The normal setting usually shifts up just above peak torque revs on normal throttle pedal settings for relaxed, economical driving. Sport mode always holds gears longer but in some boxes it also quickens the gearbox's responses to throttle pedal pressure so it shifts more readily on gentle throttle movements. The drawbacks with using sport mode are that at low speeds the changes are often not as smooth and with some boxes there is a reluctance at speed to use top, even when you ease off the throttle.

The manual change mode is often called a '**sequential' gear shift**, because you move through the gears in sequence, or '**Tiptronic**', which was Porsche's name for the first box of this type.

This enables you to shift up and down either by tapping the gear shift backwards and forwards or by pressing paddles or buttons on the steering wheel. These boxes won't let you abuse the engine, so if the change you demand would stress it, they ignore you. Most modern boxes cope so well in the automatic mode that manual mode is only of use in exceptional circumstances, like needing extra control on an unusually demanding road or in extreme off-road driving.

Insight

I find tapping up and down a sequential change tedious and rarely produces better results than the sport mode. What is often more useful is to use sport mode for the twisty or hilly bits and revert to comfort mode on the straighter sections, to make it shift into top sooner.

A few automatic boxes have a 'snow' mode or button, often marked with a snowflake icon. This is used for pulling away in deep snow and usually starts the box in second to reduce the torque being passed to the wheels, thereby helping to prevent wheel-spin (see Chapter 9 on bad weather driving).

LEARNING BOXES

Automatics with learning programmes, sometimes called **adaptive** or **active boxes,** learn from what the driver is doing by analyzing data from the car's systems. The idea is that when you drive in a relaxed way, it adapts to change up early and not shift down too readily if you apply more throttle, but if you press on along a twisting open road it adapts to shift quicker and holds gears longer.

The only thing a driver has to beware of with this sort of box is that the change in characteristics can catch you out. For example, you have driven briskly for many miles, getting used to the box shifting in a responsive way, then you get stuck behind a slow vehicle for a few miles. The trouble is that when you see an opportunity to overtake, the box has 'learned' a more relaxed approach so it doesn't change as quickly as you were expecting when you pulled out to overtake. It means you must always be prepared to use **kickdown** in such circumstances (see the next section).

Using automatics

Automatics make life easy and if you just get in, stick it in 'drive' and go it will do most of what you want, but it pays to learn how to use it properly. Read the handbook for advice on your particular gearbox, even if you are familiar with automatics, because the technology is changing fast.

SAFETY

Do something silly with a manual car, like trying to start it in gear or leaving it in gear when you take your feet off the pedals while parked, and the chances are the car will stall. Do the same with an automatic and the gearbox won't let it stall, which is why safety devices are built into them.

Modern automatics won't even let you start the engine unless the box is in the 'park' position, which locks the transmission, though some start in neutral. Most on the road today demand the foot brake is applied before they allow you to shift from park to drive. This follows lengthy litigation in the USA in the 1980s when drivers claimed automatics had run away with them when they shifted into drive with their foot on the brake. The courts eventually agreed this was mechanically impossible, but it cost the car companies involved lots of money and bad publicity.

Automatics usually have a button on the shift that must be pressed to allow the lever to move between certain positions: this varies between boxes so read the handbook. For example, it might let you move between drive and neutral without pressing the button, for easy selection at traffic lights, but requires the button to be pressed to select reverse or park so you can't unwittingly do that on the move.

If you are using a sequential box in manual mode it will automatically shift to first when you come almost to a halt, but do not rely on this at junctions. It is safer to do it manually because otherwise it may not do it quickly enough and you then pull away in the wrong gear so may be unable to accelerate as expected.

Top tip

In an automatic, it is best to engage neutral and the handbrake, or shift into park, when stopped. Most automatics creep forwards if left in drive, so if your foot slips from the brake pedal, perhaps because you were hit from behind, the car can move off even if your foot is off the throttle. In these circumstances, if your foot hits the throttle pedal, it can accelerate away where a manual is more likely to stall. In some countries the driving test demands that you leave an automatic in drive and apply the handbrake, but the danger with that is many automatics with modern high-torque engines are capable of pulling away with the handbrake still on.

KICKDOWN

There are times when you need lots of power quickly, like when overtaking. In a manual you would change down a gear or two and accelerate away. Automatics shift down in response to modest increases in throttle pressure but if you want that overtaking style of power boost, use kickdown.

This means that when you push the throttle pedal down hard, the box shifts down as many gears as necessary and the car accelerates away. It used to be literally a switch activated by the pedal, but now there are more sophisticated electronics behind it, helping to ensure smooth changes and working with the engine management and electronic driving aids.

HELPING HAND

Modern automatics' electronics cope with changing conditions well, so the gearboxes need less help than before. They may even recognize when you are going downhill – where you would once have had to hold the box in a lower gear, the electronics recognize the car is trying to go faster with no input from the driver and stop it changing up.

But don't forget about the box, especially in difficult situations, like hilly country or towing. Listen to the engine and if it seems to be working too hard, manually shift it down. Some boxes have a push button to lock the box out of top and all have positions that hold it in lower gears. With a sequential box it may pay to switch to manual mode and do it yourself.

Older automatics may 'hunt' between gears in certain circumstances, like trying to go up a slope on a fast road. This means the box can't decide what gear to be in so it shifts between two and you can hear the engine revs going up and down. If you do not help the box by changing down, it eventually overheats. Modern electronics have largely eliminated this.

CORNERING

Just like a driver, an automatic needs time to make the changes, though some modern ones are extremely quick. If you find it hasn't managed to change down for a bend, it means you need to think about braking earlier to give it time to give you the right gear to drive the car through the bend.

Many modern automatics recognize when the car is cornering, so avoid changes that might upset the car's stance, but it is a risk you must be aware of in an automatic. It is often very noticeable in sports mode when the box responds to throttle pressure by changing down more readily, which may give you more power than expected mid bend.

CVT

Continuously variable transmissions sometimes require a slightly different driving style. Older ones tend to hold a lower gear at speed unless you ease up on the throttle. It can seem odd at first that to go faster on the motorway you must ease off the throttle to get a higher gear, but when you do the engine becomes quieter and more relaxed as your speed increases.

Modern electronically controlled CVT usually drives like an ordinary automatic, but if you find the engine seems to be revving hard at speed, try easing up a little.

Driven wheels

The majority of cars are front-wheel drive, though some luxury and high performance cars retain rear-wheel drive. Four-wheel drive (**4WD**) used to be only for off-road work, but increasing numbers of road cars have it, especially high-powered ones. All these systems have different driving characteristics.

FRONT DRIVE

Front-wheel drive has become the norm because it is compact. As all the engine and transmission parts are up the front, cabin space is not stolen to run drive shafts to the rear, which usually makes it lighter, too.

Front-driven cars also have more benign handling characteristics, tending to spin off clumsily applied power without changing direction and running wide if pushed rather than swinging the back round. Over the years, suspension engineers have made them even easier to handle, largely eliminating the sometimes sharp change from running wide to tucking the nose in if the driver lifted off the throttle suddenly.

But it takes good engineering to give them sharp handling feel and allow them to cope with very high power outputs. After all, you are asking one set of wheels to both steer and propel the car.

REAR DRIVE

This was once how all cars were driven because it separated the driving and steering functions so engineering was easier. It is still used in some performance cars because it allows the power to be used to influence the car's cornering stance, helping to tuck the nose into the bend.

It is easier to make a rear-wheel drive car transfer its power to the road without losing grip, though clumsy use of power can push the back sideways, demanding engineering that helps prevent that. However, rear-wheel drive cars will still run wide on a bend if pushed.

FOUR-WHEEL DRIVE

Four-wheel drive comes in three main forms:

▶ *part-time*
▶ *full-time*
▶ *switchable road-going.*

PART-TIME

Early 4WD cars, like the wartime Jeep and most Land Rovers until 1984, had part-time systems because they were easy to engineer. On good surfaces they were driven in rear-wheel drive but when you ventured onto soft or loose ground, you engaged the front axle. These systems lack a centre **differential** ('diff', see box on page 34) to allow the front and rear wheels to travel different distances when cornering. So if you drive them in 4WD on a hard surface, the transmission winds itself until something expensive breaks. A few sports utility vehicles still have it, including some manual gearbox Jeeps and cheaper models from Korea, but it is now mostly found on pickups.

FULL-TIME

Full-time 4WD has a centre diff to allow it to be used on the road, so you get the benefits of a 4WD's increased traction and balance all the time. In performance cars it allows high levels of power to be fully utilized because it is passed to all four wheels. The most sophisticated systems use clever centre diffs, often electronically controlled, to continuously vary the distribution of the drive. So, the drive may normally be split 50:50, or with a bias towards the front or rear, but if the front wheels start to slip, it progressively moves drive towards the back and vice versa. Such systems offer extremely high levels of traction and very sure-footed handling.

SWITCHABLE

Switchable systems allow on-road use thanks to a centre diff but one set of wheels, usually the front, can be disengaged for road use. Manufacturers say this reduces wear, vibration and fuel consumption, but the effect is minimal and most cars with this feel so much better driven in 4WD that you rarely switch it off. In fact, some large vehicles with switchable systems feel positively clumsy in 2WD after being driven in 4WD.

Incidentally, the term 4×4 (four-by-four) is merely a military nomenclature for 4WD, meaning 'four wheels, four driven'. Military vehicles can even be 6×6 or 6×4.

What's the diff?

A diff, short for differential, is a system of gears that allows two **driven wheels**, or sets of wheels, to turn at different speeds. When a car corners, the outer wheels have to travel further than the inner ones and the rear wheels take a tighter curve than the front, so all four wheels are turning at different speeds. If the engine drove the wheels on a solid axle, one wheel would be spinning or being dragged by the other.

All cars need at least one diff but part-time 4WD requires one in each axle to allow the car to turn. This is adequate on soft ground, where the wheels can spin enough to overcome the front-to-rear differences, but road-going 4WD requires a centre diff to allow the front and rear wheels to turn at different speeds on grippy, hard surfaces. Without that centre diff the transmission would wind up and either break or when a wheel loses grip all the tension in the system spins out that way, resulting in unpredictable handling.

Off-roaders with road-going 4WD have a way of locking at least the centre diff or it would give a single spinning wheel all the power. Many centre diff locks are automatic but if you manually lock a diff you must remember to unlock it before returning to the road.

USING 4WD

If you own a car with 4WD you must read the handbook to find out when you can use the 4WD system and how. If you don't, you won't use it to its full ability and at worst face huge repair bills. Using it off-road is too specialist for this book and you are advised to seek an off-road driving course to learn the techniques for what is a potentially dangerous task and can be damaging to the car and environment if done incorrectly. It is worth doing an off-road driving course even if you do not plan to venture off tarmac because you will be shown how 4WD systems work and there will be times, like in heavy snow, where the knowledge is useful.

On road, you must be aware that 4WD can't defy the laws of physics. Though it provides much higher standards of traction and handling than 2WD, ultimately it is all down to the tyres' grip. If the tyres can't grip because of ice, mud or water on the road, no amount of 4WD will help you stop or go round corners. We will deal with this in more depth in Chapter 9.

High performance 4WDs often have phenomenal ability but that also means that if you do come unstuck in normal conditions you will be going very quickly and have little time to correct your mistake. In these circumstances, 4WD can be unpredictable because the way the car behaves depends on which end comes unstuck first and what the system does to try to correct it. But with most cars you would have ignored a lot of warnings that you were overdoing it.

Off-roaders are tall with a higher centre of gravity than ordinary cars so they handle differently and are more likely to roll if abused. If one of the larger ones gets away from you, it has considerable weight to try and stop and that will do a lot of damage to other vehicles. You must adjust your driving style accordingly and take care if you are new to them.

Top tip

All cars corner better if it is done under power, but this is even more the case with 4WD cars. The 4WD can only enhance the cornering stance if it has the power to do so and, with large off-roaders, failure to allow it to do its bit means their weight takes over and tries to draw them straight on. Even a modest amount of power makes a difference.

Steering

Most cars now have power assisted steering (**PAS**) to take the effort out of it. In fact, with the grip of modern tyres, steering would be very heavy without it.

Early power-steering assisted easy movement while robbing you of feedback, which turned cornering on wet roads into an act of faith because you had so little idea of how much grip the tyres had.

Modern systems are much better with most being in some way speed sensitive, reacting either to actual road speed or to engine speed. These systems vary assistance so that at low speeds, especially when parking, you get lots of help and little feedback but at higher speeds it weights up so steering needs more effort and gives more feedback. This recognizes that at speed the steering needs less movement to achieve changes in direction.

But it works better in some cars than others. It is common for there to be a certain speed, often around 40 mph, at which the steering is still over-assisted, resulting in a light, vague feel. On others you may find the steering weights up as you turn the wheel more, which can mean it feels reassuringly informative on tight bends but too light on fast, sweeping curves. But in some cars it is so well set up that you are never aware of the changing assistance.

When you get in a strange car you must take time to get the feel of the steering and learn how much feedback it is giving. Beware of false feedback, too: some power-steering is electronically varied to give a well weighted feel but it is not giving genuine feedback from the road. Artificial feel like this may only become obvious if there is no lightening of the steering feel when the wheels lose grip, like when hitting water at speed or driving on ice.

Electronic driving aids

In the beginning there was anti-lock braking, known as **ABS** from the German abbreviation for anti-lock system. ABS has gone from being an expensive extra that in the mid-1980s added ten per cent to the price of the top of the range BMW 3-Series, to something that is now compulsory on all new cars in Europe. In that time, engineers have also developed a plethora of driving aids based around the ABS sensors.

We will explain the main ones here, but new ones are being developed all the time and many manufacturers give different names to what are often the same pieces of electronics. Some systems also combine two or three functions, so stability control is often married to **traction control**. Read your car's handbook to find out what it has and any special considerations for your model.

Your car may have:

- *ABS*
- *tyre-pressure monitoring*
- *emergency brake assist*
- *electronic stability programme*
- *traction control*
- *hill descent control.*

ABS

A skid happens when the rotational speed of the wheel doesn't match the road speed of the car and the most obvious way for this to happen is when the driver hits the brakes. The worst thing about this is that when the front wheels lock up, the car becomes a toboggan with no steering control (see Chapter 9) so you can turn the wheel and continue straight towards the child in the road. If the back wheels lock they can try to overtake the front, sliding the car sideways.

ABS prevents this by detecting when a wheel is about to stop rotating and easing the brake pressure to that wheel, so it keeps turning. That not only gives you optimum braking but means you retain directional control. That sounds simple, but as explained earlier in the box on differentials, all four wheels turn at different speeds when cornering, so the system has to be programmed to know what is normal slowing down of a wheel and what isn't and it does this in milliseconds.

It is a common misconception that ABS's job is to stop you quicker but it rarely does this. Its job is to allow the driver directional control so you should be able to steer around the child in the road. The limiting factor in avoiding the child becomes whether the tyres have enough grip to cope with the steering movement, but your chances of saving a life are far greater with ABS.

When you hit the brakes hard enough to activate the ABS, the pedal vibrates or pulses, often accompanied by a mechanical buzzing sound. In emergency braking this is entirely normal and all you need do is maintain the pressure: the opposite to what you should do in a car without ABS. If you feel it activate under normal braking it means you have been going too fast for the conditions because the road is more slippery than you thought (or your tyres are too worn).

Insight

The first time you feel the ABS pedal pulse it can be disconcerting, especially in those cars in which it is accompanied by a graunching sound. So, if you are new to ABS find somewhere safe to discover what it feels like. The safest place to do it is on an unsurfaced car park or track where firm brake pressure will activate ABS at fairly low speeds. If you try it on a wet road, do it on a straight, empty one away from houses and parked cars.

TYRE-PRESSURE MONITORING

The ABS sensors are so sensitive to changes in wheel speed that they are even used to monitor tyre pressures on some cars. As a tyre deflates, the diameter of the wheel is reduced so it rotates faster. Pressure monitors alert the driver that a tyre's pressure has dropped below an acceptable level and some even show tyre pressures on a digital screen, though those may have pressure sensors in the wheels.

EMERGENCY BRAKE ASSIST

Emergency brake assist (**EBA**) has two functions: it recognizes emergency braking and increases the pressure while it also counters the effect of the tendency of most drivers to back off the pedal when they feel the ABS working. It tells emergency braking from the speed at which the driver's foot swaps pedals and when it reacts, it feels as if you hit the brakes a second before you did.

EBA is often linked with electronic brake force distribution, which balances the pressure to the brakes to match the load on the wheel. A car with rear passengers and a boot full of luggage is likely to need less brake force at the back than one carrying only the driver.

ELECTRONIC STABILITY PROGRAMME

Electronic stability programmes (**ESPs**) may also be called electronic stability control or **dynamic stability control**. This uses the ABS and other sensors to detect when a car is drifting out on a corner and then brakes the relevant wheels to pull it back into line. If that isn't enough, it tells the engine management system to reduce the power. This is always accompanied by a warning light, usually an orange or yellow triangle, which is to alert you to the fact that you were overdoing it.

ESP lights occasionally come on if you hit big bumps or potholes but at any other time it means you should slow down.

All cars with ESP have a button for turning it off. This is because ESP reacts to sideways movement and it can't tell the difference between you cornering too hard and you slithering about in deep snow or on a muddy field. With off-roaders it can seriously inhibit off-road ability, cutting power when you least need it in deep mud or as the car is nudged sideways by ruts. So turn it off on slippery surfaces but remember to turn it back on when you return to the road.

TRACTION CONTROL

Electronic traction control (ETC) is like ABS in reverse: when a
wheel starts to spin it applies the brake to slow it down. Most
systems also reduce power if that isn't enough.

Its use in off-roaders is obvious, helping the 4WD to keep you
going in slippery conditions. On the road it enables a powerful car
to pull away without spinning the wheels but it also stabilizes the
car when cornering because if a wheel spins in a bend, the car will
pull to one side.

As with ESP, a warning light shows and lets you know you are
demanding more of the tyres than they can deliver.

In deep snow and off-road, when you are struggling to keep
moving, the best technique is to apply power to the point where
the TC light comes on and hold it there, letting the system work its
magic. Progress may be so slow that you can only see it by judging
the position of something outside the car against, say, a windscreen
pillar (see Chapter 9).

HILL DESCENT CONTROL

As hill descent control (HDC) was first developed by Land Rover,
you can guess it is primarily for off-road use. Imagine descending

down a slippery slope, like a steep motorway embankment, off-road without HDC: you can use the engine braking alone to slow you down by doing it in the lowest possible gear, which can be extremely low in a serious off-roader with a 'high and low' dual-gearbox. If you try to brake, you can easily lock up wheels and, even with ABS, may find the back trying to overtake the front, which can roll the car.

HDC uses the brakes individually to slow the vehicle but brakes in a very controlled way so it applies them enough to slow you down but not in a way that lets any wheel lock up more than momentarily. It is usually accompanied by the typical ABS pulsing sound. You may be able to vary the descent speed, most often by using the cruise control buttons.

Check the handbook to find out how yours works, even if you do not plan off-road adventures, because it can also be useful if you have to descend a snow- or ice-covered hill on the road.

Security devices

Though security devices do not strictly affect your driving, they are important for your safety so you should understand how they work.

ALARMS AND IMMOBILIZERS

Most cars now have **immobilizers** and increasing numbers ally these to an alarm. An immobilizer stops the engine from starting and most now use some kind of chip in the key which the car interrogates.

Some alarms have immobilizers associated with them and in many cars the two things are only deactivated if you use the remote locking sender to unlock the car, so the alarm goes off if you use the key. Some of these combined devices also reactivate the immobilizer if you do not start the engine soon after unlocking.

If they do, you just use the sender to re-lock and unlock the car, then it should start. (Note that this can be done from inside the car.)

The best alarms have movement sensors to detect, say, a hand reaching in through a broken or open window. These give false alarms if you leave pets in the car, leave a window open (they detect air movement) or if flying insects get in. If you need to leave a pet in the car there will be a way of setting the alarm without activating the sensors, so check your handbook.

Alarms always have a signal that shows they have been set off. Find out from the handbook what this is because if you hear it you should check the car thoroughly before getting in, including looking into the back of the car to make sure nobody is hiding there.

Insight

A car that gives false alarms can be very annoying, especially as they usually do it either when you're watching something good on TV or as you nod off. The most common cause is insects, but if you can't see any, try spraying insecticide into the car. Think carefully before deactivating the alarm, unless there is an obvious fault, because thieves sometimes shake or thump cars to set alarms off, hoping the owner will do that. If something silly keeps setting it off, like a certain type of vehicle passing by, ask the dealer or an alarm specialist if its sensitivity can be adjusted.

LOCKS

Many locking systems offer the option of only opening the driver's door on the first press of the remote button. It may be a preference you have to set up and it is worth using because it eliminates the risk of someone leaping into the other side of the car as you get in.

Some systems also have an anti-hijack function which automatically locks the doors once the car is above a certain speed. They remain locked, so if you stop at the lights, or are forced to stop, nobody can get in to steal your luggage or car. Again, this may be a programmable function, so check the handbook. Once this locks the doors, it is unlocked just by pulling the door handle and has an impact-sensing device to unlock all doors in an accident.

Because car security is so good now, the most common way for cars to be stolen, especially prestige models, is by stealing the keys, so look after them, never leaving them in the car or putting them down while you pay for fuel. At home, store keys securely, hanging them in a cupboard or putting them in a drawer.

Top tip

Don't dump keys on a table near the door when you get home. Thieves know many people do that and often steal them by 'fishing' for them with a hook on a pole through the letterbox.

LIGHTS

Lights may not seem like security devices but they can be. Many cars now have interior lights that come on when you unlock the car so that you can make sure nobody is hidden inside. However, remember that this also shows a would-be attacker which car is yours in the car park, so don't unlock it from too far off.

Increasing numbers of cars have 'see-you-home' or 'door-to-door' headlights. You can set a delay on them so they stay on long enough to light your way to your front door. They usually do this only if you turn off the light switch after the ignition.

10 THINGS TO REMEMBER

1 *Read your car's handbook so you know how everything works.*

2 *Correct use of the gears saves fuel.*

3 *When you change down your throttle foot comes down before the clutch is fully engaged.*

4 *When you change up your throttle foot stays up until the clutch is fully engaged.*

5 *Automatic gearboxes sometimes need driver help to cope with awkward road conditions.*

6 *Not all four-wheel drive is suitable for on-road use.*

7 *When emergency braking in a car with ABS do not ease off the pedal when you feel it pulse.*

8 *If ABS pulses or ETC/TC warning lights come on in normal driving it means you were going too fast for the conditions, so slow down.*

9 *If your car allows it, set remote unlocking to open only the driver's door on the first button push.*

10 *Keep car keys secure because thieves know they are the weakest link in your car's security.*

Getting comfortable

In this chapter you will learn:
- *how to get the right driving position*
- *how to use the ventilation system*
- *how to optimize occupant protection systems.*

It has long been realized that making the driver comfortable is an important part of making them safe. Drivers whose attention is taken by the pain in their back or who are trying to fine tune their seating position on the motorway can't be fully aware of what is going on around them and may not even be in full control of the car. In addition, discomfort accelerates the onset of fatigue.

The fact that modern cars can accommodate such a wide range of body shapes is amazing. Designers aim for a driving position suitable for 95 per cent of people and, as cars are sold worldwide, they mean the majority of people regardless of sexual, racial or national variations, not just the majority in the country of manufacture. But having gone to all that trouble they know many drivers will not take the time to get it right.

It should be remembered that seats are as important parts of the car's safety features as the more obviously safety-orientated equipment like seatbelts and airbags. It is the seat that puts you in the right place for these things to work and it is far more sophisticated than a simple chair. Modern seats have frames engineered to take considerable stress, especially if seatbelts are integrated into them, and use dual-density foam with a soft outer layer over firmer inner sections designed to support you for both comfort and safety. For example, firmer foam in the seat cushion may be used to stop you sliding under the seatbelt in an accident. Most car seats have head restraints to protect you from **whiplash** injuries to the neck and in some cars these are 'active', moving forwards in an accident to offer more protection. Seats increasingly have airbags fitted, usually for side impact protection but sometimes to protect rear passengers from impact with the front seatbacks. But these things can't give you full protection unless used properly. Read your handbook to find out what adjustment your car offers and how to use it.

How things adjust

To accommodate such a wide range of body shapes and sizes, cars have increasingly adjustable driving features. Few modern cars now have only a sliding seat as a concession to different sizes of driver, though that was once commonplace. Now, luxury cars with 8–12-way adjustable seats are common and even modestly priced cars have seat height adjusters and 'tilt and reach' adjusting steering wheels.

When to adjust

While some seat adjusters are safe to use on the move, especially electric and ratchet operated ones, others are not, so think carefully before you try to use them. Most seat sliders completely release the seat in the runners so it can easily slide you out of reach of the pedals or crashing against the steering wheel. Japanese manufacturers still like lever backrest adjusters that completely release the back, which could lead to you falling backwards. But take care even with rotary or ratchet adjusters because some are so tucked away that there is a risk of getting a hand stuck at the wrong moment. The most sensible thing is only to adjust a manual seat when stationary.

(Contd)

While electric steering column adjusters are safe to use while driving, all manual systems completely release the column and greatly reduce steering control as the wheel flops about, so never use them on the move.

SEAT ADJUSTERS

Modern cars have seats which slide and have rake adjustable backs but adjustments for height, cushion angle and lumbar support are increasingly common. Luxury cars may also allow you to adjust the cushion length, side bolsters and upper and lower seatback angles, often electrically with memory for saving several settings.

Your handbook explains what is available in your car and how it works. For example, seat height adjustment may be by a lever you pull to unlock the seat then have to either allow it to rise or push down with your weight, but it could also be a ratchet system where you push repeatedly down to lower or pull up to rise. Some cars now have a similar ratchet system for back rake.

If the backrest has a rotary adjuster, it is usually easier to make adjustments by easing your weight off the seatback.

Insight

It is fascinating to look into a classic car and see how much safety has improved. I'm not just talking about the addition of things like seatbelts and airbags but the attention that has been given to making the whole interior safer. The most striking thing is often the size and shape of the seats. Look at anything made before the 1980s and the chances are that the seats end below all but the shortest driver's shoulder blades – a position likely to make whiplash worse. Fascias were often painted metal, with nothing to absorb the impact of unbelted occupants hitting them. Worse still, many switches and controls were metal and projected some way out of the fascia to stab unfortunate accident victims. Indeed, cars before the late 1960s had non-collapsible steering columns which could literally spear the unbelted driver's chest.

GETTING IT RIGHT

Seat specialists Recaro suggest eight points for a comfortable driving position, though some are only adjustable on the best seats.

1 *Start by pressing the base of your spine into contact with the back of the seat and then slide the seat until your knees are still slightly bent when the pedals (clutch on a manual, throttle on an auto) are fully depressed.*

2 *Press your shoulders firmly against the seat and set the back angle so you can reach the steering wheel with your elbows slightly bent. Your shoulders should still touch the seat when turning the wheel. In cars with reach-adjustable wheels you can avoid sitting too upright or having to have a shorter leg length than is comfortable by moving the wheel.*

3 *Set the seat as high as possible to ensure a natural leg position and good view of the instruments and out of the car. Tall drivers may have to compromise here. A tilt adjustable wheel can allow you to get a good view of the instruments without compromising your driving position, though with some cars tall drivers may find it impossible to see some of the binnacle without having the wheel uncomfortably high.*

4 *On seats where the cushion angle is adjustable, set it so you can depress the pedals easily and your thighs rest lightly on the cushion. When adjusting this you often have to readjust the seatback angle.*

5 *Head restraints are safety equipment and must be adjusted properly to work. They should be raised so their tops are at least level with your eyes, though Recaro says it is best if they are level with the top of your head. On restraints where you can change the angle they should be tilted to about 2 cm from your head. Only if they are high enough will they protect you from potentially crippling whiplash injuries.*

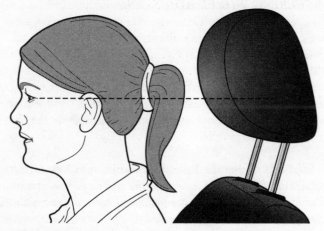

Figure 3.1 The top of the head restraint should be at least at eye level, preferably higher like this.

6 *Recaro says the ideal gap between the cushion, if adjustable for length, and back of your knee is two or three fingers width.*

7 *Adjustable lumbar support is correctly set when it supports the base of your spine in its natural position.*

8 *Adjustable side bolsters should support the upper body comfortably without undue pressure.*

If you are used to driving in an incorrect position, one set up like this may feel odd at first but give it time and see if you are more comfortable.

> **Insight**
>
> The first time an expert showed me how to adjust my driving position properly, it felt a little odd at first, even though it was not that different from my usual position. But as the oddness wore off I soon appreciated the fewer stress points the new position created on long journeys. So, if you follow the instructions here and think it feels strange, please try it for a couple of journeys before reverting to your old ways.

STEERING WHEEL ADJUSTERS

Most cars now at least have tilt-adjustable wheels but reach-adjustment is increasingly offered. Electric adjusters may even be linked to the seat's memory positions. Some luxury cars with electric wheel adjusters may also have a courtesy or access position where, when the ignition is turned off, the wheel lifts and retracts away from the driver to ease access to the car: check for this before adjusting the seat position.

Tilt-adjusters allow a basic level of positioning so you can move it to get a clear view of the wheel and so your hands are not too high. For some people, because of their height or body shape, this must be a compromise between being comfortable and being able to see all you need to in the instrument binnacle. You must decide whether you can see all that is important: you don't really need to see the speedo above 80 mph but not being able to see important warning lights could be dangerous.

For comfort, the wheel should not be so high that you sit like a begging dog, which could give circulation problems if your hands are above heart level. If you can keep your wrists fairly straight it also reduces strain on them.

Reach-, or telescopic-, adjustment is more useful. It enables you to avoid compromising either your arm or leg positions. First adjust the seat for your leg length, then pull or push the wheel until your arms are slightly bent when your hands are at 10 to 2 o'clock on the wheel. Generally, pushing the wheel in means also having to raise it; pulling it out usually also means you need to lower it.

POSTURE

Once you have all this right, check your posture. Your mum was always telling you not to slouch for good reason and at the wheel it is easy to let yourself drop into a shoulder drooping, round-backed stance. It is equally easy, especially when road conditions are difficult, to get physically tense, raising your shoulders, tensing your arms at the wheel and clamping your jaw. Such posture increases fatigue and may even cause permanent discomfort through repetitive stress.

We will look at this further in relation to long-distance driving in Chapter 6, but start as you mean to go on and get your posture right before you set off. Sit up straight, which shouldn't be difficult if the seat and wheel are correctly adjusted, and become aware of your body. If you are doing it right there should be no obvious tension as you sit at the wheel.

A common mistake is to drive with the chin up: some drivers even look as if they are reading the road through bifocal glasses. Try looking ahead of you now with your chin up and you should feel how it increases tension in the muscles running down either side of the back of your neck and into your shoulders even if your chin is only slightly raised. Now tuck your chin in to a natural head position and you should feel straight away how it is more comfortable and less stressful. It's probably also easier on the eyes, which are now looking straight out as they are supposed to.

If you can't get this right, try finding the neutral position by raising your chin until you feel the start of tension in the neck muscles, then lower it until you feel muscle tension again: the neutral position is between the two. You can use a technique like this to get most body positions right and it is a useful way of helping to relax muscles.

Insight

At one time I (stupidly) had a daily 75-mile motorway journey to work and started to get pains in my ears, but doctors could see nothing wrong. Then, sitting in a traffic jam one day I realized I was setting my jaw, which was tensing the muscles just below the ear. Doing that for long periods every day was putting stress on those muscles and once I consciously stopped doing it, what I'd thought was discomfort in my ears went away. So, if you get aches and pains, especially after long journeys or being stuck in jams, think about how you hold yourself and whether it could be what is causing your problems.

Odd sizes

If your body shape is out of the ordinary, ask your car's franchised dealer, or the manufacturer's customer service department, if further adjustments can be made. They may be able to fit things like raised, lowered or longer seat runners, or move the runners forwards if you are short legged. However, do not carry out DIY adjustments because if you go beyond certain limits you may affect the car's safety systems. Indeed, many car seats house airbags and seatbelt pretensioners – interfering with those could result in personal injury. There are many specialist companies capable of adapting cars to fit those with disabilities.

Safety gear

Modern cars are packed with safety equipment and as a driver it is important to ensure you and your passengers use it correctly. Most of the safety equipment, like airbags, is passive: you don't have to do anything with it but it is still wise to know where it is and how it works.

SEATBELTS

The most obvious safety features are seatbelts, and their use is now compulsory in most western countries. Only the very oldest cars are likely to have **static belts**, which can be very awkward to adjust so they are close enough to work but not to restrict movement. It may be wise to see if they can be replaced with **inertia reel belts**. Inertia reel belts roll in and out of a lower reel, which locks on sudden movement, so they are largely self-adjusting though heavily padded clothing can affect this.

Figure 3.2 Pregnant women (and larger people) must pass the belt around their bump.

Any seatbelt should pass the stress of impact into your skeleton, not soft tissues, so the lower part must cross the hips and the diagonal crosses the sternum and collarbone (see Plate 3).

If you are pregnant, or your belly bulges, the lower part must go below the bulge and the upper part round it. For all women the diagonal passes between the breasts or severe bruising could result.

Modern cars have adjustable upper belt anchorages to help bring the diagonal to the right point on the collarbone. The handbook explains how to do this in your car, though some adjust automatically.

Insight

For those of us over six feet, adjusting the upper anchorage is just a matter of sliding it as high as it goes. For the more vertically challenged, a general rule of thumb is that if it keeps slipping off your shoulder it is too low, and if you constantly push it away from your neck, it's too high.

REAR SEATBELTS

In the back, most cars have inertia reel belts for the outer seats but they may be combined with either a static lap belt in the middle or another three-point inertia reel. A lap belt must go across the hips and be tight enough to stop you quickly without being uncomfortable as you sit. Some three-point centre belts unclip completely from the seat to allow it to fold. They have two buckles, sometimes colour-coded. It's easier to work out which buckle goes where before anyone gets in the back – the one on the end of the belt goes in first, then the one that slides up and down is pulled across just like any other seatbelt.

Rear seatbelts not only protect the person sitting in the back but stop them flying into the people in the front, which is frequently fatal (see 'Belt up' below). Incidentally, if you are carrying heavy loads, it is safer to do up the rear belts if nobody is in the back because it supports the seat against the load in a crash (it also stops the buckles rattling).

Belt up

In most countries where seatbelt use is compulsory, only the driver is legally responsible for ensuring they and children in the car use them. However, you have a moral responsibility to your passengers to at least remind them to wear belts, which could also protect you from any claims they may make following injury. But you would also be entirely justified in refusing to carry someone who won't belt up because their unrestrained body poses a threat to the lives of everyone else in the car. In a collision at just 30 mph they are thrown forward with a force 30 times their own weight, so an adult man hits other passengers as if he weighed the same as an elephant. Front seat passengers are regularly killed when their skulls are smashed by unbelted rear passengers hitting them.

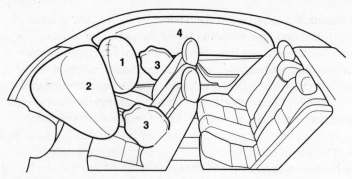

Figure 3.3 Typical airbags – 1 driver, 2 front passenger, 3 side, 4 curtain.

AIRBAGS

Airbags are important safety features but can be dangerous if misused. Your car's handbook explains where they are in your model so you can avoid abusing them. Be particularly careful not to put objects over them, like mounting a mobile phone in front of one to become a missile if the bag goes off. Even a sticker in the wrong place can deflect an airbag from its life-saving path.

Airbags have sensors which should ensure they only go off in certain types of crash. They completely inflate, do their life-saving work, then deflate in about half the time it takes to blink so don't worry about their going off distracting you at a critical time.

Insight

I have been in one accident in which they went off and, while I remember everything else about it, I have no recollection of seeing the bag in front of me. I only knew it had inflated because I recognized the distinctive 'pop' from demonstrations I've seen of them. I've spoken to others who have been in crashes and my experience is almost universal, though most did not hear the pop because the crash was so much louder. One policewoman was so convinced the bag had failed in a head-on crash that her sergeant told her to see the wreck: she found the airbag laying over the wheel with a big lipstick 'O' where her face had hit it.

If you need a baby seat in the front seat, the car's handbook explains if and how you can disable the passenger airbag. This is usually done with a key operated switch which may be hidden in the door side of the fascia or in a glove box. In cars with passenger airbags that can be disabled there are two airbag warning lights, one showing the bag has been disabled and the other showing there is a system fault, so be sure you know which is which.

Top tip

If the airbag fault light comes on it must be professionally checked as soon as possible.

CHILD SEATS

New cars have **Isofix** child seat fixing points which were designed by the motor industry working with the International Standards Organization after surveys showed the majority of child seats were not fitted properly. Isofix comprises two lower anchorages in the back edge of the car's seat with another behind the seat to which the child seat's upper anchor attaches.

The car's handbook explains which of the car's seats they are on and how to use them. In some cars the lower ones are behind pop-out or hinged covers in the seats, usually marked with an anchor or child seat icon; in others you have to feel between the cushion and lower seatback to find the loops. The loop for the upper anchorage is often on the parcel shelf in the back of a saloon but in other cars it may be on the seatback or in the boot, where it may be behind carpet cut-outs. But don't mistake load tie down points for them – check the handbook.

If your car has Isofix but your child seat isn't compatible, it is sensible to replace the seat because this fixing system is far safer, with the seat becoming part of the car's structure rather than being strapped in with the child. Non-Isofix seats install in a variety of ways so it is vital you read the manufacturer's instructions carefully. Since May 2008, all child seats in Europe have had to comply with the UN ECE 44.03 standard, which has been on sale for years.

You must also match the seat to the child. Children's body proportions change as they grow and with younger children their heads are proportionately much bigger than an adult's head (a child of four or five may have the same hat size as its mother). Because of their changing shape, the support and protection children need changes as they grow: a baby is far more prone to neck injury, because of the size of its head, than a 12-year-old. In addition, a seatbelt has to pass stresses onto the skeleton, as described earlier for adults, and this is impossible to arrange for children without the help of a special child seat.

Hugged to death

Many adults think a child is safe in their arms or sharing their seatbelt but this could not be further from the truth. In an accident the child will be crushed as the adult folds up on them and if they are sharing a belt, the child will take the full force of the adult's body hitting the belt. In addition, the babe in arms is unlikely to stay there: anyone who has been in a severe impact or roll-over accident knows you have little control over your arms against the extreme forces involved.

The correct seats are as follows (these are 'appropriate child restraints' in UK law):

▶ *Rear-facing baby seats: for children weighing up to 13 kg which should see them to one year old.*
▶ *Forward-facing child seats: for those between 9 and 18 kg, which is between about nine months and four years old.*
▶ *Booster seats: for children from 15 kg and above, which means from about four years old.*
▶ *Booster cushions: for children from 22 kg, or about six years old.*

When you drive abroad with children, check local laws – there are considerable variations, with some countries having minimum ages for children travelling in the front. In most countries, the driver is liable for prosecution if children are not safely restrained.

UK child seat laws

Children under three must use the correct child restraint (seat) in any vehicle. The only exception is in a taxi when a restraint is not available.

In vehicles with seatbelts, children must use an appropriate child restraint from the age of three until they are 135 cm (4 ft 5 in) tall. The only exceptions are:

▸ *in a taxi when a child restraint isn't available*
▸ *in 'an unexpected necessity' when one isn't available*
▸ *when two occupied child seats in the back of a car stop you installing another (it would be safer to use a proper child restraint in the front if there is no active airbag).*

You must not use a rear-facing baby seat in the front seat with an airbag unless it has been deactivated manually or automatically.

A UK Department of Transport pamphlet on child seats is available and can be downloaded from www.thinkroadsafety.gov.uk. Its safety advice should be followed in any country.

CHILD LOCKS

Child safety locks have been mandatory on cars with rear side doors for years. They usually take the form of a tiny lever somewhere near the lock on the part of the door hidden when it is closed. Some cars have something like a screw head you can insert the end of a key into so there is no chance of it being flipped by accident. A few cars have electronic locks that can be activated with a switch in the front of the car.

When they are activated, they stop the rear doors being opened from inside for two reasons: first, children have opened car doors, deliberately or by accident, and fallen from them on the move, and second they also mean a child can't open the door and rush out when it is unsafe to do so. But remember they are on – some adults panic if they can't open the door and start to exert extreme force on the handles. It is also embarrassing to ask a passer-by to let you out of your own car.

Loads

The safest place to carry objects in your car is in the boot because that separates them from the people and means their movement is unlikely to distract the driver. However, even there they should be stowed with care because in normal driving, heavy or hard objects can do considerable damage to the car and in an accident they may even break through into the passenger compartment.

Many cars now have load tie-down points and a pair of bungee straps to use with these costs very little but can save a lot of damage to the car and your baggage. Even with light objects it is worth slipping them under the straps so you are not distracted by the sound of them sliding around the boot. Some car manufacturers' accessories also include nets to use with the tie-down points, which are expensive but more versatile than bungee straps.

When carrying heavy objects, do the rear seatbelts up to help support the seatbacks in an accident. The seatbelts can also be used to restrain objects carried in the car.

If you carry anything in the car it must not interfere with the driver's access to controls or the view out of the car. It is even more important for large objects to be restrained in the cabin, and never put them on top of the rear shelf or load cover. Even a book flying the length of a car in a crash can cause serious injury because it is capable of reaching the velocity of a bullet by the time it reaches the front of the car. Small objects, like tubes of sweets, should be placed where they can't roll away because you may be tempted to reach after them on the move or they may roll under your feet or jam the pedals when you brake.

If a long object means driving with the tailgate or boot open, always open a window in the front of the car so air flows through to stop exhaust fumes being sucked in the back.

UP ON THE ROOF

Avoid using a roof rack if you can. Even empty, the drag they create adds significantly to the car's fuel consumption and can create irritating, and tiring, wind noise.

If you have to use one, loads must be securely attached. Remember, these objects have to stay up there as the car corners in what can be the equivalent of hurricane force winds (if you're doing 70 mph into a 20 mph headwind, that's 90 mph blowing over the car). Long or flat loads, like boards, should be tied down to the front of the car, as well as the side of the rack, because the wind gets under them.

Loads must not be wider than the car or stick out in front. If they stick out behind the car you must mark the end with a brightly coloured object. Make sure the ends of ropes and straps are tied off as short as possible because if they whip around they are a threat to passing pedestrians or two-wheelers, and may damage the car.

10 THINGS TO REMEMBER

1 Being comfortable helps you concentrate and reduces fatigue.

2 Head restraints can save you from crippling or fatal injury, so adjust them properly.

3 Do not slouch and avoid sitting with your chin up.

4 Seatbelts must be adjusted to cross your hips, sternum and collarbone, not soft tissue.

5 Pregnant women must route the belt around the bulge.

6 Rear seatbelts not only protect those in the back but stop them hitting those in the front.

7 Airbags save lives but can cause injury if abused.

8 Never use a baby seat in the front seat with an active airbag.

9 If your car has the correct attachment points, use an Isofix child seat for optimum safety but match it to the child's age and stature.

10 Always secure loads and do not carry things in the passenger compartment that might become lethal missiles in a crash.

4

Planning a journey

In this chapter you will learn:
- *how to plan a journey*
- *how direction signs are coded*
- *how to use satellite navigation.*

Planning a journey is important in enabling you to concentrate on the job of driving instead of worrying about where you are going. On a short trip in an area you are familiar with, this may mean nothing more than working out the best order to make your calls. On a long journey you can plan a route itinerary so you know where you are going, in which towns you make major turns and where you are going to stay if you must make a stopover.

Dangers of autopilot

Beware of the over-familiar route. The risk is that you get so used to driving it that you go into autopilot mode, letting your mind wander or failing to recognize that conditions, or even road layouts, have changed. Try taking an alternative route occasionally, but if you can't, be aware that your concentration may lapse.

This is particularly dangerous on long but familiar routes when fatigue may add risk to autopilot mode. Your familiarity can make the distances seem shorter so where, in unfamiliar

(Contd)

territory, you might take a break with 30 miles to go, on familiar ground you may decide to carry on because 'it's not far'. If you find you get to a point on the journey with no recollection of the last few miles, you must take a break because that is a sure sign of fatigue and familiarity taking over.

Direction signs

The UK's direction signing is better than most countries' in its comprehensive nature but the way it is arranged is fairly typical of the systems used around the world.

Its basis is that there are certain major towns whose names are used to navigate major routes and as long as you know the next major town on your route you should be able to follow the signs from one major town to the next. In theory, where a sign lists more than one town, the next town should be first on the list, though the capital is often the exception to the rule (probably because the people who plan all this are mostly based there and so presume that everyone else wants to go there as well).

This can also fall down in the few areas, like central Sussex, where there is a large patch with many modest sized towns but none the planners and mappers thought big enough to label as a major town. So you arrive at a junction thinking 'the next town I go through is Anytown', not realizing that the next major town is one many miles beyond that and not even on your route. However, most road atlases pick out the major towns in some way, so you should be able to see if you are entering an area like this when planning your route.

COLOUR-CODING

Direction signs in most countries are colour-coded. In most of Europe, the same colour-coding system as the UK's is used: a blue background for motorways; green on primary routes; and white with black lettering on other routes. On non-motorway routes, motorway names are picked out with a blue background and on 'other' routes the primary road numbers are shown on a green background. Tourist routes, information points and attractions are shown with a brown background.

Insight

We've all experienced 'motorway blur' where, because they tend to look the same, you suddenly find yourself thinking 'have we joined the M25 yet or are we still on the M11?' If that happens, look out for the periodic marker signs that have now been added to motorways. These replace one of the little blue and white roadside marker posts but can be read from the road and they say something like 'M11 B 1541' which tells you, and the police and Highways Agency, that you have just passed marker 1541 on the M11's carriageway B.

Paper planning

The traditional way of route planning is using paper maps. When you buy a road atlas make sure it is current and change it at least every other year. The UK's Ordnance Survey government mapping organization reckons there are around 3,000 changes a year to the UK's road system so an old atlas may mean you no longer use the best route and might get you lost. Get as large a scale and format as you can: a small book may be easier to store and carry but it is not so easy to use. Spiral binding is best because the book stays open, even when resting on a car seat.

USING THE ATLAS

Start planning your route by looking at the small scale pages that show a large area of the country with all the main routes depicted. On these it is easy to see the general direction you need to follow, but don't ignore areas without primary routes marked because there may be a quick secondary route across them. Note the major towns you go through or past.

Then turn to the large-scale pages and plan the route. Remember that a twisting single carriageway road may look more direct, but a longer dual-carriageway is likely to be quicker. Anything going through a major town will be slow during the rush hour.

Top tip

Look for landmarks near junctions. It is easy enough to know when you've arrived at your turn if it is a numbered motorway junction or in a village centre but not if is a minor road off a rural route or in a large town. If you know you go through Fordham and then take the first right after the railway, you'll know when you are near it. This is why it is useful if your atlas shows roadside restaurants and tourist attractions, even if you have no intention of using them.

ROUTE WRITING

Write your route down, remembering you may want to refer to it quickly or in poor light. If you do it on a word processor, pick an easily read font like Arial or Helvetica in at least 12 point and double space between instructions. You don't need to write the whole trip down: if you know the way to, say, the A1, just start the route with 'A1 north for Peterborough'. Always write the road number and the name of the major town. Use a consistent format like this:

▶ *'A1 north for Peterborough' means you're going in that direction but are leaving the A1 before you get there.*
▶ *'A1 past Peterborough and Stamford' means you stay on the A1 until you've passed those towns.*
▶ *'A52 into Grantham' means you enter the town to find another road.*
▶ *'A607 through Melton Mowbray' means you follow the road through the town.*

That will get you along the primary routes but then you might write:

'A607 through Melton Mowbray for Leicester, 10 ml to r/b 2nd exit, uc to Syston'.

This means you are driving along the A607 towards Leicester but at a roundabout 10 miles from Melton you take the second exit which is an unclassified road to Syston. If there is a village on the route before the junction it may help to add 'through...'

On minor country roads all you can do is list the villages and follow the signs. The trouble with maps is you eventually get to a point where to find the individual address you have to ask locally because you can't have a street map of everywhere in the country. However, there are now plenty of mapping websites on the internet where you can type in an address or postcode to see the exact location of your destination. They all allow you to zoom in and out so you can zoom out to help locate it on your road atlas and zoom in to print out the detailed map for when you get to the town. For the UK, look at www.streetmap.co.uk and www.ordnancesurvey.co.uk, while www.multimap.com covers most of the world (it will take you to your own country's page first so if you want a different country, click on the sitemap link).

TIMING

One problem with paper route planning is estimating journey times. Most road atlases have markings showing distances between points along the roads, which gives you a reasonable estimate of the distance. On out of town routes outside peak periods, if you assume an average speed of 40 mph, you won't be far out, but journeys in peak periods can be considerably slower if they pass close to large towns. Time of day and whether schools are on holiday can also significantly extend journey times, as does bad weather.

Electronic route planning

Searching a software sales website for 'route planner' revealed a choice of 48 programmes from companies ranging from mapping specialists to Microsoft and covering individual countries or whole continents. One even claimed to provide routes worldwide, even though digital mapping is incomplete outside Europe and the USA.

Such software has the great advantage that it takes seconds for it to plan a route complete with an exact mileage and an estimated journey time. However, they are not infallible and may suggest routes that use unmade tracks even in developed countries, while all fail to adjust journey times according to likely traffic. For example, their journey times are the same for lightly used motorways, where high speeds can be maintained, as for the world's busiest motorway, the M25 around London, which is notorious for its frequent congestion.

However, the better programmes allow a high degree of personalization so you can choose what sort of roads you want to use, ask them to avoid certain areas and adjust average speeds to suit your driving style. You can also set 'via' points so if you feel it would be better to go via a different town or road you can force the programme to plan a route that way.

Even then, check the route is sensible on the map before printing it out. If it doesn't print it in a font or format you find acceptable, you may be able to copy and paste it into a word processor document. With some, you can save the route and view it in a web browser, like Internet Explorer, which also allows you to change the type size before you print it.

Top tip

Some route planning programmes allow you to use them on a laptop linked to a hand-held **GPS** navigation unit, so they work like satellite navigation (see below). However, portable sat nav has become so cheap it almost certainly undercuts the cost of the GPS and programme and is easier to use in a car.

ONLINE

There are many websites offering route planning services similar to the computer route planning programmes. In the UK you'll find them at www.theaa.co.uk, www.rac.co.uk and the Government-funded www.transportdirect.info, among others. Traffic information to help with journey planning is available at www.highways.gov.uk.

These are not generally as versatile as a programme but have the advantages of being free and are likely to use more up-to-date mapping. They also take account of current traffic conditions, which isn't always a blessing: there may be a jam now towards the end of your four-hour trip but will it still be worth a detour when you get there?

Some mobile phone operators also provide online mapping for handsets with internet access. They have the added advantage of knowing where you are so they can show you maps of your current location. However, they can be expensive to download frequently.

Insight

I find Google Earth is very useful for route planning, even with sat nav. Not only will it plan a route for you, giving you a good idea of journey time, but the aerial photographs allow you to zoom in and look at your destination. This means you can see where the entrance to a large site is or find a particular building and see what landmarks are around it. It is often helpful if someone has given you directions with landmarks: if they said 'turn left after the farm shop' you may not be able to follow that on a map, but the shop may be obvious in an aerial photo. I also find that if you are going to an event at, say, a large country house, the address given is often no more than the name of the nearest village or a postcode that is actually the estate's administrative office down the road. With Google Earth you can find the entrance to the estate and plan your route to there or get a longitude and latitude reading to

(Contd)

use on any sat nav with a GPS route finding facility. Google Earth is not a website like the others mentioned here but you download free software at http://earth.google.com/ which uses mapping obtained via the web as you use it. However, you must have broadband.

Satellite navigation

Satellite navigation uses signals from geo-positioning satellites (GPS, as used by cruise missiles) combined with a built-in compass and digital mapping. It shows you where you are and where to go as well as giving voice instructions so you don't have to keep watching the map (there are cheap built-in systems with no map display which are almost useless because you can't check the route). It has become increasingly more accurate and sophisticated, though it is only as good as the digital mapping so you still need to check that the route looks sensible.

Many car makers offer built-in systems which have the advantage of being virtually thief proof, safe in an accident (they won't fly round the car) and able to integrate other car systems into the screen, perhaps using the screen for easy diagrammatic adjustments of the stereo or air conditioning. But they are much more expensive than portable systems, which can be used in any car or while on foot. They are also not so easily updated because few offer any way of adding map, software or 'points of interest' updates downloaded from the internet.

However, if you use a portable system, make sure you put it where it will not interfere with airbags going off and when you leave the car remove or hide the unit and all the cables and fixing brackets or it may not be there when you return. Leaving the bracket on view can encourage a break-in by someone hoping that the unit is in the glove box.

All sat navs have their quirks but you'll soon learn them. For some, the 'quickest route' may mean making long detours just to use more motorway or avoid going through a village, while on others the 'shortest route' might take you off a dual-carriageway only to return at the next junction, just because going through the village was 200 metres shorter. The best sat navs offer a choice of routes and all allow you to tailor routes and options.

Many built-in systems use the **Traffic Message Channel** to warn of jams and help plan routes around them. This is a service available in the UK and some other countries where the information is broadcast as a silent, coded signal alongside a normal nationwide station, though the radio does not have to be tuned to that station. Indeed, some even monitor the channel while the car is parked with the ignition turned off.

Many portable systems have a way of adding traffic information and planning routes round jams, though they usually need an internet-capable mobile phone with **Bluetooth** connection. You can also download all kinds of 'points of interest' for them, to cover everything from speed cameras and low bridges to the locations of fast-food restaurants, supermarkets and DIY stores.

Using sat nav properly has been proven to make drivers more relaxed and safer because they can concentrate on driving instead of whether they've missed their turning or arguing with their passenger 'navigator'. However, you can only use it properly if you know how it works so you can set everything up correctly and easily.

Do not try to plan a route on the move: most systems have a safety setting that only allows minor adjustments while the car is moving so don't be tempted to turn that off. Find out how you cancel route guidance because nothing is more frustrating than having it persistently telling you to turn round when you know where you're going or have changed your mind about your destination. If you need to change anything about your route or the unit, stop first.

If you know most of your route you can ask the unit to plan it before you leave and then activate the route guidance when you get close to where you leave the known route. However, if the system has real-time traffic information or speed camera locations it may be better to use it all the time.

Top tip

Most sat navs have the ability to identify your current location complete with road names and GPS longitude and latitude. It may be called a 'help me' or 'find me' facility. Knowing how to use it could save lives in an accident, not least because the GPS position pinpoints you for air ambulances.

Digital dummies

Don't let sat nav turn you into a digital dummy. There are constant reports of people blindly following sat nav directions and getting bogged down on unmade tracks, stranded in flooded fords or wrecking caravans under ultra-low bridges. It seems drivers question a spouse with a map, but accept bad advice from a machine.

Digital mapping is far from perfect and though some now differentiate between a road and an impassable track, it still makes mistakes in both directions. Sat nav does not excuse you from obeying road signs warning of narrow roads, cul de sacs, one-way streets, road closures and height limits. Above all, it does not excuse you from using common sense: it can't know that the river at a ford is a metre above normal levels, but you can see the swirling torrent.

As with a road atlas, you must keep maps up-to-date. Many manufacturers offer download updates or sell them on memory cards, CDs or DVDs, according to the system, and these are much cheaper than they used to be.

Traffic information

Traffic information has never been easier to get. At least the main roads of most European countries and the more populated areas of the USA are monitored by traffic sensing systems, backed up by people in control centres and radio stations with their own observers phoning in reports.

As we've said, some sat nav systems monitor such information, at least advising you of traffic problems on a planned route, and sometimes showing you those nearby even if no route is planned.

ON THE RADIO

If your car has an **RDS** (radio data system) radio, which displays the name of the channel it is tuned to, it certainly has a traffic programme setting (usually shown on the button and display as TP). This automatically interrupts whatever you are listening to and plays traffic information being broadcast by any other station in range. This can be very irritating because on a bad day it constantly interrupts with news of problems on routes far from yours as the local stations from two counties away may still be within range. Indeed, it may even interrupt to say there are no problems two counties off.

In Europe some countries, including the UK, have a Traffic Message Channel (TMC) which is available on some RDS radios and sat nav systems (see earlier section). This is a digital signal broadcast nationally alongside the audio signal and it delivers traffic information to some car audio systems in text form, with some even receiving and storing it when the radio is off. The messages are displayed either automatically or if you press a button. Radios can filter out those too far away to be relevant and you may be able to search by road name.

For technical information on RDS and TMC, visit www.rds.org.uk.

ONLINE

The websites mentioned for route planning also offer traffic information, though you may have to plan a route to get it. Some internet service providers, and the UK's **Highways Agency** at www.highways.org.uk can provide constant traffic information feeds to your computer by broadband.

BY PHONE

Most mobile operators offer a voice traffic information service via a dedicated number which recognizes where you are and gives local information. Most also allow you to dial in at least motorway numbers to get the traffic situation on that road. It pays to set this up with a quick dial number or with voice recognition for hands-free dialling. The same service, without the location ability, is also available on UK landlines on 08700 660115.

USING TRAFFIC NEWS

Having found out what is happening ahead, how do you use it? You must consider whether it will be easier and less stressful to sit it out in the queue or whether you should make a detour. Don't try planning a route in a traffic queue unless it is completely stationary or you may drive into the car in front.

If the alternative route is largely rural you may find it will be quicker and less stressful than waiting, but if it is urban it may quickly snarl up when others have the same idea as you. Remember, too, that it is unlikely you will be able to make up time on a route that isn't as direct as the one you were on and if you are off the motorway or dual-carriageway, driving will need even more attention. If you are worried about being late, phone ahead rather than trying to meet the deadline.

If the problem is a long way off, work out where your point of no return is and check the information when you get closer. Traffic clears quite quickly after most accidents so, unless it is a major incident, there is no point planning an alternative route if the more direct one may be moving by the time you get there.

10 THINGS TO REMEMBER

1 *Planning a journey before you leave helps make driving less stressful because you know where you're going.*

2 *Note the major towns on the roads you will be using so you know what to look for on direction signs.*

3 *Establish a standard way of writing routes to avoid confusion later.*

4 *Avoid trying to read a map on the move.*

5 *Route planning programmes are quicker than reading a paper map and can be used on any computer.*

6 *Free online route planners are often as good as costly programmes but you can only use them where you have an internet connection.*

7 *Properly used satellite navigation systems are safer than trying to read a map.*

8 *If your sat nav has a safety mode to stop you fiddling with it on the move, use it – never try to programme a sat nav route while driving.*

9 *Use your common sense and do not take an unsuitable route just because your human or electronic navigator told you to.*

10 *Programme a traffic information service number into your mobile phone with a voice tag.*

5

....

Setting out and urban driving

In this chapter you will learn:
- *which things to check before setting off*
- *how to cope with traffic*
- *about urban driving.*

Journeys start in town for most people, so that's where we'll begin. But before we take off into the traffic it is always a good idea to make sure everything is in order.

Even if you did the regular checks recently (see below) things may have gone wrong since, and town dwellers can't rule out the risk of vandalism and theft from the car. So get into this routine:

1 *Take a walk round the car looking for damage, leaks, soft tyres and potential obstructions (it is better to find the beer bottle before you drive over it).*
2 *Check lights, windows and mirrors are reasonably clean.*
3 *Ensure all luggage is safely stowed.*
4 *Make sure you have everything you need (mobile, money, credit cards, children, bags).*
5 *Get in and check everything is as it should be.*
6 *Do up your seatbelt and check passengers have fastened theirs.*

By taking an ordered approach from the start you can concentrate on your driving from the beginning of the journey rather than driving along wondering if you've remembered your briefcase or being distracted by checking whether the kids have belted up.

Regular checks

To ensure your safety and protect your car, at least once a month you must do the following checklist:

▶ *Tyres: check pressures and for tread depth and damage to the tread and sidewall. Incorrect pressures reduce the tyres' effectiveness and increase fuel consumption and tyre wear. Tyres are all that keeps you on the road.*
▶ *Oil: check level with the dipstick and top up if necessary with the correct grade.*
▶ *Coolant: check level in the translucent expansion bottle. Have sudden drops investigated.*
▶ *Brake and other fluids: never drive a car showing marked drops in the levels of brake, steering or clutch fluids because these systems may fail.*
▶ *Washer bottle: legally you must have working washers. Use windscreen washer fluid for efficient cleaning and to help prevent it freezing. (Washing-up liquid foams up too much.)*
▶ *Lights: check they are clean, undamaged and working.*
▶ *Battery: make sure the terminals are clean and tight. Check fluid levels in batteries that are not 'maintenance free' and top up with deionized water if it is below the minimum mark.*

If you need to know more about these checks and caring for your car, see *Car Buying and Ownership* in this series.

Insight

I make a point of doing these checks on the first weekend of the month because then I do not have to work out when I last did them.

Starting

Many people think they know how to start a car so they skip that in the handbook, but those who passed their tests before fuel-injection was commonplace, those switching to diesel and those with cars with security and starter safety devices may have problems.

NO FEET

Modern cars' engine management systems supply precisely the amount of fuel required for starting so putting your foot on the throttle pedal while you turn the key, as you would with a carburettor system, messes this up. It could give starting problems and certainly wastes fuel with an environmental impact.

DIESELS

Diesels have a device called a **glowplug** to warm the combustion chambers to aid starting. You turn the ignition on and wait until a warning light, with a symbol like a light bulb filament, goes out before turning the key to start the engine, with your foot off the throttle. Glowplugs normally do their job quicker than you can fasten your seatbelt. It is an essential process when the engine is cold and failure to do it in very cold weather could result in the pistons pushing against unburned fuel and acting as hydraulic rams, which damages the engine. It is not so important on a hot engine so the latest technology sees the glowplugs and their warning light only come on when required.

IMMOBILIZERS

Most cars today have engine immobilizers and a few cut in if you do not start the car within a short time of unlocking it. The car will not then start until you use the remote control to relock and unlock it, which you can do from inside. Immobilizers and alarms are usually only deactivated if you unlock the car with a remote control: they stay on if you use the key in the door, so the alarm will sound.

TRANSMISSION SAFETY SWITCHES

All automatics have a gearbox safety switch which stops them starting unless they are in the park position, which locks the transmission, though some also start in neutral. A few manual gearbox cars, mostly from America and Korea, also have a safety switch on the clutch pedal so they only start with the pedal depressed. It is a good idea to do that anyway because it lessens the load on the starter by totally disengaging the engine from the transmission.

Fuel

It's easy to forget, so get into the habit of checking the fuel gauge as soon as you have started the engine, even if you filled it last night. This way you never set off on a journey without knowing whether you need to stop for fuel and you won't be caught out by the fuel warning light coming on just after you've joined the motorway with the next services 30 miles away.

It also means you will spot if fuel has leaked out or been stolen and if you need more you can plan where you are going to buy it so can choose a cheaper filling station.

Insight

Be particularly careful to check fuel on cars with exceptionally long ranges. For example, some diesel hatchbacks can do 600–700 miles on a tank full, which makes it far too easy to forget about it, especially if you are used to less frugal cars.

Top tip

While you are checking the fuel, glance round the instrument binnacle to make sure all the warning lights have gone out after their initial starting test phase. If any are still on, don't ignore them: you may be in a hurry, but you will be delayed a lot longer if the car breaks down because you didn't check something.

FILL HER UP

When you pull in to a filling station remember that petrol is dangerous stuff, so don't smoke or use a mobile phone; a phone's signals can create sparks from metal in certain conditions. Make sure you have chosen a pump delivering fuel suitable for your car and that you pick up the right nozzle. If someone serves you, make sure they use the right pump. (Getting it wrong is covered in Chapter 11.)

It is easier to pull up to a pump on the same side as your fuel filler but most pumps have hoses long enough to stretch to the far side of all but the largest cars. Open the fuel filler before going to get the pump nozzle and take time to look at the pump for instruction notices if it is a type you are not familiar with. Most these days automatically trigger a light in the station's control desk for the fuel flow to be started but there are still a few where you must press a button first. Some pumps offer a 'pay at pump' option with a button choice to make before you can fill up.

Put the nozzle right into the filler neck: this reduces the fumes blown out and ensures the pump's cut-off will work without blowing back fuel. However, on some cars the filler pipe turns in a way that makes the cut-off work prematurely and you may need to pull the nozzle back a little to get the fuel to flow freely.

Fill the tank until you reach your price limit or the pump clicks off. If the latter, wait a few seconds, then pull the trigger again because sometimes fuel foams up and activates the cut-off early, especially with diesel, so waiting ensures it is full. But do not overfill the tank: fuel expands as it warms up and you've just pumped it from a cool hole in the ground.

You must return the nozzle to its holster to turn the pump off and make the quantity register in the pay kiosk: check the amount and pump number. Replace and lock your car's filler cap and at least take the keys with you when you go to pay, preferably locking the car to protect your valuables. (Thieves know filling stations are good places to snatch mobile phones, portable electronics and CD collections.)

Look around you

Too many drivers get a mirror fixation when pulling away, perhaps because 'mirror, signal, manoeuvre' is drummed into us when learning to drive, but you must check all around you, not just behind. Even if you have the engine running and an indicator on, a pedestrian could have stepped into the gap between your car and the next without realizing you were about to pull out.

If you fixate on traffic approaching from behind, you may not notice that cars ahead of you are beginning to stop, and in narrow roads you may have to turn out to the wrong side of the road to pull out of your drive or parking space, so you must know what is coming from that direction.

Always look over your shoulder, as well as in the mirrors, because of the blind spot which can easily hide another car or two-wheeled vehicle. It is important to 'think bike' when pulling out because they are easily missed and very vulnerable. Cyclists in particular tend to pass close to parked cars, often passing between them and moving traffic, so the slightest outward movement by your car can result in a collision. Just seeing your indicator come on could make a cyclist flinch towards moving traffic.

Signal, manoeuvre

When you are sure there is nobody likely to be alarmed by a signal, put your indicator on. Signals do not give you a right to move out, they only show your intention and you can't assume everyone has noticed them, especially pedestrians.

Keep looking around you and when you are sure you can merge with the traffic safely, pull out and match its speed as rapidly as possible. *The Highway Code* says you should not pull out unless you can do so without causing others to change direction or slow down. The fact is that in many towns you would have to wait until the end of the rush hour to join the traffic if you complied totally with that. There is no excuse for pulling out and causing someone to swerve: it is dangerous because they may swerve into the path of another vehicle. You should avoid making others slow, but with heavy traffic you may have to pull out knowing you can't accelerate away fast enough to avoid making others slow down, but by that we don't mean making them slam on the brakes.

That said, look beyond the vehicles closest to you. Most of us get annoyed when we're the last car in a line and someone can't wait for us to go by before pulling out. Drivers of large vehicles need more consideration because if they are forced to slow down, it takes them longer to pick up speed again, which is awkward for them and has a knock-on effect to the rest of the traffic. It also harms the environment because they use more fuel regaining speed.

Insight

I have a real personal bug about this because people who pull out in front of you when they only had to wait a few seconds for a clear road always seem to be the ones who drive slower than necessary. Do it to me and I'll mutter swear words at you, but not everyone on the roads is so even tempered. There also seem to be a frightening number of urban drivers who, when pulling out, fail to notice when an approaching car is towing something, even if the trailer towers above the towcar.

Eye contact and courtesy

Many people have lost the art of making eye contact with strangers, especially in cities, but it can make a difference when driving.

We all sit in our little boxes, cut off from others, and in close traffic a glance at the driver acknowledges the person within the box. Try it, if you haven't, and you will be surprised how often it results in someone responding by letting you out into traffic. At the very least it lets you know the other driver has seen you, rather than just coincidentally stopping as if to let you out.

When someone offers you a courtesy, return it with a gesture of thanks, either by waving or mouthing 'thank you' with a nod if you can't let go of the wheel.

In turn, show courtesy to others. In heavy traffic you won't get there any quicker by blocking other people's attempts to join or leave the flow, so let people in and out of turnings, drives and parking spaces, and in queues don't add to the congestion by stopping across junctions, blocking them for drivers trying to turn into them. However, don't slam on the anchors to give way to people in case the person behind isn't expecting it.

Curiously, this is one area where women as a group could improve their driving. Women, especially older ones, have been shown to be more likely to ignore those trying to get into traffic, even stopping in front of them as they edge forward or try to turn across a queue. Perhaps it's a legacy of pre-equality 'ladies first' etiquette.

Cut and thrust

For new drivers and those not used to urban driving, its cut and thrust can be difficult to cope with. There is so much going on around you it is hard to take it all in and the crowded nature of the urban environment means there isn't room to give drivers advanced warning of where their route will take them. This is made worse by the attitude of some councils that putting up road names and direction signs might encourage more traffic, rather than ease congestion by letting us all know where we are and where we're going.

CONCENTRATION

Because town traffic can be slow moving it is very easy to let your mind wander as you inch forward. Try not to let that happen because if it starts moving suddenly, or when you arrive at the junction causing the hold up, it will take you more time to appraise the situation around you. If you stay aware of your surroundings, you will be in a better position to take advantage of changing situations and avoid being taken by surprise by, say, a cyclist who has edged into your blind spot.

So, keep a check on your mirrors even while stationary and don't be distracted by things that are nothing to do with the traffic, like shops or passers-by.

OBSERVATION

Observation is the key to good town driving. Use mirrors frequently because things are happening close to you, but for the same reason do not rely on them entirely because things that are close may only be in the mirror for moments. Make sure you always glance over your shoulder before moving over or changing lanes because the traffic around you is likely to be moving at the same speed as you, so something can stay in a blind spot for a very long time making it easy to forget you had seen a taxi there a while ago.

Don't forget you can also look through other cars and if you drop back from them it will be easier to see round them. Don't forget to look under them, too: many a day-dreaming pedestrian has been saved because a driver saw their feet as they walked out between parked cars.

Windows in buildings can also give you a useful view ahead. For example, if you are stopped behind a large vehicle, you may get early warning of the queue moving by checking the reflections in shop windows.

But remember there is more to urban streets than traffic. You must keep aware of the whole street scene so you notice cars coming out of premises along the way, pedestrians looking as if they plan to cross the road and cyclists ignoring the law by pedalling the wrong way up the street.

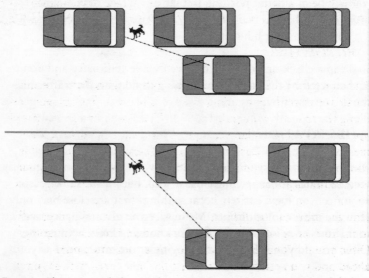

Figure 5.1 If you pass parked cars wide, you improve your view between them.

His fault?

Someone may have put themselves in danger by doing something stupid or against either the law or the accepted rules of the road but that doesn't absolve you from a moral and social responsibility to protect them from injury. In addition, it is *your* car that the cyclist going the wrong way round a roundabout will damage and *your* journey that will be interrupted while you sort out the accident.

BE POSITIVE

The motto for town driving could be 'Who dithers, loses' because the driver who hesitates about a move is likely to find someone else filling the space they intended to use. That doesn't mean cut people up, but don't signal a lane change or turn, start to move across then pull back. Not least because it confuses other drivers about your intentions: do you really mean it or have you just forgotten your indicator is on?

However, this can be difficult if you are new to a town, especially in the rush hour when everyone else knows where they're going. Often you don't get enough warning that your route turns ahead and you need to be in a particular lane (even with sat nav) and if this happens you can only signal your intention and try to create an opportunity to go where you want by slowing and easing over. But in the end you rely on the goodwill of others to let you do it so you must make your intentions clear, using a (polite) hand signal for emphasis if necessary and thank everyone who helps.

Unfortunately, in some complex one-way systems you may find there is so much traffic between you and your exit that you have no alternative but to go round again. Whatever you do, never stop suddenly or on a roundabout. Taking another lap on a roundabout is easy, but signal your intention and be aware that others may not expect you to do it, so they assume you're going to follow the flow.

Insight

It is annoying when someone suddenly decides they're in the wrong lane and needs to move over so everyone in the jam has to give way to them, but be considerate. You may know you need the left lane before the bend to get onto the motorway, but a stranger guided by inadequate road signs does not. Just remember, it will happen to you in a strange town one day.

RIGHT OF PASSAGE

In narrow roads drivers often have to give way to each other, perhaps by pulling into a gap in the parked cars. In general, the driver who has right of way is the one staying on the correct side of the road. However, you must be reasonable: if you have somewhere to pull in and they don't it makes more sense for you to pull over. Car drivers often cause problems for drivers of large vehicles, or those towing trailers, by expecting them to pull over even though there are only car-sized spaces along the road. It is usually easier for a car driver to find somewhere to pull in and it is certainly easier to reverse a car. Indeed, in town it can be very dangerous for a truck or towcar to reverse because they have a vast blind spot behind them and would often be unaware if they backed into someone.

Find calm and escape

Town driving can be very frustrating but getting flustered or angry only makes it more so. If you find it is getting on top of you, it may be wise to turn into a side street and find somewhere to stop while you cool off.

Try to do the same if you get lost. Once lost in town it can be very difficult to orientate yourself if you keep moving. If you turn off the main route, make sure you take note of the name of the road. If you have a town map you will find it easier to locate yourself by stopping near a junction where you can see both road names. If you have an internet-capable mobile phone, most service providers give links to mapping services that show you where you are and can even plan short routes, so you might be able to get it to show you how to get back to the through-town route you want.

Speed

It is in town that the misuse of speed can have the most dire consequences because it is here that different types of road user are in closest proximity and most likely to come into contact. Indeed, two thirds of injury accidents in the UK happen on roads with speed limits under 40 mph.

The UK urban speed limit is 30 mph and it is approximately the same in most countries. Many people think going 10 mph over this limit doesn't matter, but British research suggests otherwise. An adult pedestrian hit at 20 mph has a 95 per cent chance of survival, at 30 mph it drops to 80 per cent but at 40 mph they only have a 10 per cent chance of survival. Surprisingly, the survival rate for children at 40 mph is 10 per cent higher.

However, it is worth pointing out to the supporters of spending vast sums of money on speed cameras that according to government statistics, 'excessive' speed is involved in only one in five fatal accidents. But it must be remembered that speed can still be excessive even if you haven't broken the speed limit (something speed cameras ignore) because there are times when even 30 mph in a town is too fast.

The 30 mph limit may be too fast in narrow streets with parked cars down each side, outside schools at the start and end of the day, in heavy traffic, in poor visibility and in places where there are lots of pedestrians, especially if it is raining so they're hiding behind hats, hoods and umbrellas. A speed limit is just that, a limit, and it is up to the driver to judge whether they are driving at a speed sensible for the circumstances. Ask yourself:

- *Can I stop in the distance I can see?*
- *Will others have the time to see me?*
- *Is the speed preventing me taking in everything that's happening around me?*
- *Do I have space to take avoiding action at this speed?*
- *Am I able to stay far enough away from vulnerable road users?*

If the answer to any of these questions is 'no', you should slow down.

You must also be aware of changing circumstances, especially in town. Driving up a shady street at 30 mph may be perfectly safe, but when you turn into the sun and its glare is reducing your ability to see what is on the road ahead, is it still safe?

Insight

Some sat nav systems have the ability to warn you if you exceed the speed limit and the mapping's speed limit coverage is improving all the time in the UK. The great thing about it is that you can spend more time reading the road instead of constantly checking the speedo and, in unfamiliar places, it highlights changes in speed limit that have been poorly signed or that you missed.

Steering

No matter how tempting, never drive with only one hand on the wheel or elbows resting on the door because if anything happens you won't have full control. Drive with your hands kept at about 'ten-to-two' or 'quarter-to-three', always returning them there after changing gear or using any other control. The grip is light, preferably with thumbs outside the rim which stops you gripping too hard and means that if the road wheels hit anything, like a pothole or debris, the steering wheel spokes won't injure your thumbs if the steering kicks back.

Police drivers are taught to never cross their hands on the wheel and always feed it through their hands in a smooth push and pull motion. Though many drivers find this awkward at low speeds and unnecessary when making minor steering adjustments it is wise not to cross your arms because once they are crossed you can't make further adjustment if it is needed and there is a risk of getting your hands tangled up.

So to turn left you slide your left hand up no further than 11 o'clock and as you pull the wheel down to the left, your right hand slides down to five o'clock. You then grip with your right hand and push the wheel round as your left slides back up. Turning right is the opposite motion starting with your right hand moving up to one o'clock.

Slide the left hand up

Pull wheel down with left hand slide right down

Push wheel up with right hand, slide left up

Push wheel down with left hand, slide right up

Figure 5.2 Push pull steering reduces the risk of getting arms tangled.

Schools

Children going to and, particularly, home from school have their minds on other things and often don't have the experience to accurately judge vehicle speed and distance. Because of this, they are vulnerable.

Many towns now put lower speed limits around schools but even if they haven't you should slow down near them at times when children are about, especially in poor weather (rural schools usually turn out earlier than urban ones). Slowing down not only means the children have a better chance of survival in an accident, as explained earlier in the chapter, but you give yourself more chance to see them and can stop quicker.

Insight

Beware of the school-run parent. They often seem to see driving to the school as a chore of as little consequence as washing up so they usually have their minds on other things, especially with a car full of kids telling them about their day or arguing. Look out for them pulling out as they signal (or without signalling) or driving down narrow roads with little regard to whether they have right of way over those coming the other way.

As children no longer seem to walk anywhere, another danger at school day beginning and end is the vast numbers of cars dropping or collecting children, stopping with little regard to road safety or allowing other drivers to go about their business. If you are a parent making the school run, it is safer to let them walk a little further than to endanger lives by blocking drivers' view of school gates and crossings.

Keep back

Many drivers who are conscious of keeping a safe following distance on faster roads let it lapse on urban ones, though this is unwise because things can happen very quickly in towns.

You also have to consider the convoy effect: when you have a line of vehicles the effects of anything that the vehicles in front do is exaggerated as it goes along the line. So, if the car in front slows down, the next driver has to react to that and slow down too, but needs to slow a little more to make up for the reaction time. This ripples down the 'convoy' with each driver having to compensate for reaction time until the person at the end has to brake hard or ever stop. Get too close, and the fact that a driver ten cars ahead of you had to slow to let someone turn off could see you driving into the car in front.

You can still occasionally apply the two-second rule (see box below) in town when the traffic is moving, but keeping a safe distance also applies if you are stopped or crawling along. If you have allowed space it shouldn't cause you problems if the car in front stalls, breaks down or rolls back.

A simple rule of thumb for keeping your distance in queues is that when you stop you should still be able to see the back wheels of the vehicle in front. Use common sense, though: if it's a truck with huge wheels you could stop underneath its back bumper and still see the wheels. Similarly, if you drive something with a tall bonnet, like a substantial 4×4, stopping so you can still see the wheels of a low sports car in front could mean stopping a long way back.

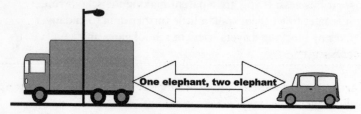

Figure 5.3 The car should pass the lamp-post two seconds after the truck.

Safety from elephants and fools

The simplest way of maintaining a safe following distance is the two-second rule because it doesn't involve judging distances and it adapts itself to your speed.

The old advice used to be to maintain a metre gap per 1 mph of your speed, so at 30 mph it was 30 metres and at 50 mph it was 50 metres. Trouble is, most of us couldn't accurately estimate 50 metres when standing still, never mind while driving at 50 mph, so the idea of timing it was put forward.

If you keep a two-second gap between you and the vehicle in front, it gives you time enough to react – the distance will automatically be greater at 50 mph than at 30 mph. There are many phrases you can use to time two seconds by saying them at normal talking speed: two favourites are 'One elephant, two elephant' and 'Only a fool forgets the two-second rule'. In the rain you can extend them with an extra elephant or two or by adding '… especially in the rain'.

So, as the car in front passes a 'marker', say a sign or a mark or shadow on the road, you start saying the phrase – if you pass the marker before you've finished, you should back off. We'll be referring to the two-second rule in other chapters as well.

Helping the car

The stop-start nature of urban driving can be stressful to the car as well as the driver, so give it some help.

GEARS

Some drivers think you can be lazy about gears in town, especially in queues where they may only be moving a short distance at a time. But incorrect use of the gears puts strain on the car's transmission and engine while increasing noise and fuel consumption, which harms the environment as well as your pocket.

If you were driving on a clear road you wouldn't dream of holding first gear for any longer than necessary: it's supposed to be the gear to get you moving. We all know that changing up reduces the engine speed making the car quieter but it also allows the engine to work more efficiently because you are maintaining the same road speed at lower engine revs. So, if you do even 50 metres in second or third gear instead of first, the effort of the gear changes will be rewarded with less noise and vibration and reduced fuel costs. The improvement in economy is small, but over a long trip or a week's commuting, it adds up.

However, using too high a gear is just as harmful, if not more so. Many cars will pull at just over 30 mph in top gear so the temptation for mechanically unsympathetic drivers in town traffic is to stick it in top and put up with the occasional judder when they let the speed drop too low. That judder is the engine's insides vibrating as it tries to pull the car forwards without being able to develop the torque (pulling power) needed for the job asked of it. It isn't good for the engine or fuel consumption. In addition, using top gear robs you of some of the control a lower gear gives, so the car's speed more easily increases without you being aware and then it won't lose it quickly enough when you come off the throttle, so you have to brake harder.

By dropping a gear you give the engine more leeway to cope with slight changes in speed and you grant yourself more control.

Insight

That judder is also irritating to many passengers and if they are more mechanically sensitive than you it lets them know you are not a driver who takes pride in the task or cares anything about the car or the environment. In short, it reduces their faith in your abilities on the road.

The right gear is something you have to learn. Nobody can tell you what the right gear for a given situation is because there are too many variables. It is affected by the gear ratios, the rev range over which the engine develops usable torque, what load the car is carrying, your road speed and whether the road goes up or down. Listen to the engine: if it sounds busy, try changing up; if it sounds as if it is struggling, change down.

The most efficient gear is usually the one that keeps the engine a few hundred revs either side of the point at which it develops peak torque (check your handbook), though some cars, especially diesels, develop useful torque over such a wide rev range that they can pull efficiently from very low revs.

EQUIPMENT

Modern cars have a lot of electrical equipment on top of all the vital electronics running engines and driving aids. At tickover, the **alternator** (the car's generator), which is driven by a belt from the engine, may not be spinning fast enough to provide all the power the equipment needs, so the demand starts to drain the battery.

Over a long journey this does not matter too much because you should drive part of it at a high enough speed for the alternator to provide enough power to run the equipment and charge the battery. But if all you do is short, urban journeys you could end up with low battery charge problems, perhaps finding it won't always start on dark, damp days.

So, when you are in slow traffic, turn off things you don't need to reduce the load on the alternator. For example, a heated rear screen uses as much power as full-beam headlights, so turn it off as soon as it has done its job. Keep the heater fan boosting to the lowest speed that does the job and don't play with electric windows.

Power usage also affects fuel consumption by putting extra load on the engine. A rear wiper only increases fuel consumption by about 0.2 litres of petrol an hour but run five unnecessary items like that and it's a litre an hour that could be saved. Having said all that, don't put miserliness before road safety.

Turn off pollution

Look at the average traffic jam and you'll see a line of cars ticking over and going nowhere. Those cars are all pumping exhaust gases into the atmosphere for no reason and they are not helping to disperse it like they do when they're moving.

So, if it looks like you may be stopped for any length of time by traffic or, say, at level crossing gates, switch off the engine if you can. To reduce emissions, increasing numbers of cars do this automatically as soon as you put the gearlever in neutral and apply the handbrake, restarting when you touch the throttle or clutch pedal. But if your car doesn't have this 'stop-start' technology, you can do it manually to save fuel (and it often has the magical effect of making the traffic move again).

However, don't do it at night or in poor visibility – you need lights for others to see you are there, or you may need the heating and fan to keep the windows from steaming up. Stop-start systems usually take account of such things.

Junctions

Junctions create the maximum opportunity for accidents because they bring opposing streams of traffic together, therefore it is vital that you make your intentions clear and are observant about what others are doing. Never assume someone is going to do something at a junction: just because someone signals to turn into the road you're trying to turn out of, it doesn't mean they will, so don't pull out unless you're sure they're turning. They may have forgotten their indicator is on or be turning into premises just beyond your road.

The information here assumes you are driving on the left. When you are driving on the right the rules suggested for turning right become the rules for turning left (that is, across the oncoming traffic) and vice versa. In countries that drive on the right, roundabouts go counter clockwise so you turn right to get on and off them, which means you reverse the signals given here (though in many countries, signals seem rare on roundabouts).

Room to turn

When any vehicle turns, the back takes a tighter line than the front and therefore passes closer to things on the inside of its turn. The front-to-rear difference grows with length so while modest cars need little turning space to allow for it, on long cars, like limousines and some seven-seat 4×4s, the rear wheels may be far enough over to clip kerbs if you turn as you would in a small car. That doesn't usually do much damage at low speeds if it's just a kerb, but if you do it in the wrong place it might be enough to damage your car or another vehicle, or to run over someone's feet. Remember this if you tow anything or hire a truck or longer car than you're used to.

With longer vehicles, including cars and trailer outfits, the difference between front and rear turning lines is significant. With a long lorry the driver may have to leave a car's width on his nearside to allow turning space and you get into that space at your peril. As the lorry turns it blocks your way out while the driver may not be able to see you in his mirrors until it is too late (see Plate 4).

LEFT TURNS

Left turns are the least feared by new drivers because they are simple to execute and are least likely to bring you in conflict with other traffic. But you must still be cautious because, particularly in towns, you can't see much of what is in the road you are turning into.

Check your mirrors, remembering to look along the passenger side for cyclists and motorcyclists. As you turn, particularly if it is a right-angled turn rather than into a sliproad, your vehicle will slow considerably so the cyclist you've just passed could easily catch you up. If you are not sure you can get far enough ahead of him to turn without risking broadsiding him, you'll have to slow and let him get ahead. If you do that, signal to let him know why you have slowed down: if you're lucky it might be a rare cyclist who is polite enough to speed up for you.

Remember that slowing down is part of the manoeuvre, so signal first. This lets the drivers behind know you will slow down.

Look out for pedestrians approaching the road you are turning into. They may not be aware of your intentions or have noticed you approaching from behind and may step out in front of you. Remember that children and other non-drivers may not recognize drivers' intentions from their changes in speed and road position as another driver would.

Be prepared to stop quickly as you turn into narrow town streets because there may be cars parked close to the corner or someone approaching the junction close to its centre line.

When to signal

In general the faster you are going the sooner you should signal, but in urban environments this must be treated with caution. You need to signal early enough to allow others to see and react to it, but not so early that you confuse people.

Look at what is between you and your junction. If you signal now, might you make someone think you are turning into the road before? Let's say there is someone waiting to come out of a filling station just before your turn: might they think you intend to turn into the same station and so pull out?

So, we can't say 'signal so many metres from the junction'; you must signal in good enough time to inform others but with due regard to the risk of misinforming them if you do not observe the situation before flicking the switch.

On wide roads with more than one lane of traffic in each direction, try to move over to the relevant lane far enough back to make two stages of it. So, you check the mirrors, signal and move over, drive along without an indicator for a short way, then mirror, and signal for the turn. That reduces the risk of cutting people up and of not seeing two-wheelers travelling on the other side of the lane you are turning from while giving others time to adjust to your intentions.

Insight

There is a school of thought that says you should only signal if you can see another road user who needs to be informed. While there may be a case for this on quiet country

(Contd)

roads, I think it unwise in town because the more crowded environment makes you more likely to miss someone who needs to know your intention. By signalling every time you maintain a good habit and alert those you can't see or haven't noticed, who may be dangerously close to you.

Right turns

Right turns usually frighten new drivers and with just cause. It brings you into conflict with two flows of traffic and correct positioning on the road is vital if you are to complete the turn safely and easily.

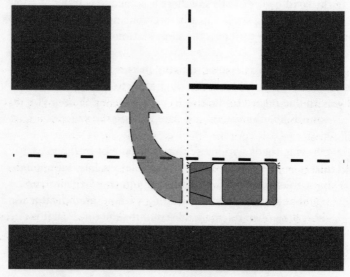

Figure 5.4 When turning right, stop in line with the side road's centre line.

GET SET

It is vital you know what is going on behind you because you are going to have to move out towards the centre of the road and then turn across it. You don't want to do either of these things into the path of someone who is overtaking you. Indeed, just because you are stopped in the middle of the road with your right indicator on, don't assume that will stop anyone being stupid enough to overtake you – there are those who just can't wait for others to move out of their way. So, check your mirrors, looking out for anyone with right turn indicators on.

When it is safe, signal and move towards the centre of the road. Don't do this too early: you frequently see people who hog the right lane of a dual-carriageway, stopping everyone from overtaking, simply because they are turning right two miles down the road. In town, though, you may get little warning of your turn ahead and if it is unsafe to move across you may have to go on and turn back.

POSITIONING

Many drivers fail to understand where they need to stop to turn right. Obviously you need to be to the left of the centre line of the road you are on, otherwise you obstruct traffic coming the other way and risk someone driving into you. But you must also be positioned to allow you to easily turn into the road you want to take.

To do this, imagine the centre line of the road you are turning into projecting out across the road you are on and stop just short of that line. Unless it's a very narrow road, that should allow the space to make the turn a right angle rather than a loop. With narrow roads you should stop further back and if they are single track roads you stop level with what will become the driver's side kerb.

Your indicator should be on all the time to draw attention to your car and show your intentions. If you have a long wait it may be sensible to apply the handbrake and put the gearbox in neutral, but if there is nobody stopped behind you, keep your foot on the brake pedal so the brake lights draw attention to the fact you are stopped.

⚠ Warning!

When you stop to turn right, try to do so with your wheels pointing straight ahead. If you stop with your wheels turned and are hit from behind you will be shunted into, or across, oncoming traffic with little chance to get out of their way. If your wheels are pointing straight ahead and are struck you have more chance of staying on your side of the road.

CROSSROADS

The correct way for two right-turning vehicles to pass at a crossroads is right side to right side, looping round each other. This means each driver has a clear view of traffic approaching them and the traffic can clearly see them.

However, not everyone seems to know this, so you may be forced to do it wrong and then need to take care. If you can't see enough, think carefully before edging forwards because oncoming drivers may not be able to see you and might not expect the nose of your car to project beyond the car blocking their view. You may be able to see through another car's windows, but if it is a large vehicle it may block your view and it is then safer to let them turn first.

Insight

Think before pulling into the junction. If there is a huge truck or a car towing a trailer planning to turn right from the opposite direction, it will need a lot of space and will block your view so it may be more sensible to let them make their turn while you hold back. But keep your signal going so that people behind you are aware of why you are in the middle of the road – and don't be surprised if someone behind you starts sounding their horn because they've looked no further ahead than your taillights.

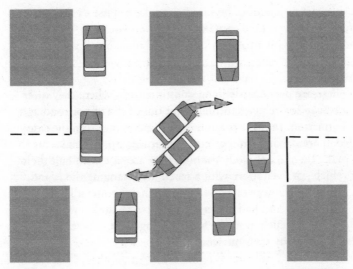

Figure 5.5 At a crossroads, turning driver's side to driver's side means they don't block each other's view.

On narrow crossroads and staggered ones it may be impossible to turn correctly. Some large junctions have right-turn lanes painted on them.

RIGHT-TURN REFUGES

Some larger junctions and dual-carriageways have what is known as a right-turn refuge: a gap in the central reservation, or in a specially built island, for vehicles turning right. These make right turns much safer, but only if they are used correctly. A very common, and dangerous, driving fault associated with this type of turn is the driver who stops as soon as his seat is level with the island, forgetting that a metre or two of his car is still overhanging the carriageway.

This is dangerous because a following driver may not expect you to be so careless and either hits your car or swerves into someone else to avoid it. In addition, at night a turning car's taillights viewed side on may not be visible enough for approaching drivers to see them in time.

At this sort of junction, be sure you make full use of the refuge. However, take care not to position your car so that road signs, which grow profusely on some islands, block your view.

> ## Insight
>
> These are particularly dangerous junctions where they offer a refuge for vehicles turning right out of the minor road at a T-junction. In this situation drivers emerging from the side road are driving straight into the refuge gap, which seems to make them more likely to think they are safe with half their vehicle, or even more with a truck, overhanging the island. I used to live near one and I and my neighbours all had near misses and had all seen accidents: we all knew never to assume a vehicle heading for the refuge would be entirely out of the way by the time we got there.

BOX JUNCTIONS

A box junction is one where a diamond grid of yellow lines is painted on the road. The aim is to keep the junction clear of traffic queues to avoid it grid-locking. You must not enter the grid unless your exit is clear, even if traffic lights are green, though you can stop to turn right in one. These are increasingly painted in front of fire and ambulance stations where blocking them could threaten lives by delaying emergency responses.

Roundabouts

The roundabout is common across Europe though rarely seen in the USA. Properly designed, and used correctly, it can maintain traffic flow without the use of lights. Note that roundabouts rotate clockwise where you drive on the left and counter-clockwise in countries that drive on the right. Most, if not all, countries now follow the UK lead that traffic on the roundabout has priority over those entering it.

APPROACH

On your approach to the roundabout, get into the correct lane
for your intended exit as soon as you can, making full use of
mirrors and signals as well as looking over your shoulder. This
can be difficult for town roundabouts where signing may be late
or inadequate and traffic heavy. Try to be aware of what others
are doing around you and in very slow-moving traffic look out for
those sneaking in where you least expect it.

On roundabouts with two approach lanes you normally use the
left lane to turn left or go straight on and the right lane for exits
beyond straight on. However, if the exit is a dual-carriageway it is
acceptable to use the right lane if there is slower traffic on the left,
though you must allow lorries extra turning space and keep a check
on what vehicles to your left are doing: it may be someone intending
to turn right who didn't get in the right lane in time.

On three-lane entries the left lane is for left turns, though
slow vehicles may use it for straight ahead, especially on dual-
carriageways. The centre lane is for straight ahead only and the
right lane for exits beyond straight ahead.

You do not have to stop at a roundabout if it is clear, but give
yourself time to judge the speed and distance of anything on it and
remember the danger of windscreen pillars hiding bikes and smaller
vehicles coming round.

If you are second in the queue to join a roundabout, always keep an eye on the car in front. It is far too easy to get engrossed in traffic coming round the roundabout and to try to drive into a gap forgetting there is someone in front of you who may be slower to take advantage of the opportunity to move off. In the same way, don't assume that because they have started to move off they will complete the exit: they could stall or stop because they feel they have misjudged the speed or position of oncoming vehicles. Most rear end shunts on roundabouts happen in one of these ways.

Open wide

There was a time when road planners thought the way to increase traffic flow through roundabouts was to increase the width of the road around them; they now realize that this makes it harder for drivers to judge when it is safe to enter it. This is because oncoming cars towards the centre of the roundabout appear further away and in terms of the roundabout's radius, they are. Unfortunately, the distance that matters is how far away from you they are in terms of the roundabout's circumference, because that determines how quickly they close on you. So take special care on wide roundabouts: take a good look at vehicles approaching you as you enter and beware of drivers entering unwisely as you go round (see Plate 5).

SIGNALS

If you are turning left you simply keep your left turn indicator on during the approach and through the roundabout, remembering to check it has cancelled as you leave.

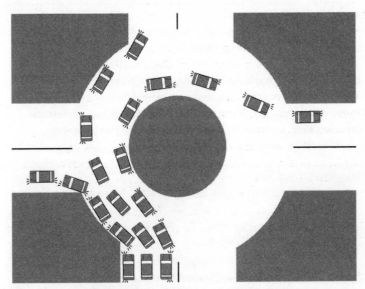

Figure 5.6 The correct signalling methods for roundabout exits.

For years the advice for straight on has been that you enter the roundabout with no signal and use the left turn one as you pass the exit before yours and for turning right you enter and go through the roundabout indicating right, then swap to left as you pass the exit before yours. Some road safety experts suggest it is better to use a right turn indicator for any exit other than left, so everyone knows you haven't just forgotten it. It is certainly sensible to treat any exit after 180 degrees from your entry point as a right turn.

Top tip

Make sure you do not signal too early, especially where the exits are wide or close to each other. If there is any risk that drivers might think you plan to take an exit before yours, delay your signal or someone may pull out in front of you.

OBSERVATION

It is essential you stay aware of what is happening around you and be prepared to slow down or change your position. Roundabouts are not a race you must win and though another driver may have been stupid or lax about correct positioning and signals, that is no reason to block them or let them drive into your car.

Keep checking mirrors and looking around, and certainly check the mirrors before changing lanes or turning off. Assume that drivers who don't get in the right lane to turn right are not the observant type so can't be trusted to know there is someone alongside them or to use the correct signals.

Insight

One of the really irritating things at roundabouts when you are towing a trailer, or driving any long, slow vehicle, is the person who comes onto the roundabout at speed then blasts his horn at you for being in his way. The fact is that as you are already on the roundabout, you have right of way. The person making the mistake is the 'horn jockey' because he has not taken into account the length and speed of the car and trailer and so assumed that it would be out of his way when he entered the roundabout. When you join a roundabout you must not assume all the vehicles going round it are doing the same speed or are the same length – large vehicles cannot speed up just to let you on quicker. Failure to give large vehicles time can mean you are forced to stop in the roundabout, making yourself vulnerable, often with lots of witnesses to the fact you were in the wrong.

EXIT

Always check your left mirror, before your exit, for vehicles and two-wheelers on that side, especially for any exit beyond a first exit because people may have entered the roundabout without you noticing.

Be prepared to adjust your driving style as you leave because the road may be different to the one you entered on: it could be one lane instead of two in each direction or very narrow. Check around you for others leaving the roundabout, just in case someone is trying to squeeze past (very important where there are two lanes out of the roundabout coming down to one).

Remember to also check that your indicator self-cancels.

MINI-ROUNDABOUTS

Many towns have mini-roundabout acne but that is because they are a cheap way of improving traffic flow and generally work. Treat them as if they were an ordinary junction, so there is no need to signal left on exit unless you are actually turning left. Legally, traffic on a mini-roundabout has priority over those entering, just as on the full-sized ones, but some are so small that this is not enough in practice. Over the years an unofficial first-come-first-in priority has developed in many places so drivers take their turn in entering the roundabout, but don't expect everyone to use them that way, especially in cities.

Traffic lights

Traffic lights are used all over the world and always take the form of red for stop and green for go. Most countries also use an amber light to warn that the light is changing to red and in the UK you are supposed to stop on amber unless you have crossed the stop line or if stopping might cause an accident. In the UK, amber is also used with red to warn that the green light is about to come, though the combination still means 'stop', but many countries go straight from red to green. In those countries drivers are often quick to show displeasure at those they feel have not reacted quickly enough.

Flashing amber is also used differently. In the UK it is used at light-controlled pedestrian crossings to indicate that drivers may go if there are no pedestrians on the crossing (it means the same as the orange **Belisha beacons** on zebra crossings). However, in many countries flashing amber at a junction means proceed with caution.

There are two main sorts of traffic lights:

▶ *those controlling junctions*
▶ *those for pedestrian crossings.*

JUNCTION LIGHTS

Follow the rules for turning left and right but only do so when the lights are green. If you are going straight ahead and there is no specific lane for it, stay in the left-hand lane. There is nothing to stop you using the right lane if the arrows on the road show straight ahead and the lane continues on the other side of the junction, but if someone turns right in front of you, you may have to wait behind them.

At complex junctions, green arrow filter lights are used to allow drivers to make left or right turns (a white filter arrow is for trams). Take care not to get into filter lanes unless you want to turn: if you do it by mistake you may be forced to make a turn you don't want to. (In the USA drivers are allowed to turn right against red lights if it is safe to do so, but this is not allowed in most other countries.)

There is nothing wrong with watching the opposing lights to see when they turn red so you are ready for your green, but do not assume this means yours are going green straightaway. There could be an all-red phase for pedestrians to cross or filter lights may operate.

When the lights go green, put your car in gear and release the handbrake but do not start to pull forwards until the car in front of you starts moving. It is too easy to assume the car in front will move when the driver may not have seen the change or may have a pedestrian in front of them that you can't see.

Green for danger

Though *The Highway Code* stresses that you must look to see if the way is clear before moving off on a green light, most drivers see it as a 'go' signal giving them right of way. The danger of this is that if someone has skipped a red light, stalled in the junction or failed to make a right turn, you may drive into them. In addition, some pedestrians may not have seen the change or may not have been able to cross quickly enough.

Nobody should ever skip a red light but people do through inattention or thinking they can beat the lights. However, if you find yourself crossing the stop line on red, you must think quickly: you've already broken the law so safety is now paramount. On smaller junctions it is usually better to keep going than to skid to a halt in the middle of the junction with the 'green for go' brigade bearing down on you. On larger junctions you must judge whether you can clear it before traffic on the other side catches up with you.

It may be safer to stop and reverse back towards the stop line, or even stay where you are in the middle of a very wide junction, if others can get round you.

KEEP CLEAR

Even when the lights are green, stop at the stop line if your exit from the junction isn't clear otherwise you may find yourself stuck across it when the lights go green for cars crossing your road.

If you are turning right behind other traffic it is often better to wait your turn at the stop line rather than risk being stuck out in the junction because the person ahead of you couldn't make the turn or took longer than expected.

CYCLISTS

In many towns, when cycle lanes meet traffic lights there are two stop lines with a coloured section of road between them for cyclists to stop in. Take care when these lights turn green because some cyclists are slow to set off and many do not consider it necessary to signal their intention to turn right, expecting drivers behind to know they plan to stop again a few metres beyond the stop line.

TIMING

Many roads have timed traffic lights that operate in a synchronized way to smooth out traffic flow. When you get a green light, drive at the speed limit and you'll get a green light at every junction along the road while the boy racers get stopped at every set.

Pedestrian crossings

There are many types of pedestrian crossings with and without lights. In most countries they give pedestrians priority but in the UK the law is very strict about pedestrians having right of way over drivers, especially on uncontrolled crossings.

On any pedestrian crossing you must not drive on if people are still on the crossing, even if they have passed you. Apart from being illegal on uncontrolled crossings, it worries the more vulnerable pedestrians, may confuse those unable to see or hear and is dangerous because other drivers seeing you moving may assume the road is clear, perhaps overtaking you when they are unable to see children on the road beyond your car.

If the crossing has an island it is usually treated as two crossings, one for each side of the road, but take care when children are approaching the island because they may not stop.

In traffic queues, leave the crossing clear, so pedestrians do not have to weave through cars, but remember that on light-controlled crossings pedestrians seeing you stop may think the lights have changed and step off the kerb, so take care when driving on.

LIGHT-CONTROLLED

Traffic light-controlled crossings in the UK vary in style and layout but all work in the same way. As well as the light phases used at junctions, they have the addition of a flashing amber phase during which pedestrians have priority, but if the road is clear, cars can go. Even when the lights are green you must make sure the road is clear because pedestrians may have misjudged it or been physically incapable of crossing in the time allowed.

> ### ⚠ Warning!
>
> Never stop at pedestrian lights on green for blind people waiting to cross as this causes confusion, especially for guide dogs. The big danger is that other drivers may not realize you have stopped, or see why, so overtake you. The sound of your engine can mask the sound of the overtaking vehicle from the blind person while a guide dog has no chance of seeing cars coming up on the outside of you. Most pedestrian lights bleep to let blind people know they are red for the traffic.

Best known in the UK as zebra crossings, pedestrians on them have absolute right of way. In addition, it is an offence to park on the zigzag lines either side of the crossing or to overtake the last vehicle before the crossing.

Approach crossings with care because pedestrians you haven't seen may also be approaching them and the elderly and children are often bad at judging vehicle speed and distance so may step out when you have little chance of stopping.

Stopping for pedestrians waiting to cross is a peculiarly British thing (don't expect it when walking around any other European country). It is commendable, but always check your mirrors before doing it because someone following close behind may not be expecting you to do it. You could argue it is daft to stop with nothing behind you when the pedestrian would only have to wait a few seconds more, but it is safer than having an impatient child step out at the last moment. That said, never wave someone across: let them assess whether all the traffic has stopped because they can see and hear more than you.

Night driving

Though night driving in town is generally easier than in the country, because there are street lights, you must be aware of the variation in lighting and the way it can create deep shadows from which things suddenly emerge. This is why you should always drive with headlights on in town at night, because they help to span the pools of light and shadow. They also give a light source to pick out reflective signs and clothing, which only reflect light back towards its source, and help others see you.

Take particular care when going from a brightly-lit main road into a poorly-lit side street because your eyes need time to adjust to the difference. There is no reason why you can't use beam headlights, if there is nobody else in the street, but you may find they cause glare from reflective road signs at close quarters.

In crowded areas, especially after the pubs turn out, slow down when passing revellers because they may not be aware of the world around them, or able to do anything about it.

At junctions look out for un-lit cyclists and pedestrians wearing dark colours who can be particularly difficult to spot among correctly-lit vehicles.

Top tip

In the UK it is illegal to use your horn between 11.30 p.m. and 7 a.m. in a built-up area except when another vehicle poses a danger, though it is unlikely you'd be prosecuted for sounding it to save a pedestrian from harm. It is also illegal to use a horn on a stationary vehicle.

Parking

Think before you park. Obviously, if you park where it is illegal, you will have problems, but careless parking even where it is legal can cause difficulties for you and others. In fact, if your parking causes an obstruction, it becomes illegal in most places and you may return to find your car has been removed.

CHOOSING A PLACE

When choosing a parking place you should consider:

▶ *is it legal?*
▶ *is it safe?*
▶ *is it secure?*
▶ *is it big enough?*

Is it legal?
In the UK, *The Highway Code* lists all the places it is illegal to park. Yellow lines in the kerb indicate restrictions that should be shown on signs nearby.

It is illegal to park:

> ▶ *on motorways except on the hard shoulder in emergencies*
> ▶ *on the zigzag lines around pedestrian crossings*
> ▶ *in various types of 'clearway', which have signs at the beginning and end, and notices showing restricted times*
> ▶ *on roads with double white lines up the middle, except to pick up or drop passengers*
> ▶ *in active bus and cycle lanes*
> ▶ *where there are red kerb lines in urban 'red routes'.*

The use of lights when parking at night varies a lot from country to country. In the UK you must show parking lights in roads with speed limits over 30 mph, even if parked in a lay-by. Cars can be parked on roads with limits up to 30 mph without lights if they are more than 10 metres from a junction and are in a recognized parking place or lay-by.

Is it safe?
Parking safely is mainly common sense and boils down to whether others will be able to see your car and see round it.

That means you don't park on or near blind bends and brows, remembering that if you do you may force drivers of slower, larger vehicles to put themselves and others at risk by passing your car on the wrong side of the road. You also may not give others enough time to avoid your car once they have seen it.

If you park within 10 metres of a junction, you restrict the view of drivers coming out of the junction and may make it impossible for drivers of large vehicles to turn in. Parking opposite a junction also makes it harder for turning vehicles. The same applies to stopping opposite anything that restricts road width, like an island or another parked vehicle, including creating a tight slalom by parking just a little away from it. In these cases, if your car is restricting a turn, or forcing large vehicles to weave awkwardly, there is a good chance it will get damaged. Remember, too, that you could block the road to emergency vehicles.

Look out, too, for drop kerbs that indicate a vehicle access from properties or a route for those with wheelchairs and pushchairs. Apart from being discourteous, parking in front of them may force the users into unsafe routes over the kerb or even strand wheelchair users in the road.

Top tip

On a hill, always leave a manual car in gear and an automatic in 'park' to back up the parking brake by engaging the transmission. If the car is facing uphill, select first gear in a manual and turn the steering wheel away from the kerb so the front wheels roll against it if all else fails. If facing downhill, put the gearbox in reverse and turn the steering wheel towards the kerb.

Is it secure?

Security is important, especially if you are returning to the car in the dark. Look for lighting and CCTV cameras, especially in urban car parks. In streets, thieves love people who park by the end walls of houses, where nobody can overlook them at work. In car parks, choose a well-lit, central area, not a dark corner or somewhere near bins, where attackers may hide.

Busy areas and those overlooked by houses and businesses are generally more secure, though somewhere outside rowdy clubs at closing time is best avoided.

Is it big enough?

Naturally, the space needs to be long and wide enough for your car, but look around it, too. You need to be able to open the doors enough to get out and there must be enough space around the car for pedestrians to get past without banging into it. If you park near a large vehicle make sure you leave enough space for them to get out, not least because if the driver gets it wrong your car is likely to come off worst.

GETTING IT IN

There are three ways of parking:

1 Parallel *parking where the car is parallel to the kerb.*
2 Inline *parking, as in a car park with cars lined up facing in or out.*
3 Herringbone *parking where cars are parked at an angle to the kerb.*

....

Top tip
Always check your mirrors and signal when parking, even in a car park. Never reverse back into a space without checking it is clear. In large vehicles you may have to get out and check behind. In cars with electric mirrors, it may help to adjust them so you can see kerbs or white lines marking parking spaces.

....

PARALLEL

This is the hardest to master because you have to avoid a kerb you can't really see and may have other vehicles in front and behind your spot. New drivers should only try to do it where the space is plenty long enough. It is wise to park on 'your' side of the road otherwise you have to leave the parking space in the face of oncoming traffic, with a restricted view of it. In the UK it is illegal to park on the side of the road facing the direction of traffic at night and in some countries it is always illegal: it is never sensible because of the difficulty getting back out.

Judging the space length is best done by halting alongside it. How much longer than your car's length you need depends upon your skill and the car's shape. It is easier to park a square-bodied 4×4 than a smaller saloon because you can see where all four corners of the 4×4 are but the boot of a saloon may be completely invisible to the driver, so you need margin for error.

Top tip

Parallel and reverse inline parking works on the basis that the front of the car is steered making it more manoeuvrable than the back, so if you get the back in first, you can fiddle the front about to get it in. In both cases it pays to know where the rear wheels are in relation to seats and windows to help with starting turns.

Once you have judged the space's length, the parallel parking strategy is as follows:

1 *Pull forwards alongside the car in front of your space and about a metre out from it.*
2 *Reverse back. On most cars you start turning the tail in when your rear wheels are about level with the back of the car alongside. If your car is different, find a point on the rear side windows that works as a turn marker. In narrow roads, keep a check on the front of the car as it swings out, to ensure it doesn't obstruct oncoming traffic or touch obstructions.*
3 *Aim to turn the tail in at an angle that will bring it to about the right distance from the kerb as the nose of the car clears the car in front.*
4 *When the nose is clear of the car in front, start turning the steering the other way to bring the nose in. Reverse back as far as possible.*
5 *Edge forwards, turning the wheel towards the kerb to bring the nose right in. In tight spaces you may have to move back and forth several times to get straight and close in.*

Leave the car with the wheels straight, unless you are on a hill (see page 119), so you know where they are when you return and so they do not get caught by vehicles and two-wheelers passing close by. Make sure the car is secure (see later section on personal security) and check the mirrors before opening the door.

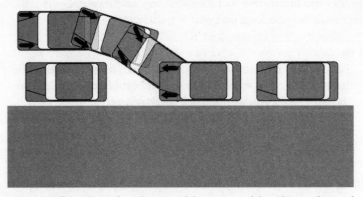

Figure 5.7 Parallel parking takes advantage of the manoeuvrability of a car's front end.

INLINE

Many drivers seem to view driving nose first into inline parking spaces as the 'easy' option, but it isn't, unless you are so short that your view of the car's extremities is limited. Again, the rear of the car is less manoeuvrable than the front, so if you tuck it in first you can swing the front about to finish the movement.

A properly performed reverse park is one movement where forwards parking often requires a wide sweep or lots of backwards and forwards adjustments. In addition, reverse parking makes it easier and safer to get out, because you can see what is coming (see Plate 6).

The principles involved in reversing into a parking space also apply to reversing into a garage or drive. If you have no turning space, reversing into a drive means you come out forwards with a better view of the road.

Reverse parking also saves fuel because you drive straight off rather than manoeuvring with a cold engine.

> ### Insight
> Unfortunately some people drive round car parks not
> thinking that anyone else is likely to be parking their car, and

they too often seem to get behind me! These people generally
find reverse parking perverse and do not appear to notice
indicators and reversing lights. So beware of the person
who, no matter how carefully you signal, pulls up behind
you. If they can't or won't back up, move on slowly to the
next parking space and, as well as indicating, open your
window and point at the space you intend to use. If they still
don't get the message either let them past or have a polite
word about intending to reverse park. Oh, and don't do the
same to others: leave people in front of you room to park.

In one-way car parks, if you can pull up diagonally across the
access way it makes reversing into the parking space easier, but
beware of people behind you trying to overtake as you stop.
Indeed, always keep an eye out for people doing that because some
do not realize that as you go back the nose of the car will swing
out. In one-way car parks it pays to drive down the middle of the
road to stop people trying to do that.

Once you have found a suitable space:

1 *Check your mirrors and indicate.*
2 *Stop at least a metre out from the next car along, further out
   if you can, and about half a car's length from your parking
   space (more if your car isn't very manoeuvrable).*
3 *Reverse back and start turning towards the parking space
   just before your rear wheels come level with the edge of your
   space. In a car with a long rear overhang, you may need to
   start turning a little earlier.*
4 *Check your mirrors to ensure you are not passing too close to
   the cars on either side of your space. In saloons, take care to
   leave enough room for the boot to swing round.*
5 *As the nose comes round in line with the space, straighten
   the steering.*
6 *You should still have space to adjust the position of the tail
   within the parking space as you go back, checking the mirrors
   to judge how far you are from the cars on either side.*
7 *In most cars, anything behind you disappears long before it
   is close to the car. There is no easy way of judging this, so be*

prepared to get out and look, especially in a car you are not used to.

8 *If you finish too close to cars on either side, or overlapping the space's lines, check oncoming traffic, pull straight forwards and reverse back, correcting your line.*

9 *If you have to pay before leaving, take the keys with you. Make sure the car is secure before leaving it.*

PARKING BY MIRRORS

You always use door mirrors when parking but if you are short, drive something with limited visibility or have the back packed with luggage you may have to park using mirrors alone, as truck drivers do. If necessary readjust your mirrors so you can just see the extremities of your car and remember that mirrors sometimes give a false impression of how far away objects are, so compare the view in them with what you can see by turning round. Always check the space you are reversing into before reversing on mirrors, getting out of the car if you need to, because you have a huge blind spot behind you between the mirrors.

As you reverse, check both mirrors to get a better idea of whether you are straight. As it can be difficult to judge distances in the mirrors if you are not used to it, be prepared to lean out of the window or door, or get out and look.

Some cars automatically tilt the passenger side mirror down when reverse is engaged, which can be useful for seeing the kerb when parallel parking but stops you seeing behind for other manoeuvres. Check your handbook because on some cars it can be programmed and on others you disable it merely by turning the mirror adjuster selector to that mirror.

Top tip
Protect your mirrors when parked. Many cars now have electric folding mechanisms on door mirrors but even those that don't can usually be folded manually. At least fold them in tight places. For example, in a narrow, busy street it is sensible to at least fold the mirror on the traffic side.

Narrow gaps

Car drivers are often amazed at the narrow gaps truck and bus drivers can squeeze through, often in reverse, but most professionals use a very simple trick. Once you have made sure the gap is wide enough for the car and have the car presented straight at it, you only watch one side of the car, apart from giving the mirror on the other side an occasional check to make sure nobody is doing anything stupid over there. Think of it this way: if you know the gap between two gateposts is 30 cm (1 ft) wider than the car, by keeping the driver's side 15 cm away from the post on your side you know the other post is 15 cm away from the car's passenger side, so you don't need to keep looking at it.

Insight

If your car has reversing sensors that bleep as you get close to things, do not get over reliant on them and remember their limitations. Before reversing into a parking space or up to any obstruction, check there is nothing there the sensors might miss. A friend of mine wrecked the rear lights on his new car because he relied solely on the sensors to reverse up to a wall that had an empty window box bracket projecting from it.

Personal security

You must be aware of your own and your vehicle's security in towns, even on the move. It is easy for someone to throw a door open at the lights, steal a bag and run knowing you are unlikely to be able to give chase, or if you do, their accomplice can probably steal your car.

Read your car's handbook to see what security it offers. Many now offer programmable locking so the driver, or a garage, can adapt the way the car locks itself. A common one is for remote central locking to only open the driver's door on the first press of the button, which means nobody can leap into the other side. Some cars have automatic re-locking when the car gets above a certain speed, the doors re-lock so nobody can get to you at the lights or by forcing you to stop. This also protects your luggage from snatch thieves. On some cars you can also remove the boot from the central unlocking so it stays locked when the other doors are opened and is only unlocked on a second button press, with the key or by a switch in the car.

But all this is wasted if you give the thieves your keys. Theft of keys is the commonest way for cars to be stolen now, especially prestige models, because security has become so good. This can mean burglary or robbery for the keys but it also means a driver has been stupid enough to leave them in the car while paying for fuel or going into a shop. Don't expect sympathy from your insurer if you do this. In fact, with so many of us carrying mobile phones, hands-free kits, portable sat navs and laptops, it makes sense to lock the car while you pay for fuel.

OUT OF SIGHT

Don't advertise valuables in your car. Tuck bags, especially handbags and laptop cases, down behind the seats when you are driving because one left on the passenger seat next to you is very easy to grab in seconds through an open or broken window. In some cities, thieves do this from motorcycles where they especially look out for convertibles.

If your car has a load cover, use it. If it is a five-door without one, carry a dark coloured rug to throw over things in the boot. The thieves will still be able to see there is something there but won't know if it's a top-spec digital camera or rubbish bound for recycling.

Even low value items left on display can tempt thieves: cheap sunglasses can be sold to supplement pocket money. In addition, the thief doesn't know that a CD case or designer shop bag is empty until after he's broken in, and you can be sure he'll have a good search round having taken the trouble. For the same reason, never leave gadget-mounting devices on show in a car because thieves recognize what they are and know there is a good chance that the portable sat nav, or whatever the device is, may still be in the car.

If you must leave valuables in the car, take care people don't see you putting them into the boot.

RETURNING TO THE CAR

As you return to the car, keep a look out for anyone hanging around it and avoid unlocking it from too far off because it shows anyone watching which car you are going to. Most cars now light up their interiors as soon as the doors are unlocked. This is not just a welcome 'courtesy' but a security matter, allowing you to check the interior is clear, seeing that there are no signs of break-in or, even, of someone hiding in the back (see Plate 7).

If you have something to put in the boot, keep the keys in your hand so that if anyone approaches, you can shut the boot and jump into the car.

Modern highwaymen

Car-jacking is on the increase, especially of prestige cars and of cars obviously loaded with luggage. So, if anyone signals you to stop, be careful and certainly don't stop anywhere secluded. If you must stop, lock the doors, keep the car running and talk to the person through a small gap in the window.

If you do get out of the car, pocket the keys. A common ploy is to put something in the road, or in the entrance to someone's drive (like their wheelie bin) knowing they will leave the car running when they get out to move it.

If you can't get away, repeatedly sound your horn to attract attention. But when confronted by armed assailants it is sensible to hand the car over, though make sure you save your mobile phone so you can call the police straight away.

Emergency vehicles

It can be very difficult in towns to tell where a siren is coming from, so if you hear one keep an eye on the road around you. In queues, the first clue that an emergency vehicle is coming from behind may be that larger vehicles start pulling over because, being higher than the rest of the traffic, the drivers can see further.

If you are stationary or moving slowly, try to move right over to let the emergency vehicle through. But if you are moving it is very important that you do not just slam the brakes on. The chances are that the emergency vehicle is already closing on you fast and braking hard without getting out of their way means they are closing even more quickly and may not be able to avoid you.

Get out of their way as quickly and safely as you can, signalling your intention to move over. But do not take risks or break the law, for example, by skipping a red light. If you speed up to let them past and exceed the limit you are technically breaking the law. It's unlikely a police officer would penalize you for it, within reason, but don't expect a speed camera authority to be so understanding.

Take care when pulling back out again in case another emergency vehicle is following them, or other drivers who are using the gap they have created to get ahead.

10 THINGS TO REMEMBER

1 *Make monthly checks on tyres and other essentials a routine.*

2 *Get into the habit of running through our six-point checklist before setting out.*

3 *Read the starting procedure in your car's handbook.*

4 *Use mirrors before pulling out or changing direction but beware of what is in your blind spot.*

5 *Learners have 'mirror, signal, manoeuvre' drummed into them, but many drivers forget braking for, say, a turn, is part of the manoeuvre they should have mirrored and signalled before.*

6 *Do not let your mind wander in town traffic because things can change quickly.*

7 *Keep a two-second gap between you and the car in front when moving.*

8 *Signal in plenty of time before junctions and learn the right signals for roundabouts.*

9 *Think when choosing a parking place: is it legal, safe and secure?*

10 *You are the weakest link in your car's security: lock it or lose it.*

6

Dual-carriageways and motorways

In this chapter you will learn:
- *how to use dual-carriageways*
- *how to cope with speed*
- *the risks of long-distance driving.*

Though dual-carriageways and motorways are generally our fastest roads they are also our safest. This is because they separate traffic going in opposite directions and remove much of the risks involved in overtaking. Because they make it easier to overtake they also reduce the likelihood of frustrated drivers taking risks to get past slower moving vehicles. In addition, many have all junctions designed so that opposing traffic flows pass over or under each other.

However, because driving quickly becomes easier, and many of these roads are boringly featureless, it is too easy to become complacent and to forget just how fast you are going.

Insight
Because driving on motorways and dual-carriageways is so similar, from now on we'll refer to motorways, except where something is unique to non-motorway dual-carriageways. To save confusion we will also number the lanes:

> ▶ *lane 1 is the nearest to the car's passenger side of the road (the left lane in the UK)*

- *lane 2 is the next one over and ...*
- *lane 3 is the next (and so on).*

American readers should note that in most countries on multi-lane roads, overtaking is only allowed on one side, so you can only overtake a car in lane 2 by moving into lane 3, unless the traffic is in slow-moving queues.

Using sliproads

The problem with joining a high-speed road of any kind is matching your speed to that of oncoming traffic. In the case of motorways, the speed difference can be very great and the consequences of someone being forced to swerve or brake can be disastrous. This makes it important that you do not just glance in the mirrors, but truly look, giving yourself time to judge the closing speed of oncoming vehicles and to see if anyone is moving into the lane you are planning to occupy (some people do this even if you are indicating your intention to join the road).

If you pass over the road you plan to join, take a quick glance along it. This can give you an idea of the weight of traffic to expect before you turn onto the sliproad.

On modern roads the sliproads themselves are designed to be quite fast, with gentle bends and banking, but on older roads they can become deceptively tight. This is more of a problem on exit when you have become used to fast, straight driving, so don't assume it is a well designed one unless you can see all of it.

Insight

Many people forget that the sliproad is usually legally part of the motorway so all the motorway rules apply and you are breaking the law if you stop on one or if you or your vehicle are prohibited from motorways.

OBSERVATION

On a sliproad with a good early view of the road you are joining, the temptation can be to concentrate on the traffic on the main road, which is a sure way of driving into the truck in front of you. If there is traffic on the sliproad in front of you, you must keep an eye on it and regulate your speed to give them room, not least because they may be concentrating on the main carriageway, not a car coming up from immediately behind. Give space to trucks in particular because of their limited view of what is close around them and the fact that they need more room to join a fast road. If you have to slow down behind a truck while you both join a motorway, you will soon be able to pick up speed and pass him, but if a truck is baulked on the sliproad he will have extreme difficulty picking up speed to safely join the carriageway.

When you look down the motorway in your mirror you are looking for what is in lane 1, how close it is to you and how quickly it is gaining on you. You also need to be aware of what traffic in the other lanes is doing: is anyone signalling to change lanes towards you or appearing to be changing without signalling? If anyone is signalling to move out of lane 1 to help you on, make sure they are intending to do that (not just forgetting an indicator) and are going to be able to complete the manoeuvre before they get to you.

Finally, glance over your shoulder to make sure nothing is alongside you in your blind spot. Do this even if your car has blind spot mirrors because a motorcyclist can still escape those.

Top tip

Get into the motorway habit of regularly scanning the mirrors so you know what is happening around you. In that way you build up a picture of what is going on so that if you look in the mirror prior to changing lanes you will recognize if a vehicle is 'missing' and know that it might be in your blind spot. If anything untoward happens you'll also have an idea of what must be avoided from behind as well as in front.

Plate 1 Mirrors often have a wide angle area marked by a line (arrowed).

Plate 2 An advanced automatic box with its 'sport' mode position on the hook-end of the J-shaped lever slot and manual paddle shift (inset) behind the steering wheel.

Plate 3 This correctly adjusted seatbelt passes over collar and breastbones and hips, avoiding soft tissue.

Plate 4 Look how the long truck's cab passes much wider than its tail.

Plate 5 Wide roundabouts make it harder to judge the distance and speed of vehicles on them.

Plate 6 Reverse parking gives you an easier view on leaving a parking slot.

Plate 7 Car interiors light up on unlocking so you can check for intruders.

Plate 8 The driver of the red car is sensibly slowing down to join the dual-carriageway behind the camper van.

Plate 9 The green sign shows one sliproad lane becomes a new dual-carriageway lane so the arrowed car should not move over.

Plate 10 Get into the deceleration lane as quickly as possible when leaving a dual-carriageway.

Plate 11 The Jaguar driver has pulled over to let the Jeep past because it is able to go faster on this bumpy narrow road.

Plate 12 It is hard to see the car in the shade without lights but easy with them.

Plate 13 Side winds curling over tall vehicles may draw you towards them.

Plate 14 The difference in size and shape of space saver and road tyres shows why the former has a speed limit.

Plate 15 Marker post on a motorway.

SIGNALS

Some people take the view that if you are coming down a sliproad it should be obvious you intend to move onto the motorway. While that is true, an indicator draws attention to your car and reminds those on the motorway that you will be moving over. In some situations, especially in poor visibility and at night, it can be difficult for drivers to pick out what cars are on the main carriageway and what cars are moving over from the sliproad, but an indicator clearly shows this, and lets others know that you may be going slower than cars already on the motorway.

You don't need to indicate all the way down the sliproad and on longer ones it may confuse people behind you. However, you should certainly be indicating by the time you are parallel to the motorway.

JOINING IN

Pick up speed as soon as you can but don't look on it as a race. You haven't got to get into lane 1 before the red truck and it may be safer and easier to slow down a little so you can get on behind him. The idea is to filter into the traffic, not force a gap (see Plate 8).

Always keep an eye on how much **acceleration lane** is left in front of you so you don't get taken by surprise and get forced to stop before it runs out.

Once you are on the main carriageway, check your mirrors to see what is happening around you. If you are not planning to overtake anything, cancel the indicator.

Top tip

On some motorway junctions, the sliproad becomes an additional lane on the motorway (a new lane 1). This is always clearly marked with a large sign bearing a diagram of however many lanes the motorway has with the new lane angling on from the side, yet many motorists fail to recognize the meaning of this and unnecessarily move over to lane 2 (see Plate 9).

Speed

Motorways are built for speed so maintaining high cruising speeds is not difficult and it can be too easy to pick up speed without realizing. So, keep checking your speedo especially on sections that are downhill. Equally, check your speed on uphill sections to make sure you are not slowing down, which others may not expect and which uses more fuel when you speed up again.

Many cars now have **speed limiters** and **cruise control**. Limiters allow you to set a speed above which the car will not go, which is especially useful in quiet, powerful cars. Cruise control automatically maintains a set speed and is of most use on motorways. However, it is best avoided on crowded roads where the situation may change suddenly and if you are on a dual-carriageway you should always take back control on twisting sections or where you pass through junctions with cars waiting to join the main road.

Active cruise control (**ACC**) uses radar to keep a safe distance from other vehicles but even this should not be trusted on very busy roads where the traffic situation changes quickly. Some ACCs allow you to vary the gap it keeps but read the handbook to find out which setting is closest to a two-second gap. Be ready to use the accelerator on bends where the radar beam may go across a neighbouring lane because if it picks up vehicles you are overtaking it might suddenly slow the car down.

Because cruise control maintains a steady speed, it can help reduce fuel consumption.

Be aware that on long motorway trips, speed becomes deceptive. After a few hours at 70 mph, 50 mph feels very slow, but may not be slow enough in certain situations.

Insight

Cruise control reveals how many drivers speed up when they notice a car overtaking them. What usually happens is that you are on cruise control in lane 2, steadily gaining on a car in lane 1 until a few metres short of it, then find you are no longer gaining. The other driver probably doesn't even realize they're doing it, though they should be checking their speed. In these circumstances it is probably safer to increase your speed a little to get past, so you're not stuck in the other driver's blind spot, then settle back to your pre-set speed. You almost always find that you are now pulling away as steadily as you were gaining on the other car before they noticed you. Make sure, however, that you do not do this when people are overtaking you.

Keep your distance

Because speeds are higher it is important to keep your distance from vehicles in front. This is especially so on busy motorways, where traffic can suddenly slow right down or even stop because of an event far ahead of you; this is due to the convoy effect mentioned in the last chapter. It is worth remembering that at 70 mph you are travelling at 31 metres a second, so if it takes you a second to react you will have covered the equivalent of the length of seven Ford Focuses before you even touch the brakes.

So, use the two-second rule (see previous chapter) to check you are far enough back and if the road is wet allow even more space.

Many countries, including the UK, are now at least experimenting with the French chevron idea for judging distance on motorways, at least in places where bunching occurs, perhaps because of hills or congestion. Chevrons are painted at intervals along the road and you keep at least two between you and the car in front. The French have now moved on from that using gaps in the white lines at the carriageway edges, which obviously saves paint instead of using more on chevrons, but it works in the same way.

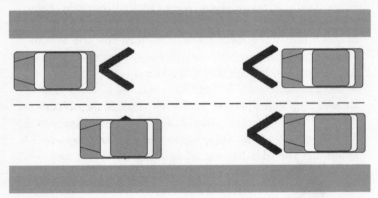

Figure 6.1 *By keeping two chevrons apart, cars in the top lane are a safe distance apart.*

Try to avoid slowing down on a motorway by just coming off the throttle. This gives no warning to those behind you that your car is slowing and so delays their braking. You do not need to brake hard to make the brake lights come on: any use of the pedal is usually enough to trigger the lights. Check how much pedal pressure it needs when you are parked in front of something that reflects the lights.

Hazards on the move

The only time it is legal to use **hazard warning lights** on the move is if you are being forced to stop suddenly at the end of a motorway queue. It is well worth getting into this habit because it gives drivers behind you a clear indication, especially at night, that you are stopping or slowing down significantly rather than braking gently.

Some cars have automatic activation of the hazard lights on hard or sudden braking. Take care with these because in the aftermath of a heart-stopping incident it is easy to overlook that the hazard lights are still going.

Looking ahead

Do not get fixated on the car in front. Look well ahead: the faster you go the further that needs to be. Yes, you must be aware of the car in front, but if that is as far as your attention goes, things will take you by surprise, especially in heavy traffic. In addition, that driver may not react quickly enough to an incident ahead, which leaves you even less time to react.

Look out for vehicles coming down sliproads to join the motorway and if you can safely do so, signal and move into the next lane to let them on. This not only helps them, particularly drivers of slow vehicles, but is safer for you because it removes the risk of someone misjudging your speed, or just being awkward, and pulling out in a way that forces you to brake or swerve.

Don't ignore distant brake lights because if they are stopping, rather than slowing down, you'll come up on them very quickly. If you reduce speed now, you may not have to slow down as much as they are later because you counter the convoy effect.

Blue flashing lights ahead make it obvious there is a problem, but truck drivers slowing down can also be a hint of trouble to come because they can see a long way ahead.

Lane discipline

In most countries, including the UK, the motorway lane discipline is that you stay in lane 1 unless you are overtaking.

In some countries this is legally enforceable but in the UK there is nothing to stop you becoming a member of the 'Centre Lane Owners' Club' other than your conscience. Indeed, on the busy motorways in the London area, staying out of lane 1 is virtually standard practice leading to the daft situation where you often see lane 1 almost empty while the others are packed. Such centre-lane hogging is rare anywhere north of the Tropic of Cambridge.

The reason this behaviour is illegal in many countries is that it clogs up the motorways. Trucks and vehicles towing trailers are not allowed into lane 3 so if a slow car driver refuses to move over, there is no way those drivers can legally overtake.

So, instead of having one lane of slow moving traffic, you now have two, with only one lane open for overtaking. Truck and towcar drivers may then be tempted to overtake in lane 1 or risk moving into lane 3.

Insight

Centre-lane hoggers seem to take the attitude of 'why should I get out of his way?' and wonder why lorry and towcar drivers get so irate. The reason is simple, with heavier vehicles it takes a lot more time, fuel and, often, driver gear changing effort to regain lost speed than it does in a solo car, so by slowing these drivers down you are not just being inconsiderate and annoying them, but you are costing them money and harming the environment. Anyone doing this is also likely to be holding up more than one lorry, multiplying the additional fuel used as they all return to their cruising speed.

Changing lanes

Changing lanes should be seen in the same way as joining another road from a junction. You are moving into another flow of traffic, so others need to know what you are going to do and you should not do it in a way that might cause others to swerve or brake. Many motorway accidents are caused by sloppy lane changing: you don't have to hit another car, just make the driver swerve into another lane or brake hard with the inevitable chain reaction.

OBSERVATION

Naturally, you have been keeping an eye on the mirrors so you should have a good idea of what is around you. As you approach a vehicle you might want to overtake, pay more attention to your mirrors and give yourself plenty of time to check them before you need to make the manoeuvre. Remember, cars coming from behind may be going considerably faster than you are so look at them long enough to judge how quickly they are gaining.

Look for people indicating their intention to move out from behind you or to move from an outer lane into the one you want to move into. Glance over your shoulder to check your blind spot.

SIGNAL AND MOVE

As speeds increase, signals become more important and, ideally, need to be given further ahead. How long should you signal for? You need to give people time to see and react to it so six seconds of indicator is ideal: you would cover about 185 metres at 70 mph in that time. However, that is six seconds BEFORE you start moving over: if you change lanes as you flick the indicator on, nobody has time to react to the signal, especially the motorcyclist you didn't see in your blind spot.

Most cars allow you to hold the indicator on for lane changes, which makes it less likely you will fail to cancel it. Some modern cars with touch-on indicator stalks, where you just tap it up or down rather than clicking it through a gate, have a lane change facility where it stays on for three seconds. That is too short a time to be effective and because it usually cancels before you have even started the lane change, it may make others think you have changed your mind.

Aim to flow smoothly at a shallow angle into the next lane rather than jinking across like a skier in a slalom. That way you are less likely to upset the car's balance or to take anyone by surprise and if you have failed to spot a car nearby, you both have time to react. Cancel, or let go, of the indicator as soon as you are in the new lane.

Top tip

Take care if you are new to a car with touch-on indicators because it is very easy to tap those straight from right to left: some allow you to cancel them by touching in the same direction, so if you are indicating right you tap it right again. All allow you to hold them on for a lane change and then cancel as soon as you let go, which is

the easiest way to use them on a motorway. A few are
programmable to driver preferences. Check their operation
in the handbook.

Large vehicles

Drivers of large vehicles need consideration because they do not
always have the visibility or acceleration car drivers take for
granted.

It can be difficult in a long vehicle to judge how far behind a car
in the next lane is, so a truck may not pull out when signalling to
do so or pull out when you are too close. You must watch out for
both of these. It is polite to allow a truck to pull out if you can't
get past him quickly because he needs more time, and fuel, than
you do to regain lost speed. However, it will help him to know you
are doing this if you flash your lights.

The Highway Code says flashing your lights is merely a way of
saying 'I'm here' but in this context it is generally taken as meaning
'go ahead' or 'you are past me' if the truck is overtaking. This does
mean, however, that it is unwise to flash your lights if you are
warning a truck driver not to pull out because you are too close:
use your horn, but be prepared to brake.

If you are alongside a truck when its indicators come on, the driver
may just be signalling his intention to pull out when you have
passed. If you are almost past, speed up if you can to get out of his
way. If you are further back, a polite toot of the horn will ensure
he knows you're there.

Top tip
> Don't box yourself in alongside trucks. If there are several
> trucks to be overtaken on a two-lane dual-carriageway,
> wait until the vehicle in front of you has almost passed them
> *(Contd)*

before pulling alongside them, especially if it is a lorry ahead of you who may not be able to see you are there. This way, if anything goes wrong, you will not be trapped alongside the trucks.

Overtaking on the left

In the UK you are allowed to overtake on the left if:

▶ *other vehicles have indicated their intention to turn right*
▶ *the traffic is queuing and the lanes on the right are moving more slowly.*

That was probably clear-cut when first introduced to *The Highway Code*, but they didn't have multi-lane motorways then.

It is generally considered unacceptable, if not illegal, to overtake on the left if the traffic is flowing freely. But if you are doing 70 mph in an empty lane 1, while everyone else is doing 60 mph in lanes 2 and 3, you may take the view that the second point in *The Highway Code* applies. However, the danger is that the drivers in lane 2 may not expect it and so might pull across into lane 1, not realizing you are gaining on them. Then you would have to argue in court that you were not doing anything against the advice of *The Highway Code*.

Where it does seem nonsensical is on four-lane motorways where there may be an empty lane between you and the inattentive lane hog. If you apply *Highway Code* thinking you would go from lane 1, across lanes 2 and 3, overtake in lane 4 and then come all the way back again. Obviously, if the outer lanes are busy enough to be seen as queues, you are doing no wrong to overtake in lane 1, but if it is a lone car out there, what you are doing may be safe and sensible but is, strictly speaking, against current *Highway Code* advice.

Naturally, there is nothing wrong with going faster than cars on the main carriageway if you have entered a filter lane, for example, where motorways diverge. Technically, the traffic on the motorway you are leaving has indicated its intention to 'turn right' by staying over there, but look out for those making a sudden move over when they realize, too late, that this is their turn.

Roadworks

The presence of roadworks is usually signed well ahead on motorways, even if it is a temporary 'mobile' works, which is usually preceded by a truck with huge flashing amber beacons and a large 'move over' or 'lane closed' sign.

Lane closures and speed limits for roadworks may be annoying but they are essential for the safety of people working in unpleasant and potentially dangerous situations. As we've said, at motorway speed you cover tens of metres a second so half a second's inattention by a driver in roadworks can instantly put vulnerable workers' lives at risk. Yet, amazingly, there have even been fatal crashes caused by impatient drivers trying to overtake by weaving through the bollards of contra-flow systems.

When you see signs saying there are roadworks ahead, get ready to pull over if you are in a lane shown as closed. Don't leave it until the last minute because it increases risk and if traffic is heavy you may even have trouble filtering over.

TEMPORARY SPEED LIMITS

You may see two types of speed limit sign in roadworks in Europe. Where the limit is shown on a round sign with a red border it is legally enforceable. Where it is shown on a rectangular sign with a black border, it is advisory, for example, suggesting a lower speed through a lane change or bend with **adverse camber**. Adverse camber means the curve in the road surface tilts the vehicle the wrong way for the bend, increasing the effects of centrifugal force instead of countering it like banking on a fast bend.

It is sensible to keep to the enforceable speeds because, apart from breaking the law if you don't, the roadworks have been designed with that speed in mind, so bends and enforced lane changes are designed to be taken at that speed. In addition, you are likely to find narrower than normal lanes, missing road markings, uneven surfaces and ramps, not to mention debris and dirty water from the roadworks. For the same reasons, it pays to keep your distance, which also reduces the likelihood of being hit by stones thrown up by the wheels of the vehicles in front.

Though your car may be able to go through lane changes faster than an advised speed suggests, be aware that trucks and cars towing trailers may not be able to and may even slow down more than the sign suggests if the driver has livestock aboard or an awkward load like bulk liquid. Truck drivers also get a much better view over roadworks signs and bollards than most car drivers, so if they start slowing down for no apparent reason, don't go hurtling past them.

Look out, too, for vehicles that may be connected with the roadworks, such as tipper trucks; they may need to slow down a lot to enter the works.

Insight

Narrow lanes in roadworks often show how little idea some car drivers have of the width of their cars. Someone in a small hatchback will hold everyone up because they are too scared to overtake a lorry and when they finally get out of the way, a large 4×4 passes with no trouble at all. If you are in a car, the lanes will be wide enough for you. If you do not have enough faith in your driving to overtake in narrow lanes, don't stop others doing it: you'll just have to pull over and sit behind the truck until you reach the end of the roadworks.

JUNCTIONS IN ROADWORKS

If you think your junction may come up in roadworks, pay special attention to the signs. You may need to get into a particular lane a long way before you reach it, for example to avoid a contra-flow system for through traffic only. It may pay to stay in lane 1 even if there isn't a contra-flow because signs for the exit may not be as numerous or easily seen as usual and could be completely hidden if you are passing a truck at the time.

Indicate your intention to leave as early as possible because you may have to slow down more than expected if the bollarded-off exit is shorter than a normal sliproad.

Night driving

Night driving on motorways and dual-carriageways is generally easier than on other roads for the same reasons they are safer. However, on un-lit rural motorways, speed can become deceptive in the dark, especially when the roads are quiet – you have so little to judge it by, so be careful that your speed isn't creeping up.

Be prepared to slow down, too, because the width of the road means it can sometimes be disorientating in the dark, making it difficult to see where it goes ahead, especially if it curves just after a bridge.

LIGHTS

People are often confused about the use of beam headlights on motorways, but the rules are the same as on any other road: don't use them if they would dazzle someone. Be particularly careful on bends where the beam swings across the other carriageway, not least because lorry drivers can be affected by your lights long before you see them – their lights are hidden by the central reservation but the driver is sitting high above them. Even on straight roads, beam lights can dazzle those on another carriageway even if it is some way off: don't ignore others flashing their lights in protest to your beam even if you think they are unjustified. So, really the only safe time to use them is when you are sure there is nothing ahead of you or a bend takes your lights away from the other carriageway.

However, if you suspect there is something up ahead, a quick flash of beam may reveal it without causing too much distress to others and is certainly a safer prospect than risking running into something, or someone, on the road.

Be prepared when driving on beam to dip them when approaching bridges and large signs. Very pale bridge supports and large reflective signs can reflect back a considerable amount of light from beam headlights, which may stop you seeing beyond them.

Many motorways now have lighting at major junctions or on new sections, which is useful but when you leave those sections you are often plunged into darkness. It takes your eyes longer to adapt to sudden darkness than it does to sudden light, so be prepared to slow down if you cannot see. Blinking can help the eyes recover more quickly.

Leaving motorways

Motorways and some major dual-carriageways have numbered junctions and life is a lot easier if you know the number of the one you want. If you know you want junction 20 you'll know it's the next one when you pass junction 19 or 21, depending upon which way you are going. It is also easier at complex junctions where the number of the road you want might be a long way down the list.

Motorways also have signs usually at a mile then half-a-mile (2 km and 1 km) in advance of the junction, then **countdown markers** for the junctions starting with three diagonal bars at 300 metres, then two, and then one, which is 100 metres from the start of the sliproad.

Move into lane 1 as soon as you can and certainly not later than half a mile back, unless there are a lot of very slow vehicles in it. Try not to get caught out by overtaking slow vehicles immediately before the junction because you could easily get stuck in lane 2 and be tempted to swing across too close to vehicles you are overtaking.

Start indicating to leave at the 300 metre marker and keep the indicator on until you are well into the sliproad. That helps to stop people blindly following you, thinking you are still on the motorway, especially at night or in poor visibility.

If there is traffic behind you, do not slow down significantly until you are in the **deceleration lane** (see Plate 10). Check your speed because you may be going faster than you think if you have been on a clear stretch of fast road for a while. Also beware on older motorways and dual-carriageways that some sliproads have tight bends in them.

Check the signs on the sliproad because they show you which way to go at the junction ahead and, therefore, which lane you must be in.

ROUNDABOUTS

On dual-carriageways roundabouts are no problem if they are frequent but the danger when you come upon one after many miles of fast motoring is that you approach it too fast. Many, but not all, have the same countdown marker as sliproads to help drivers, but when you know you are approaching one check your speed, especially if you are going straight on because you may not be mentally attuned to the idea of going round something.

See the previous chapter for how to signal on roundabouts and make sure you get into the correct lane as soon as you can, especially if turning right.

SIDE ROADS

Some older dual-carriageways still have side roads with little or no deceleration lane. Get into lane 1 early and indicate at least 300 metres in advance to make sure everyone behind you knows you are taking the next exit and will slow down. Check your speed because you do not want to be braking hard while trying to take a 90 degree turn.

If turning right across the central reservation at these junctions you can emphasize that you haven't just forgotten to cancel an indicator when you moved into the right hand lane (swap left and right here if you drive on the right) by taking it in two steps. Indicate and move over, cancel the indicator for a few metres, then indicate right again. Make sure you pull all of your car into the right-turn lane and leave no part of it hanging over the lane you have just left.

Service areas

The danger with service areas is that you are coming straight from a fast road into what is effectively a car park. We've already stressed the importance of checking your speed when leaving the motorway at a junction but it is even more important in service areas because you have all the hazards of car parks, with cars going in and out of parking spaces, drivers trying to find the exits, people walking about and parked cars restricting your view.

People, especially children, intent on finding food and toilets may not be paying attention to crossing roads, so you must look out for them and be going slowly enough to avoid them.

COOLING OFF PERIOD

Be kind to your car when you pull into a service area. You have just been cruising down a high speed road with the engine working hard so don't just pull up and turn it off. Let it idle for at least 30 seconds to help the oil and coolant dissipate some of the heat first. This is particularly important with turbocharged cars where the turbo gets extremely hot at high speeds and relies on the flow of oil to cool the bearings. In fact, if the turbo is hot enough, switching off too quickly can lead to the oil being carbonized in the bearings, which isn't good for the turbo's longevity.

SECURITY

Service area car parks are large and when they are busy you may have to park away from well-lit areas. Service areas are easy places for thieves to steal from cars and be a long way off before anyone realizes what has happened. So take a few moments to hide valuables, or take them with you, especially easily removable high value items like portable sat navs (and their mountings), laptops and mobile phones.

If you have a lot of luggage in the car, it may be sensible for someone to stay with the car.

Insight

Most of us use service areas purely for their convenience in areas we do not know, but if you don't like them or their prices, there is an alternative if you have portable sat nav. There are several websites now where you can download 'points of interest' (POI) which include restaurants and supermarkets, so you can see if there are any close to your route. Start by looking on your sat nav manufacturer's website. Some supermarkets' websites' POI links allow you to choose between all their stores and just ones with filling stations. Also try putting 'points of interest' into a search engine which reveals hundreds of free and pay sites offering all kinds of POI.

Long-distance driving

What distance qualifies as a long drive depends very much on how much motoring you do. A three-hour trip would be nothing to a transcontinental truck driver but would be a tiring long haul to a new driver who has never ventured out of town before.

Your physical condition also has a bearing: if you have been unwell, stressed or had a bad night, you will tire sooner. Traffic and weather conditions add to fatigue by demanding more concentration and creating a frustration factor to crank up the stress. Even your car has an effect because a long trip is much less tiring in a quiet, luxury car than in a noisy, uncomfortable one.

Time of day also affects us. We are at our lowest ebb sometime between 2 a.m. and 5 a.m., but an early riser will cope better with an early morning drive than a late night one, while a night owl type will find late night driving less tiring than setting off at dawn.

You must be honest with yourself and not think that because you feel tired and unable to concentrate after an hour you should press on just because your partner finds two or three times that easy. At the end of the day, fatigue is a killer because it affects your concentration and judgement. The ultimate danger is going to sleep at the wheel because you only have to nod off for a fraction of a second to veer across the road. That is a truly frightening wake-up call and if you have reached that stage, you have serious problems and should get off the road as soon as possible.

PREVENTION

Prevention is better than cure when it comes to driver fatigue, and a lot safer. Try not to set out on a long journey if you are tired or stressed. As explained in Chapter 1, illness, bereavement, anger and work-related stress all have significant effects on your ability to drive well and for long periods, so if you have to drive at these times take extra care.

Take time to get comfortable in the car and plan the journey (Chapters 3 and 4) because if you start off feeling relaxed and know where you are going, it gets you in the right frame of mind. Avoid setting distance targets: if you decide 'I'll have lunch when I get to Boston' and it takes longer than you expected, you'll keep pushing on instead of taking a break. Instead try to take a break every two hours or so, even if it is only to pull into a lay-by and walk about for a few minutes, and do your best to have meals around your normal times.

Take drinks and high-energy snacks with you so you can have them when you need them rather than when you find somewhere to buy them. It is certainly sensible to keep things like this in the car in extremes of weather because being stuck in a motorway jam in sweltering heat or freezing cold with nothing to drink or eat is pretty grim.

Incidentally, the old idea of opening the windows and getting some fresh air to combat fatigue is now largely discredited, though a stuffy car doesn't help.

FOOD

Don't over-eat and certainly don't drink alcohol if you face a long trip because both make you drowsy. Fatty food and high-energy food should help, though starchy foods do not, so the traditional English fried breakfast is probably better than a continental one with lots of bread and pastry.

Caffeine helps but don't overdo it because it can affect judgement and make sitting still for long periods difficult.

EXERCISE

Even modest stretching exercises can help fight fatigue by increasing the blood flow to tired muscles, preventing the onset of aches. But when you stop, don't leap out of the car and start running around because that is a sure way of pulling muscles and tendons. Gentle stretching is a much better idea and can even be done while driving or stopped in traffic. If any exercise or stretching hurts, stop doing it because it's the body's way of saying 'no'.

In the car, try the following exercises (you don't have to do them all every time, but vary them):

▶ *Shoulder rolls to free shoulder and neck muscles: Sit or stand with your shoulders in a relaxed position then slowly rotate them up towards your ears and round. Do this several times in each direction.*

SHOULDER ROLL

▶ *Neck stretches to relax neck muscles: Looking straight ahead, tilt your head to one side until you feel mild tension in the muscle running down towards your shoulder and hold this for ten seconds. Then do it the other way. Do this three times for each side.*

NECK STRETCH

▶ *Shoulder pulls to stretch muscles running over the shoulder joint: Bend your right forearm across your chest in the old cowboy film 'big chief' style. Bring the left arm up with the forearm vertical and place the right wrist behind the left forearm: now use the left arm to pull on the right and create mild tension in the right shoulder. Hold this for five seconds, then swap arms. Repeat this once more for each arm.*

SHOULDER PULL

▶ *Hand stretches to relax hands and wrists: Straighten your arm down towards your knees (both arms if you are parked) and stretch your fingers until you feel mild tension. Hold that for ten seconds then relax the fingers at the knuckles for ten seconds, then repeat both.*

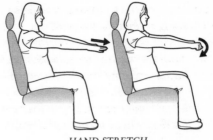

HAND STRETCH

▶ *Ankle rolls to ease ankles held in pedal positions: Only when stopped and the handbrake is on, take your foot off the pedal and rotate the foot at the ankle in both directions for ten seconds each, then do it with the other foot (in most cars there isn't room to do both feet at once).*

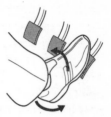

ANKLE ROLL

When you stop for a break, warm up with the shoulder rolls and neck stretches in the car, then step out and try these:

▶ *Shoulder stretch to flex muscles that have been holding arms to the wheel: Stand up straight with your shoulders relaxed. Gently raise your outstretched arms to the same angle as the natural slope of your shoulder (it helps if you can see your reflection) and hold it for five seconds before slowly lowering it. Do five of these with your palms down and five with your palms up.*

SHOULDER STRETCH

▶ *Leg stretch to flex and straighten leg muscles: Stand up straight then slowly raise one foot off the ground in front of you (keep your supporting knee slightly bent because it is harder to keep your balance if you lock it). Slowly stretch your leg out to point the toe forwards and hold it for five seconds, then slowly swing the leg out to the side and hold it, then behind and hold it. If you lose your balance, touch the foot to the floor. Repeat this with the other leg.*

LEG STRETCH

▶ *Back bends to ease back and shoulder muscles: Stand up straight and imagine you are standing with your back against a wall. Peel your backbone away from the wall starting by tilting your head and then letting the movement roll down your back, allowing your head and arms to dangle, until you at least look as if you are trying to touch your toes (don't force it if you can't). Hold it for five seconds and slowly build the back up again to return to the upright position. Do this twice more. The idea is to gently stretch the back, not violently touch your toes.*

BACK BEND

If you feel too self-conscious doing this, just go for a walk and gently stretch your arms and back out.

When you are in the car try to make yourself aware of tensions creeping in. Consciously sit up straight, unclench your jaw, drop your shoulders, lower your chin and ease your grip on the wheel.

DANGER SIGNS

If you find yourself getting bad tempered, making mistakes, failing to see things or not remembering part of the journey, you are getting seriously fatigued and must stop at least for a rest. If you must continue your journey, take more frequent breaks.

Beware of 'nearly there' syndrome, especially when homeward bound. It is the tendency to carry on instead of resting when you need it because you are now in the same county as your destination, back on familiar ground or there are 'only X miles to go'. A fatal mistake is always a fatal mistake whether it happens far from home or just a few miles from your door.

10 THINGS TO REMEMBER

1   As you join motorways from sliproads, take care to observe
    what the traffic approaching you is doing.

2   Keep checking your speed: motorways are built for speed
    so it is easy to go faster than you think.

3   Keep your distance because you need a lot of space to stop or
    avoid something at speed.

4   Look well ahead, not just at the vehicle in front, to avoid
    surprises.

5   Treat lane changing like joining a new road, signalling
    for about six seconds before moving over.

6   Treat large vehicles with consideration because they need more
    time and fuel to pick up speed if slowed down.

7   Do not hog the centre lane because not all vehicles are allowed
    into lane three to overtake you.

8   When leaving a motorway, signal at the sliproad's 300 metre
    marker.

9   Always check your speed when leaving a motorway, but
    especially when entering a service area.

10 Do not take risks with fatigue. If you are tired or start making
    mistakes or losing your temper, leave the road and rest.

7

....

Rural roads

In this chapter you will learn:
- *how to cope with our most dangerous roads*
- *safety issues in country driving*
- *danger signs to look for.*

Good rural roads are the most pleasant to drive on because of their sheer variety and the fact that they are often quiet enough for you to simply enjoy the freedom of driving. But they are also our most dangerous because they demand more of the driver, give you more opportunity to get it wrong at speed and bring a variety of road users easily into conflict. In addition, some are not perfectly designed for modern traffic, having their roots in a time when even horse-drawn transport was infrequent.

It doesn't help that our traffic authorities are also inconsistent, so while one county may put up warning signs for everything, chevrons on almost every bend and speed cameras every few miles, others seem to keep their chevrons for main roads and only replace missing road signs when enough insurance companies have threatened them with legal action. Indeed, there are some places where you don't need a sign to tell you you have crossed a county boundary because the sudden deterioration in the road makes it obvious.

In short, on rural roads you must be prepared for ever-changing driving conditions and road standards. Nature also plays its part: trees may change the road conditions by creating shade or dropping leaves; mud may wash off surrounding land in heavy rain; in areas with fine soils the wind may create 'dunes' of slippery loose material where you least want it and animals have little road sense.

Top tip

The days when every village had at least a one-pump fuel outlet are long gone so before leaving the main roads, make sure you have enough fuel. Running out in very remote areas can be dangerous, especially in bad weather.

Speed

A national speed limit usually applies to rural roads, which is 60 mph in the UK and around that speed in most other countries (normally 100 **kph**). However, rural roads are fine examples of how a speed limit is no more than a maximum. There are plenty of exceptionally good rural roads where you could safely top 100 mph, if the law allowed, but there are also many where half the speed limit would be too fast. Speed of itself is not dangerous but the misuse of speed on rural roads often is. You must judge what is a safe speed and by that we mean a safe speed for you in those conditions. A skilled driver who knows the road and has, say, an advanced four-wheel drive sports car may be able safely to go considerably faster than even an experienced driver who does not know the road and has an older, more modest car. If things seem to be coming up too fast and you regularly have to brake harder than expected, you are probably going too fast for the road and your abilities. If your car's electronic driving aids are regularly being activated, you are certainly going too fast.

However, don't stop others driving at the speed they feel safe. If you or your car, or even just your mood, mean you are driving slowly it is more than just polite to let others past if the road stops them overtaking. It is also safer because they won't be tempted to take risks to get past you or drive too close to you. You may think their driving is unwise, but it is not for you to enforce common sense, or the laws of the road, and you do not want to be involved in their accident. Just signal and pull into a lay-by, gateway or passing place when you can. In some northern European countries it is illegal not to pull over if you have three or more vehicles behind you: it's a shame that's not a universal law.

Vacant vacationers

Anyone who has lived in a tourist area will tell you that too many holidaymakers forget to pack their brains and their manners.

Please remember when you visit the countryside that not everyone there is on holiday or having a nice day out. You may be relaxing, but they have appointments to go to and work to do, so don't get in their way. The person behind you in a big hurry could be a doctor or vet trying to get to an emergency.

If you show consideration you often get it in return. For example, tractor drivers are more likely to pull over for the person who follows quietly at a safe distance than someone who hassles them.

If you want to admire the view, always check your mirrors first and only stop where it is safe, which doesn't mean the middle of the road or after a blind bend, no matter how quiet the road seems. Never use field gates as parking places because farmers need access to their fields at all times, especially if there are animals in them. They have every right to move your car if it is an obstruction, particularly if lack of access affects animal welfare.

Observation

Observation is critical on rural roads, especially at speed. Hedges and field walls can considerably restrict your view ahead but it is still possible to glean information. A flash of colour through the trees tells you something is coming the other way or may be moving slowly beyond the corner. Recently disturbed puddles or water splashed across a dry road suggest there is something not far ahead. Animal droppings that are still shiny suggest a horse-rider or someone driving cattle has recently come that way.

Look out, too, for changes in road surface. Older tarmac may offer less grip while a dark, damp area that never sees the sun under overhanging trees could be slippery, especially on frosty mornings. On more minor country roads, look out for surface damage that will certainly be uncomfortable and might damage the tyres.

Insight

Keeping an eye on changing road surfaces comes naturally to motorcyclists, who are more vulnerable to its vagaries, but it is also a skill it is worth car drivers developing. It is part of recognizing that road conditions are always changing, which also helps stop you becoming complacent when driving a regular route. Recognizing that something is different could be the difference between getting safely to work and sliding into a ditch.

HUMPS AND DIPS

Humps and dips in the tarmac also need caution at speed. Humps can even send taller people thumping against the roof while a series of them can seriously upset the composure of some cars, especially softly sprung ones where the suspension may still be reacting to the first lump when it hits the second. If this happens, avoid braking hard because that can bring the nose down on the next hump.

Dips that run along the direction of travel affect some cars more than others. Those with wide, **low profile sports tyres** often follow these indentations, particularly under hard braking or acceleration, which is called 'tramlining' because old cars with narrow tyres did it on tramlines. It can be very disconcerting at speed, especially if it is road edge subsidence which twitches the car towards the edge. Resist the temptation to snatch the steering back, not least because the car rarely has any intention of going seriously out of line. This is where a relaxed hold on the wheel helps you feel what the car is doing. It will feel less worrying if you slow down.

THE WAY IT GOES

The tree line and, to a certain extent, telegraph poles can help guide you to the route the road follows, but don't rely on them too much. The trees may follow an older route while the utility company might have decided it was cheaper to run the line across a field instead of following the road.

Take care in flat and featureless countryside like the English Fens, Holland and northern France. The lack of features often gives the impression that a road is straighter than it really is and this is made worse by the fact that in these areas roads often are straight for many miles before kinking to avoid a feature of the landscape. Even worse, these features often contain deep water to finish off the unwary (such a road in Suffolk claimed eight lives in a year). These areas are particularly dangerous at night because you have little to judge speed by and can see the lights of other cars a long way off so you may think the road between you and them is straight when it isn't.

BEHIND YOU

Don't forget to check your mirrors. If you know what is behind you, you won't be surprised if you are overtaken or pull out to overtake just as someone is overtaking you. You also know that you need to signal earlier for junctions if someone is close behind and that you can't suddenly stop if you miss a turning. In narrow

roads the passenger side mirror can also help to give you an idea of
how much clearance you are giving the road edge on that side.

Insight

Country roads are not like town streets where all the roadside
'furniture' is safely set back from a distinct kerb. Road
edges may be broken, or simply merge with the mud, and
rocks, trees and other natural obstructions are not a uniform
distance from your door mirrors, especially on sunken roads.
So, don't drive too close to the road edge and remember
that after heavy rain and storms some of these natural
obstructions may have moved. If you have to pull well over
to get past something, keep an eye on hedges or banks on
your nearside for obstructions, or ask your passenger to.

Overtaking

Overtaking is at its most dangerous on rural roads because of
the changing nature of the roads and the closing speeds involved
if it goes wrong, so it must be carefully judged. You should only
overtake where you can be sure you will be safely back on your
side of the road in the distance you can see is clear.

LOOKING AHEAD

A common mistake when trying to overtake large vehicles is to
drive too close to them. If you back off, you'll be able to see past
them more easily and you won't have to move out so far to see
round them. Look at it like this: if you hold your hand a few
centimetres from your nose you can barely see anything round it,
but if you stretch out your arm you can see more the further away
your hand is. The only problem with this is that if you drive a low
powered car you get to the point where the advantage of seeing
further is lost by the fact that it takes you too long to catch up and
overtake, so you must compromise.

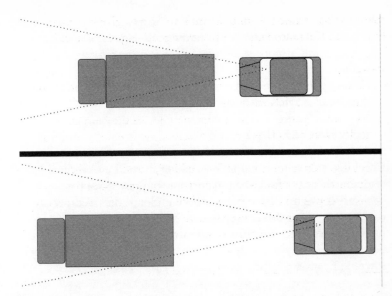

Figure 7.1 By pulling back the driver extends his view past the truck.

Top tip

By dropping back you also make it easier for the drivers of large vehicles, including cars towing trailers, to see you. They are relying entirely on their side mirrors so if you can't see those mirrors, they can't see you or your signals.

But don't just look at what is coming. Also consider the following:

▶ *Is there anything in front of the vehicle in front? You need more space to overtake two vehicles instead of one.*

▶ *What is the lie of the land? If it goes uphill a truck might slow right down but will you still have the power to overtake?*

▶ *How much of the road can you really see? Hidden dips can hide oncoming vehicles that are very close to you.*

▶ *Is there anyone ahead signalling to turn across you?*

▶ *Are there side turnings someone might emerge from as you overtake?*

▶ *Is it legal? Look for 'no overtaking' signs or solid white lines. The reasons for the latter may not be obvious, like a hidden dip or poor sight line, which is often why they are there.*

▶ *Once you have overtaken, will you have enough road to slow down again for any bends ahead?*

LOOKING BEHIND

Checking your mirrors before overtaking should be obvious, but also remember to check them before moving out to see past a vehicle – if you do that while someone is alongside, the cars may touch or the other driver may swerve because they think you are pulling out further. This is very important in a queue where more powerful cars may overtake from further back to exploit distances it would be unsafe for drivers of slower cars to use.

By constantly checking your mirror you build a picture of what is behind you so you know if anyone looks as if they plan to overtake.

SIGNAL

Signal before overtaking because it warns the overtaken driver of what you are planning to do and lets anyone behind you know you are going to move out so, in theory, they won't. You don't signal before pulling back in because it should be entirely obvious to everyone that you will be doing that and if there is a junction approaching it could give the impression you are turning off.

GEARS

You know your car so you should know whether you need to change down and whether it needs to drop one or two gears. The aim is to be in a gear that allows you to accelerate quickly from your current speed to one that is fast enough to overtake quickly. If you can complete the manoeuvre in one gear, so much the better because it makes it a quicker, cleaner operation with no opportunity for a poor gear-change putting you in danger. But don't stretch the engine beyond its useful rev range. For example, many diesels accelerate well from just below 2,000 rpm to about 3,500 rpm then performance trails off, so changing up a gear to stay in that rev range maintains good acceleration.

With automatics you use the kickdown facility for overtaking. This is a throttle switch, activated when you floor the pedal, which tells the box to drop a gear or two. Be prepared for a surge in power, especially in turbocharged cars. Automatics should keep you in the most effective rev range, though CVT boxes (see Chapter 2) may need you to ease off the throttle to get them to change up.

OVERTAKING SPEED

You need to get round the car ahead as quickly as you can but be aware that you are still breaking the law if you exceed the speed limit. Check your speed after overtaking – you won't have had time to check it while you were overtaking and it is very easy to forget, especially if you are 'celebrating' getting round something you've been stuck behind for miles.

Animals

Unfortunately, animals and cars frequently come together with disastrous results. There is often little a driver can do to avoid them and in some cases harsh decisions must be made. Slamming on the brakes or swerving might be a natural reaction to a cuddly bunny in the road but doing so could put you and other road users at risk, so try to resist the temptation. Quite often drivers harmed through trying to avoid a small animal wouldn't have hurt it anyway because the car would have passed over it.

With larger animals you may have no choice. Something the size of a deer does considerable damage and will come through the windscreen if it is leaping as you hit it. Indeed, even a large bird, like a goose, can take the windscreen out of a car. By the time you get to large animals like red deer, elk and horses you are talking of life-threatening crashes. A car hitting these animals usually knocks its legs away, or may even sever them, and the body crashes into the car across the windscreen pillars. Many cars are now built to withstand this impact, but it can bring the roof down on the car's front seat occupants.

If the animal is injured, rather than killed, you must call the police, animal welfare or forestry services to kill it humanely or take it away for treatment. In the UK and most other countries you must inform the police if you have been involved in an accident with any domesticated animal and with deer. Oddly, cats are usually an exception from this.

AVOIDING ANIMALS

Always pass animals slowly because they are unpredictable and even if they are not frightened by your car, something else may spook them as you go by. Above all, don't expect animals to stop and look both ways when they cross the road: if you see one heading towards the road (or the eyes glowing in the dark) assume it is going to cross.

Take particular care if a herd animal crosses in front of you. Things like deer rarely travel alone, so if one bounds across a few metres ahead of you, you'll probably get there just in time to hit the rest of the herd if you do not brake. Even domesticated animals that wander free can get worried if the herd is split as they cross the road or if a youngster is separated from its mother, which can lead to them taking risks without warnings that would be apparent to those unused to them. If farm animals and horses get out of a field, they do not usually do so alone, so one cow encountered on the road is likely to be followed by others.

Birds are also prone to this: pheasant 'harems' often follow the cock bird across the road only for the last in the line to do a U-turn as the car gets close. Should you decide such a victim would make a good dinner, make sure it's dead before you put it in the car as a panicking pheasant is not a safety conscious passenger.

With any animal bigger than a rabbit or pigeon, always check the car for damage after an impact. They often dislodge pieces of trim and may even damage wiring and brake pipes as they go under the car.

We will deal with domesticated animals again in Chapter 8.

Top tip

Prey animals like rabbits, hares and some ground birds often run along in front of a car. This is because predators prefer to hit them from the side (watch a film of lions chasing zebra) so by avoiding turning they feel safer. Generally, if you slow down a little to give them room, they will turn into the countryside.

Bends

Bends are one of the things that make rural roads different and more challenging. Interestingly, drivers have been found to push the car closer to its limits on tight bends than they do on fast open bends. This is because we all have an inbuilt perception of what speed we feel safe at and though the car might safely take a sweeping bend at 70 mph, we perceive that, say, 50 mph is as fast as is safe. If that is the case, the same driver may happily take the car through a tighter bend at 40 mph where the car's safe limit is 45 mph. So, just because you slow down more for a tight bend it doesn't necessarily mean you are any safer.

On a road you don't know, choosing a safe speed for a bend is a matter of erring on the side of caution because you don't really know it is safe until you are round the bend. This is something we have to learn by experience but what you are doing without realizing it is looking for a point of convergence where the two sides of the road appear to meet. If you are doing it right, that point should stay the same distance ahead of you all the way round the bend. If you are going too fast, or the bend tightens on itself, that point will appear to be getting closer.

POSITIONING

If you watch racing drivers, they try to take the straightest line through a bend, using up the whole width of the track. Unfortunately, this technique is not suited to the road because racing drivers don't have to worry about things coming the other way. There is no reason why you can't mimic their racing line through a bend on a narrow road where you can see a long way ahead (even then don't do it on your driving test) but there are few roads where you can safely do that.

On the road, you want to increase your view round the bend as much as possible. Even sticking to your side of the road, just moving to left or right can extend your view ahead by many metres, depending on the width of the road. So, if you are taking a right-hand bend, enter it as far to the left as you can safely go and if it is a left-hand bend, move over to the right. You can still straighten the line once you can see through the bend.

However, you must remember that moving towards the centre of the road brings you closer to oncoming traffic, while getting too close to the edge is not always wise on high-sided or wooded country roads where not all obstructions stop at the kerb and some rocks and branches may stick out far enough to damage your car.

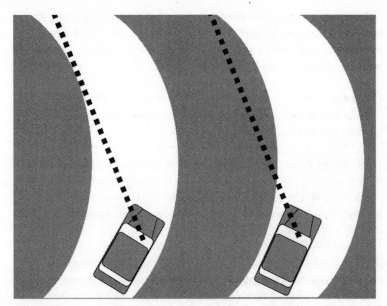

Figure 7.2 By entering a left-hand bend to the right of your side of the road, you get a better view round it.

POWER

Only an idiot would coast around a bend in neutral because you have no control over the car, but it is surprising how many people allow a car to drift round bends with their foot off the throttle, which is called being on a '**trailing throttle**' and isn't much better. You are turning the steering to ask the car to change direction but without power you remove the means for it to carry out your command.

In effect, you are using the car's weight and momentum to take it through the bend and the problem with this is most obvious in large vehicles and in cars towing trailers. On a trailing throttle many 4×4s feel as if they want to drift out, because that's what their weight wants to do, while a towcar often feels as if the trailer is pushing it straight on, which is effectively what is happening. In either case, the slightest use of power counters this effect by driving the car through the bend, allowing it to take command of its weight or pull the trailer instead of being pushed. Indeed, in anything with four-wheel drive, the power enables the expensive technology you have paid for to actually do its work and the car should feel much more balanced.

The fact is that while it is most obvious in large vehicles and towcars, it happens in all cars and even the smallest will feel better cornering under power.

THROTTLE CONTROL

Aim to slow down early enough for the bend to allow you to change down, if necessary, then come back on the power to drive through the bend.

When you are past the apex of the bend, heading towards the exit you can ease on more power to drive you away from the bend and regain your cruising speed. Indeed, if you are unsure of a bend, apply the old rallying adage of 'slow in, fast out': the point being that if you enter slowly you won't be correcting for nasty surprises so will be in a position to regain speed quickly as you leave.

Avoid sudden applications or reductions in power while cornering as both upset the car's balance and can lead to serious handling difficulties. We'll be covering skidding in Chapter 10, but if the car runs wide try to avoid the temptation to snatch your foot off the throttle because that makes the situation worse. In some cars it can change their stance so completely they switch from drifting nose out to swinging the back round as the weight is transferred forwards by the sudden drop in power (almost like you being thrown forwards by braking). Four-wheel drive vehicles and rear-engined sports cars are particularly prone to this.

RIGHT GEAR

Nobody can tell you what the right gear for a bend is because there are too many variables. It depends on the car, the tightness of the bend, whether it is going uphill, your speed and your load.

Many modern cars offer extreme flexibility and can comfortably take country road bends in top gear, but you must also consider control. It is easier to maintain control in a lower gear because when you ease off the throttle the car slows quicker and when you apply the throttle it picks up speed faster. Indeed, some six-speed automatics, notably turbocharged ones, may feel like they're picking up speed when you ease off the throttle on the approach to a bend.

More importantly, if you use a lower gear there is less chance that you will be caught out when you try to apply power, either to correct a problem mid-bend or to make your exit. Having to change gear mid-bend also upsets the car's balance.

By putting the car in the most effective gear, you also save fuel. As explained in Chapter 2, if you keep an engine at the revs in which it develops its workable torque, it pulls with the least effort. Most modern automatics do this very well, but you may need to help some in unusual circumstances, like uphill bends, or if you want to maintain more control on very twisting, undulating roads.

Junctions

Rural junctions often come up very quickly and can be difficult to see, or see out of, so they need special consideration. Remember that slowing down for a junction is part of the manoeuvre – you should have mirrored and signalled before, otherwise the driver behind isn't going to expect you to slow down and may overtake if you do not signal that you are going to turn across the road. So, check your mirrors and signal in plenty of time.

Take care when turning right because your view of oncoming traffic may be limited and traffic coming from behind may have little time to react to you being there. See Chapter 5 for how to position yourself correctly but remember it is even more important not to turn your wheels while waiting at the centre line because the speed of approaching cars is higher on rural roads so any impact is more serious.

LEAVING SIDE ROADS

Visibility at junctions in rural areas is often limited because of undergrowth and sight lines that have been created by accident rather than design. You may get a better idea of how busy a road you are joining is from further back, so keep an eye to either side as you approach.

If the roadsides are very overgrown you may have to edge forwards to see out, but take very great care because if you can't see up the road, oncoming drivers may not be able to see the nose of your car until it is too late.

Take time to judge the speed of oncoming vehicles, which may be high. Remember to look both ways, too. If you are turning left (in the UK) the temptation is to only look right, but what if someone is overtaking something approaching from your left? You could turn directly into their path.

Take care about crossing or turning in front of a large, slow moving vehicle. Someone following it, looking for a chance to overtake, may not even be aware of the junction ahead, never mind expecting you to be there when they pull out. So, don't cross or turn in front of a slow vehicle unless you are sure there is nothing behind it. Equally, don't take risks to get out in front of a slow moving vehicle to avoid being held up by it: you'll be held up a lot longer if you cause an accident.

Top tip

Don't turn out of a side road into a narrow road if you can see something coming towards you that you won't get past, even if it is some way off. If you are in a side road, the other vehicle can pass you safely but if you pull into the narrow road you'll have to find a passing place, so waiting may turn out to be quicker, too.

Single track roads

The most rural of roads is the single track road weaving its way across untouched countryside. These can be a pleasant drive across open land, like the Scottish highland moors, where you can usually see what is coming, but nerve racking where they are closely bordered by hedges or walls, or where they have become sunken roads. They are probably most dangerous where they are close to cities and in tourist areas where instead of meeting locals who know the risks you meet townies who think you drive everywhere in the countryside at 60 mph.

There is nothing wrong with driving quickly along a single track road with good sight lines as long as you remember they tend to feature adverse cambers, sudden bends, hidden dips and blind summits, most of which are not marked with warning signs. So it is vital that on these roads you do not drive at a speed that means you can't stop in the distance you can see and that you do not become complacent. If anything goes wrong, you have nowhere to go and it could be a long time before anyone finds you if you leave the road.

Don't be afraid to occasionally use your horn to warn others of your approach on bends, but don't treat it as giving you right of way.

Insight

Look out for wild and domestic animals on single track roads because you have very little room to avoid them. Never try to squeeze past horse-riders, people leading animals, cyclists or pedestrians, especially those with children or dogs. If they are coming the other way, it is much safer if you stop and let them pass you. If you are going the same way, slow down until they are able to get out of your way into a gateway or passing place.

PASSING PLACES

Many single track roads have small lay-by-style passing places, often with a sign saying 'passing place'. Most people accept that if something is coming the other way they either pull into one of these or stop opposite one until the other vehicle has passed. However, a source of great frustration to locals, especially in tourist areas, is how few visitors realize that if someone comes up behind you they are obviously going faster than you want to so you should pull in to the next passing place to let them pass (see Plate 11).

Though the usual etiquette is that the driver nearest to a passing place reverses back when it is necessary, this may not always be possible. You can't expect any driver to reverse round a blind bend. It is also far easier for a car driver to back up than it is for a truck or towcar driver to reverse even a short distance on a narrow road, because their view behind is so limited and their vehicles lack manoeuvrability. In addition, some passing places may be too small to accommodate a long vehicle.

As can be seen, these passing places are important to the free flow of traffic so never use them as parking places. In some areas, the police are empowered to remove cars left in passing places.

CATTLE GRIDS

Single track roads often feature cattle grids, particularly where they cross moorland or traditional heathland. These are a trough the width of the road overlaid by a grid of steel poles (sometimes old railway lines) that are set just far enough apart to stop cattle, sheep and horses crossing them but close enough for vehicles to drive over. They are an alternative to having gates on roads across land where animals roam free.

Never cross one at high speed because they can be slippery and the less well-maintained ones may damage tyres or its bars may even bounce up under the car. However, if you cross them too slowly you'll feel every bump rather than a quick buzz as the tyres skim across the grid.

Take them as a signal that there may be animals on the road ahead.

Loose surfaced roads

Though rare in the UK, stone and gravel roads are common in the more remote areas of many countries, even those with sophisticated infrastructure elsewhere. This is often because these surfaces stand up to it better than tarmac in places where the soil moves because of its make-up or because it regularly freezes and thaws. They can range from surfaces that feel almost as smooth as tarmac, like Finland's gravel roads, to badly potholed tracks.

Smooth gravel roads can be deceptive because the car feels fine in a straight line but drifts alarmingly when you try to turn into a bend. This is particularly so in vehicles with sophisticated four-wheel drive which moves the power according to how much grip the wheels have, so compensates for the changing surfaces in a straight line but can't force tyres to grip on bends. So, always drive with caution on these roads and slow right down for bends.

However, sometimes it pays to go faster. If these roads are not regularly graded they can build up a washboard effect on the surface caused by the natural frequency of compression and rebound in vehicles' suspension forming regular ripples. On these roads there is a 'harmonic speed' at which the frequency of the ripples harmonizes with the natural frequency of your car's suspension and so the ride appears to smooth out. If it is safe to do so, maintaining this speed is less wearing on the car and its occupants.

On these roads always keep an eye on the surface just ahead of you because it may deteriorate suddenly with potholes or banks of soft gravel. But remember that on these remote roads you rarely need to stick to one side of the road, so you should be able to avoid crashing wheels into obstacles. As an African 4×4 driver put it: 'In England you drive on the left side, in America you drive on the right side, but here you drive on the good side.'

If you come across other vehicles, slow down because you and they are throwing up stones and dust. Do not follow too close behind another vehicle for the same reason and because stopping and avoiding action are difficult. In addition, in dry conditions vehicles create lots of dust so show consideration by slowing down as you pass other vehicles, people and animals.

Loose chippings

When tarmac roads are resurfaced it is usually done by spreading tar on them then small stones called chippings. Until these stick down and the surplus is swept up, the road should be treated as a gravel road because you will slide on them. Indeed, most gravel roads have far fewer loose stones than a newly surfaced tarmac road.

In addition, loose chippings can do significant damage to the bodywork and glass, so keep your speed down to about 20 mph. Above this speed your wheels are more likely to throw chippings high into the air which not only puts other people's car windows at risk, but your own when they bounce back off other vehicles. Also, if someone else is going too fast, you reduce the impact of chippings on your car by reducing the closing speed between your car and the other car or the chippings it throws up.

It is also wise to close your windows, at least on the side facing oncoming traffic, so you don't get hit in the face by flying stones.

Tar spots can be removed from paint and clothing with white spirit.

Hills

The steepest hills tend to be in rural areas and where most of us master pulling away on modest slopes as learners, because it is part of the driving test, steeper hills need special consideration.

Top tip

Engine power drops with altitude as the air gets thinner so a given volume contains less oxygen. The odd few hundred metres will make little difference, but in mountainous areas you will notice the drop in power and so may have to hold lower gears longer. Indeed, on high altitude passes you may not even be able to use top gear on flat sections of road.

PULLING AWAY

Pulling away is largely a matter of balancing the application of power with releasing the handbrake. Many cars now make this easier with automatic handbrakes and **hill start assist**, which hold the brakes for a few seconds after the brake pedal is released. These work well in most circumstances, but be careful the first time you use them on extremely steep slopes in case it is more than they can handle.

Pulling away in an automatic involves no more than applying enough power to stop it rolling back as you release the handbrake and then pull away by applying more power. On modest hills an automatic will usually hold itself on tickover power.

With a manual gearbox you can use the rev counter to help you pull away on steep hills. As we've said before, torque (pulling power) is what gets the car moving, so if you set the engine revs at around the peak torque speed (see your handbook) it should pull away efficiently. The mistake many people make, though, is to try juggling clutch and throttle pedal, when they only need to use one. This is how it works:

1 *Put the car in gear with the handbrake on and clutch depressed.*
2 *Use the throttle pedal to raise the revs to around peak torque (say 2,000 rpm on a diesel and 3,000 rpm on a petrol).*
3 *Now gently raise the clutch until you feel the transmission take up the car's weight (the bonnet will rise a little).*
4 *Ease off the handbrake while raising or lowering the clutch pedal gently to keep the revs around the peak torque point. (Hold the throttle pedal steady.)*
5 *As the car picks up speed you should find you are able to fully raise the clutch as you increase the revs.*

Don't be tempted to change up too early because on a steep incline a higher gear may not be able to keep the engine in the right torque range so you may stall and have to start again. It's better to stay in a lower gear and climb more slowly.

CLIMBING HILLS

Climbing hills requires lots of torque and means using higher revs for the road speed than you would on a flat road. It is easier on you, the engine and the transmission if you anticipate the slope and change down before you get to the point at which the engine starts to labour. That way you keep up your momentum and don't have to try to change down on the hill. With an automatic, apply more power before you start climbing, rather than when it slows down.

What gear you use depends on the flexibility of the engine, the spacing of the gear ratios, altitude, the steepness of the slope and how heavily loaded the car is. So, a lightly laden diesel with plenty of torque may sail up a hill in fourth or fifth, but a small petrol car with five people and their luggage aboard may require second or third. It is often better to hold a lower gear and climb more slowly than risk changing up and finding the engine cannot cope, so you have to change down again and regain speed.

Modern automatics usually cope with hill climbing on their own but listen to the engine and if it seems to be struggling, shift the box down to a lower gear. On twisting hills even modern automatics have trouble as they try to shift up and down for the corners, especially as the slope in a hairpin bend is often momentarily steeper than the climbs in between. In these conditions an automatic may need driver help, perhaps holding a lower gear all the time or pulling it down a gear before turning into a bend.

Take care not to change up quickly when you get to the top of a steep hill. The sudden change in torque as you lift off the throttle to change gear can destabilize the car, which could cause problems in bends, on slippery surfaces or when towing. Once you get to the top, reduce the throttle smoothly before changing up.

DESCENDING HILLS

In mountainous areas you can always tell the tourist cars by the way they take long descents with the brakelights on all the way. This is a recipe for brake fade as the brakes overheat by being used so much with little chance to dissipate the heat.

You can ease the burden on the brakes by selecting a lower gear and, with your foot off the throttle, using the engine's resistance to slow the car down (this is called engine braking). You may still need to use the brakes on steep slopes, but not as often as you would in a higher gear.

Many modern automatics recognize you are going downhill because the car is trying to gain speed with no driver input. They then refuse to change up and may even shift down. However, even these boxes may need manual help to select the right gear for the slope.

Top tip

With an automatic in hilly areas, especially on twisting roads, it often pays to lock it out of top gear, which is sometimes done with a push button 'overdrive off' facility. If you don't do this you may find the box repeatedly shifting in and out of top gear, which is annoying and can make it overheat.

Night driving

What makes night driving on rural roads different to night driving elsewhere is that it's dark. Towns and even motorways are not truly dark: in towns you obviously have street lights but on busy main roads the volume of traffic creates a significant amount of light that is enough to help you see which way the road goes for some distance ahead. Even in a crowded island like the UK, there are still plenty of places where your car's headlights are the only source of light, so make sure they are clean.

Top tip

Do not assume it is safe to drive at speed on a twisting country road because the lights of oncoming vehicles will give you plenty of warning of their approach. You still get drivers who are reluctant to use beam headlights and if their lights are not as powerful as yours you may not see them. In addition, there are plenty of things that don't have lights, like stray cattle and broken-down trucks.

BEAM ME UP

Modern headlights are very powerful and provide good light even on dip. The most modern beam headlights can light up a road like a little patch of daylight, even having a similar colour balance to help your eyes. But this makes it even more important that they are used properly. This is not just courtesy to others – if you have blinded the person coming towards you, you could be involved in the resulting accident.

Try to dip your headlights a fraction before an approaching car comes round a bend, but remember that your field of view will be suddenly cut short so you have to take in what is between you and the bend. Also dip your lights if you come up behind another driver. It is difficult to say how far ahead they need to be before you can use full beam without causing problems, because it depends on the power of your lights and size of their mirrors, but if light is being reflected back by their number plate and reflectors, you probably need to dip.

It is obvious you should dip your lights for pedestrians and cyclists coming towards you but it is also safer to dip them when you are close behind them. Beam headlights create huge shadows in front of them that may stop them seeing potholes and kerbs.

Though beam headlights generally let you see further ahead, they don't always. Unless your car has twin headlights with dipped beam staying on with main beam, when you crest a hill or humped backed bridge you plunge into darkness. However, if you switch briefly to dip as you go over the crest, the light will shine down into the road below. On some cars where dipped beam is strongly to the passenger side, it may also help you see into bends turning to that side. Beam headlights also reduce visibility in fog and snow by reflecting back off the water droplets or snowflakes (see Chapter 9).

DIPPING MIRRORS

Most cars now have manual or automatic dipping interior mirrors. In unlit country roads it is safe and sensible to leave these permanently in the dipped position, though when you re-enter a town it pays in some cars to return to the undipped position for a clearer view out, unless you are dazzled from behind.

Try to avoid readjusting door mirrors to cut glare from behind because you may forget you have done it and on dark roads it may not be obvious that you are no longer seeing what is behind you. Except on cars with very big mirrors, you can usually avoid glare in door mirrors by tilting your head.

10 THINGS TO REMEMBER

1 Rural roads can be demanding and dangerous.

2 Observation is important if you are to avoid surprises such as which way the road goes.

3 Overtaking must be treated with caution and only carried out where you can complete it in the road you can see before pulling out.

4 Encounters with wild and domesticated animals are always a potentially dangerous risk on rural roads.

5 Never assume a herd animal crossing the road is alone.

6 If you are constantly having to brake hard or bends seem to tighten up on you, you're probably going too fast.

7 Avoid taking bends on a trailing throttle.

8 Sight lines at junctions may be poor on rural roads.

9 Never park in passing places on single track roads or in field gateways to which farmers may need access.

10 If someone has gained on you on a single track road, pull over when you can to let them pass.

8

....

Vulnerable road users

In this chapter you will learn:
- *how to recognize vulnerable road users*
- *what consideration they need.*

Not all road users are drivers but as we sit in our cars it is easy to forget the needs of those we share the road with who do not have a protective box around them.

Consideration for these people is not just courtesy, it is a question of safety – yours and theirs. It is also your moral responsibility to remember that your car has the potential to cause distress and even to kill if you do not use it properly.

Fire and water

People outside your car are vulnerable to anything coming from it so think carefully before washing the screen as you pass someone, or throwing out cigarette ends.

Apart from the distress this causes it can be a real road safety risk if someone is blinded by eyes full of washer fluid or a shower of smouldering cigarette ash. Indeed, discarding cigarettes this way is thoroughly irresponsible because of the risk it creates to people, their property and the countryside: if you don't want to use the ashtray, don't smoke in the car.

(Contd)

For similar reasons, make sure anything carried on your car is firmly attached and that the straps used to tie it down are tied off short so they do not whip around in the slipstream.

Pedestrians

Pedestrians often do not realize how vulnerable they are on the roads and we've all done it. Most of us have walked along a poorly-lit road dressed in dark clothes or crossed where it might not have been sensible. In addition, not all pedestrians drive so they may not have the road awareness you might expect, not realizing how drivers can't see them in certain conditions or how much time a car needs to stop.

In rural areas, pedestrians often have to walk in the road, even in villages. Slow down and give them room and do not attempt to squeeze past when something is coming the other way because you leave yourself no room for manoeuvre.

Top tip

Be aware that in bad weather, pedestrians may not be paying attention to what is coming as they try to keep the rain or snow out of their faces. Those wearing glasses may have vision substantially reduced by water on them.

CHILDREN

Children are particularly vulnerable because they do not have the experience of life to fully recognize the dangers around them or that might result from their own actions. They are frequently not even aware of anything beyond the game they are playing or their friends, so do not assume a child approaching the kerb is going to stop.

Always drive slowly near play areas and past schools at times when children are on the move. Look out for signs of them at play, like toys in or near the road or a ball bouncing out.

Never stop for children to cross the road unless you are certain vehicles around you will do the same. Children won't look past your car and may cross while someone is overtaking you. For the same reason, never wave a child across the road because they won't think to check for vehicles you may have missed or been unable to see.

Insight

In many countries there is an increasing use of extra low speed limits in areas where there are large numbers of children, such as near schools, parks or in residential areas. In the UK the usual urban speed limit of 30 mph is reduced to 20 mph. Try to observe these speed restrictions because it gives you a far greater chance of seeing a child about to do something silly and a child's chances of surviving an impact are greatly increased at 20 mph. Remember, that while 20 mph may seem unnecessary when going past a school when the children are inside, people will have become used to traffic being slower in that area.

THE ELDERLY

Elderly people on foot may not be as sprightly or traffic aware as they once were and, sadly, may not realize that. A lot of the considerations for children apply to the very elderly with the addition that they do not have a child's agility to get out of the way if anything goes wrong.

Do not assume that an elderly person crossing some way in front of you will be out of the road by the time you get there. Do not try to hurry them across the road if the lights change in your favour: if they were on the crossing before the lights change, they still have right of way. Driving on while they are still on the road makes them vulnerable because other drivers may not see them in time.

Take special care in poor light, including places where an elderly pedestrian is looking from sunlight into the shade, because old eyes are not as good at adapting to changes in light as younger ones so they may not see a car that doesn't contrast markedly with its surroundings. This is one reason why **daylight driving lights** are being adopted across Europe.

Remember too that their hearing may also be impaired. This is a particular concern if you drive an electric car or a hybrid that runs on its electric motor at low speeds: while youngsters may be able to hear the high pitched noise of the motor, older people lose the ability to hear higher pitched sounds.

Elderly people are not as good at judging speed as younger adults, which is why elderly drivers often have problems using roundabouts or pulling out of junctions and may pull out at the wrong times. Elderly drivers tend to drive more slowly because their reactions are slower, which can be frustrating if you are stuck behind them on a twisting road, but hassling them won't help. If you do anything stupid they may not be able to react quickly enough to avoid an accident.

Insight

Most of us would say that an elderly driver who recognizes their reactions are not as good as they were and slows down is wise, and, if we're honest with ourselves, we hope we are similarly sensible as age takes effect. But it is a shame that while many elderly drivers admit they are slow, few ever consider pulling over to let others past. Age does not excuse you from courtesy, so if a traffic queue forms behind you, be considerate and pull over when you can.

Retire gracefully

If you are an elderly driver, be honest with yourself about whether you are still safe. In the UK it is up to you to tell the licensing authorities if health or infirmity mean you can no longer drive. If you regularly have near misses, fail to see other vehicles or frighten passengers, you should seek your doctor's advice about whether you are fit to drive. If you think relatives' criticisms of your driving are unjustified, why not get an independent view by taking a 'lesson' with a driving school?

Disabilities

Our cities are increasingly being designed to be more friendly to people with disabilities but our society often needs to adapt in the same way. Make allowances for people who cannot do things as well, or as quickly, as you and probably they, would like.

When parking, or in slow moving traffic, have consideration for the blind and those with mobility problems. Many city streets have lowered kerbs with pimpled paving to help wheelchair users get across and blind people to find safe crossing places. If you obstruct these places, the most vulnerable pedestrians will have to find a way round your car.

BLIND

While blind people need consideration, trying to help them in the wrong way can cause them even more problems. A common complaint is drivers stopping to let them across the road when traffic would not normally stop, for example, when lights are green. This may give the blind person a false impression of whether the lights have changed while your engine can mask the sounds of vehicles that are still moving.

Doing this can also confuse guide dogs into crossing the road when it is unsafe and because they are low down, they won't be able to see anything overtaking you.

Do not be surprised if a blind person stands at the kerb after lights have changed in their favour; they are waiting for the bleeping signal to start, so give them time.

DEAF

It is not usually obvious that someone is deaf, so it is best to treat everyone as if they are. Do not expect someone to hear you coming especially as many modern cars are so quiet that the crunch of gravel under the tyres may be all you hear of them. Some people with perfect hearing may not notice that, so what chance does a person with poor hearing have?

WHEELCHAIR USERS

Anyone in a wheelchair needs time to cross the road and because they are low down they may not have a good view of the traffic around them.

Do not assume that when they reach the kerb after crossing they will be able to continue as quickly as they were while they crossed the road. Wheelchairs are not easy to control as they mount obstacles and even some drop kerbs are not the perfect height for all wheelchairs to negotiate, so the user may have to slow or even stop to manoeuvre over the obstacle.

Wheelchair users also need more space to get past things than walking pedestrians do. Therefore, in roads with parked cars they may not be able to go straight across and may find when they get to a gap that they can't get through it because of something they could not see from the other side of the road, like a towbar or debris in the road.

Top tip
Wheelchair users need at least a metre of space to get themselves and their chairs into their cars so do not park too close to a car with signs saying it belongs to a wheelchair user or which has obvious adaptations.

Two-wheelers

Motorcyclists and cyclists are vulnerable because they are easily overlooked by car drivers and come off worse if they are. Both need road space because their machines are inherently unstable and are vulnerable to road surface faults. Indeed, in British law a test case decreed that a cyclist was 'entitled to his wobble'.

MOTORCYCLISTS

Motorbikes can have acceleration that would leave even the fastest cars standing and many car drivers are not prepared for that. The bike pulling out of a junction half a mile down the road from yours may already be going very quickly and be close to you by the time you get out in front of him.

Bikes are also relatively small and easily hidden by a car's blind spots, so make sure you move your head to look round windscreen pillars before pulling out of junctions, especially roundabouts where a bike coming round is often obscured by the pillar.

In traffic queues, remember that bikes may be moving between the queues, so keep an eye in your mirrors for them and if you can, ease over to give them more space to pass. That isn't just courtesy, you now no longer have a bike behind you that might find its way into your blind spot.

Bikes are more sensitive to changes in road surface than cars, so may need to move out to avoid something that could destabilize them. Often car drivers would not even notice these things: polished manhole covers, diesel spills, patches of shiny tar and unduly raised Catseyes can all unseat a motorcyclist. For the same reason, never follow one too closely because if he comes off you will be hitting a largely unprotected person.

Top tip

If a motorcyclist comes off in front of you at speed, watch the rider, not just the bike: too many motorcyclists are killed by drivers trying to avoid the bike. If you can, use your car to protect the rider from other traffic as he slides along the road. Use your hazard warning lights and when you stop, turn the car's wheels so that if it is struck it will turn away from him. Never try to remove a motorcyclist's helmet after a crash because it can make serious neck injuries worse.

CYCLISTS

Sadly, cyclists are often their own worst enemies on the road. They are not trained like motorcyclists so are often totally unaware of the dangers they pose to themselves, such as not wearing high visibility clothing and cycling in poor light in dark clothing and without the legally required lights. Indeed, some don't even consider they should obey the rules of the road and may cycle the wrong way up one-way streets and round roundabouts. Unfortunately, while they may be in the wrong, it is your car they'll damage (often without insurance).

But even the responsible ones are still vulnerable. They are easily overlooked and on rural roads may be going considerably slower than approaching traffic, so you must be prepared for them and check your blind spots.

In town, look out for cyclists on your nearside when you turn and accept that there may be times when to turn safely you will have to slow down behind a cyclist to let them clear the junction ahead of you. If you overtake and cut across them, there is a real risk they will cycle into the side of you, through no fault of theirs.

As we've said, you should never pass cyclists close but that especially applies in rural roads where your car's speed is high and just the slipstream from it can destabilize a cyclist, especially in wet weather when spray is added to it.

Insight
Cyclists who are sensible enough to make themselves visible on the road often fail to do the same when they use a rear mounted bike rack on their car. If the bikes obscure the number plate and/or lights you are legally required to have a light board with a number plate and lights that plug into towing electrics. Sadly, in the UK this is not enforced as rigorously as in other countries and too many cyclists do not seem to have the common sense to realize that if their lights are hidden, nobody knows if they are indicating or braking.

Horse-riders

Unlike most road users, horse-riders do not generally want
to be there. Riding a horse on the road is not fun, because you
have to be on your guard all the time, but, particularly in the
UK, provision for riding off-road is, at best, fragmented and land
access rights mean that if you can't drive a car there, you can't
ride a horse either. In fact, while cyclists and pedestrians can use
bridleways, horses aren't allowed on cycleways or footpaths.

Unfortunately, too many drivers treat horses as machines,
especially if they are pulling a carriage, and some try to overtake
them in spaces where they wouldn't even get safely past a cyclist.
If you look at the width of a horse and the rider's legs you'll
see that they are as wide as a small car, but the big difference
is that small cars are not easily frightened. Even a sensible and
experienced horse is unpredictable and no matter how good the
rider and how calm the horse, sudden movement and loud noises
spook them. It may be nothing more than a blackbird bursting
from a roadside bush or your tyres splashing through a puddle,
but it is enough to put the horse out in front of you.

They generally spook away from whatever worried them, often
swinging their rear out so they can see whatever they are concerned
about. If you see a horse starting to do this, don't try to pass it. A
spooked horse can move a couple of metres sideways in one step.

Sadly, some drivers take the attitude that if the horse and rider
can't cope they shouldn't be on the road but if you don't care
about the horse and rider, just think of yourself. If you hit a horse
you generally take the legs from under it (or even off it) and the
body, with rider, comes crashing down on the windscreen pillars
or roof of your car. These usually collapse under the impact of
half a tonne of kicking, screaming horse. In addition, horses
involved in road accidents usually have to be put down and riders
are often seriously injured, so you can expect prosecution and a
huge insurance claim. Courts, especially in horsey areas, generally

take the view that drivers should have the sense to treat horses as unpredictable so the drivers are usually to blame for accidents.

Amazingly, one of the most common horse accidents is a driver trying to overtake a horse in a narrow road with something coming the other way. Remember, if a horse-rider is asking you to slow down it may not just be for their own benefit: they have a much better view of the tractor round the bend than you have.

So, when approaching horses:

▶ *slow right down: 30 mph on a single track road is still too fast*
▶ *give the rider time to get out of your way in narrow roads*
▶ *pass as wide as you can*
▶ *stop if the rider asks you to (it's one of the oldest motoring laws)*
▶ *on wet roads take care not to splash horses*
▶ *be prepared to stop and turn off your engine if the horse spooks*
▶ *don't let children lean out of the car or try to pat the horse as you pass. They may frighten it or get crushed between it and the car.*

Top tip

If you have to follow a horse until a safe passing place can be found, stay well back. Horses will kick out at anything that gets too close behind or that they can hear behind them and not see. If you touch a horse's back legs it will either kick or sit down on your bonnet. Horses can also stop suddenly and can go into reverse without stopping. In any of these circumstances, any insurer will take damage to be your fault, so stay two or three car lengths back.

Farm animals

In some areas, farm animals may wander free and are generally very used to traffic. In fact, some may be so used to it that they no longer treat it with respect, so don't expect them to get out of the road when they see you coming. As we said in the previous chapter, many herd animals can become distressed if separated from the rest of the herd, especially youngsters, so if part of a group crosses in front of you, it is safer to let them all cross.

Drive with care in areas where animal roam free because you never know where they may be next. It is common for these animals to lay on a warm, dry road in damp weather and they don't necessarily do it in sensible places.

Never feed animals in areas where they roam free because it encourages them to hang around the roadsides and try to approach cars. (They are also likely to bite if they don't like what you've offered or think there should be more.)

You may also come across animals being herded along the road, most commonly cows going to be milked. Don't try to hurry them along or push your way through them because you affect the herdsmen's ability to keep them under control and a panicked animal could easily run off towards a main road. In addition, if you push through even small animals, like sheep, there is a good chance of your car being damaged.

You will just have to slow to their pace or stop until they have passed. If you don't, you could be held up a lot longer while the herdsmen round them up or you have to deal with an accident.

Remember, all domesticated animals belong to someone, so if you are involved in an accident with one, you must inform the police locally, if you can't inform the owner.

10 THINGS TO REMEMBER

1 Not all pedestrians are drivers who understand what you can see and do.

2 Children are vulnerable because they do not have an adult's experience or awareness of the world around them.

3 The elderly need time to cross the road and react to traffic, which they may not be able to see or hear properly.

4 Stopping in odd places, like when lights are green, endangers rather than helps blind people.

5 The person apparently ignoring your car's presence could be deaf.

6 Wheelchair users need space to get up kerbs or get into their cars.

7 Cyclist and motorcyclists are easily obscured by your windscreen pillars, so check round them.

8 Look out for bikes moving between traffic queues.

9 Pass horses slow and wide and expect them to be unpredictable.

10 Do not try to hurry farm animals being herded along the road.

Bad weather

In this chapter you will learn:
- *how to cope with fog, snow, ice, rain, wind and heat*
- *when to use lights in bad weather*
- *when to stay at home.*

When the weather is good, driving is a pleasure but when it is bad the shortest journey can become a nightmare. Unfortunately, you can't always choose to avoid the worst weather, perhaps because a journey is essential or because conditions worsened unexpectedly when you were already on the road. Even a sunny summer's day can turn sour if the temperature climbs too high with the inevitable effects on roads, vehicles and tempers.

Whatever the weather, the essential thing is to accept that you have to alter your driving style to match the conditions and that your journey may take longer. To do otherwise is to put yourself at risk by getting frustrated or trying to meet a schedule that has become impossible: that opens the door to potentially fatal mistakes.

Insight

As someone who has been rained on in the Californian desert and seen frost in Florida, I may be pessimistic about the weather, but try to be prepared for the worst. If you do experience freak weather for the area you are in, take particular care because roads may not be designed for it and local drivers may not know how to cope with it.

(Contd)

In California, the desert roads did not have enough **camber** to rid themselves of the sudden downpour and their surface, which was fine in dry weather, quickly became slippery. Floridians obviously did not realize that what looked like a wet patch might be ice on a frosty morning.

Before you go

If the weather has clamped down before you set out, the first thing you must ask yourself is: 'Do I need to make this journey?' Fetching urgent medicines might justify the risk but while your mum will be disappointed if you don't visit on her birthday, she'll be distraught if you have an accident trying to get to her.

If you really have to go, allow more time than the journey usually needs. If it is windy or raining you won't have to allow much more time, but fog and snow significantly reduce your average speeds and increase the likelihood of hold-ups. Also consider your route: if you are in a low-lying area and it is snowing lightly, think twice about a journey that takes you through the mountains where it may be snowing much harder. Most of us know the local quirks of the weather so think about likely changes in conditions: if you live on the side of a hill and it's misty, is it likely to be thick fog lower down? Is a particular road liable to flooding or snowdrifts? There are plenty of television, online and telephone weather information services you can use to check the forecast locally and nationally before setting out.

Bad weather driving can be very tiring, so be prepared to take more frequent breaks. But you must also be more careful about where you stop because in bad visibility there is always the risk of someone running into you. Certainly, avoid stopping on the road and if you pull into a lay-by it is wise to use hazard lights because of the risk of other drivers following your lights into the lay-by without realizing you are stationary. The safest idea is to pull into a service area or detour into a town and find a car park.

Defrosting

In freezing weather you may have to clear frost and ice
from your windows before setting off. Do not skimp on
this because it severely restricts vision, and driving with
only a small area cleared is illegal in most countries.

Use a de-icer spray because, except in extremely low
temperatures, it helps prevent ice reforming. While you
are spraying it on, make sure you spray some along the
wiper blades' contact with the glass and on the washer
nozzles. Use a squeegee blade to wipe the excess off the side
windows and the wipers to clear it from the windscreen.

It helps to run the engine so you can blow air up the
windscreen and run the heated rear screen. However, keep
this to a minimum because it is not best for the engine or the
environment: ideally you should drive off soon after starting
but this may not be possible in frosty weather. If you run
the engine, do not leave the car unattended because thieves
know frosty streets are a good hunting ground (insurers call
this type of theft 'frosting').

Take de-icer with you because, apart from defrosting glass
for your return, you can use it as an emergency screen wash
if the washers are frozen.

BE PREPARED

Are you sure your car is up to it? Correct tyre pressures are even
more important in poor weather because you need the maximum
grip and don't want to be out there changing a wheel. Setting out
with worn tyres in heavy rain or snow is asking for trouble. Lights
are essential in bad weather so they must all be clean and working.
On wet and mucky roads you are likely to need the windscreen

washers more than usual, while windows that are clean on the inside are less likely to steam up. Fuel consumption is likely to be higher if you have to use lower gears and are in stop-start traffic but in very severe weather service stations may be closed. Check your mobile phone is fully charged and take a car charger with you.

If you have any doubts about the car's condition, don't set out, especially in sub-zero temperatures where a dead car with no heater could become your tomb. If you need to know more about caring for your car, see *Teach Yourself Car Buying and Ownership* in this series.

It pays to have water in the car in hot weather and high-energy snacks in cold weather. In snow, carry a fold-up shovel and tow rope.

> ### Top tip
> Always take clothing suitable for the weather, regardless of how short your journey is. In sub-zero temperatures you can get hypothermia in a broken down car a few miles from home just as easily as on a transcontinental journey. Make sure you have shoes suitable for walking and even in summer, take a coat in case the weather changes. The gods of motoring ensure you rarely have punctures and breakdowns on nice, sunny days.

Lights

New drivers often ask how they should know when to use their lights in poor weather. The simple answer is that if you find yourself wondering if you need them, you probably do. If you drive a dark car, or a silver one that blends in with fog, spray and snow, you should err on the side of caution even more.

Also look in your mirrors to see how well the cars behind you show up. In winter, when the sun is low behind you, the cars coming towards you may be well lit by it, giving you a false impression of how easily you can be seen. With the sun behind you, your car may blend into the morning mist or the shadows of roadside trees (see Plate 12).

In most European countries, including the UK, you are also required by law to use lights in rain, fog and falling snow. It is also wise to use them on wet roads when spray can suddenly reduce visibility: remember, the lorry driver you are passing is relying on his mirrors alone to see you in the cloud of water droplets.

Fog lamp abuse

Don't misuse fog lamps. All cars in Europe are required to have rear fog lamps and many cars have front fog lamps fitted. These lights, as the name suggests, are for use in fog: they are not 'slightly misty lamps'. In the UK you can only legally use them in fog and falling snow if the visibility is below 100 metres. That is the distance between motorway marker posts.

Rear fog lamps cause glare to drivers behind, particularly in poor light and on wet roads. That means following drivers often can't see past you and may not be able to see when your brake lights come on, especially if your car doesn't have a **high level brake light**. In addition, if someone is not far behind you in the dark, they can almost certainly see your ordinary lights.

If you can see a car's ordinary lights some way off, you almost certainly don't need rear fog lamps. It is also courteous, day or night, to turn off rear fog lamps in traffic queues because they create a lot of glare close up and someone stopped a few metres behind you can see you even in the thickest fog. Don't forget to turn them off if the weather clears.

Vision

Be careful not to carry your own 'fog' round with you. Fog, rain and snow (except in very low temperatures) means a high water content in the air which not only settles on the outside of the glass but makes the inside of the windows more likely to steam up. It can be very difficult to tell whether the screen has misted over, inside or out, in fog.

Fog droplets, light rain and snow may not settle on the outside quickly enough to warrant using intermittent wipers, so remember to use flick-wipe every so often. If your car has rain sensing automatic wipers, do not rely on them to clear the screen when necessary in these conditions because the sensors don't normally detect fine misting on the glass.

Give the ventilation system priority to demisting the screen and front side windows and if in doubt just check by touching the glass with your finger to see if it leaves a mark. This is also one of the times to use air conditioning in the winter. As air conditioning cools the incoming air, much of the water in it condenses out so it reduces the amount of moisture being sucked into the car. That does not mean driving round with cold air blasting out because, even on the simplest systems, you can warm the air with the heater (read your handbook to get the best from the system).

Don't forget to use heated front and rear screens and heated door mirrors, if fitted. If you don't have heated mirrors you can buy long lasting preparations which stop the glass misting up, but wiping them with washing up liquid or any kind of liquid soap or shampoo does the same thing, making the water form a film instead of opaque droplets. Don't use these things on the windscreen in case it smears.

Fog

Even the most confident drivers fear fog more than most weather conditions. It robs you of all chance of protecting yourself by driving defensively because you can't see likely sources of danger. At its worst it can be so disorientating that you end up with no idea where you are in a road you are entirely familiar with.

Sadly, you can't rely on others being sensible even in fog. There will still be those who drive on sidelights or no lights at all, who drive too fast and stop in stupid places. All you can do is give yourself more time to avoid them and drive in a way that reduces the risk to you both if the worst happens.

LIGHTS

Lights are essential in fog. They do not help you see further but they enable other people to see you. However, they must be used correctly, especially at night, or they will cause problems for you and other road users (see 'Foglamp abuse' above).

You must use headlights as soon as visibility is affected. However, at night in anything thicker than light mist it is likely that beam headlights will restrict your vision rather than enhance it because the light scatters back from the water droplets in the air. Just flick them on and see if you can see further with or without them.

Front fog lamps are less likely to cause problems and help make your vehicle clearly visible without causing glare. If you are buying them as an accessory, do not confuse them with auxiliary driving lamps, which are designed to augment beam headlights. Fog lamps emit a thin, fan-shaped beam, spreading light out to the sides of the car, not vertically. They help you to position yourself in the road in fog, especially at night, by lighting up kerbs and lane markings. They can also help you to find your drive or side turning in thick night-time fog. In some countries they can be used alone at night in fog, because they create less scatter back than headlights, but in the UK you are required by law to use headlights, too. On most cars they will only come on with the headlights and many cars have switches that bring on front fog lamps first then rear fog lamps.

With the abuse of rear fog lamps so common, if you find yourself at the back of a queue of stationary traffic on a fast road in fog it is even more wise than on a clear day to use hazard warning lights in case someone mistakes the brake lights for fog lamps on moving cars.

DRIVING STYLE

It is obvious that fog restricts your vision. That means you get less warning of hazards and so have less time to avoid them. You have to give yourself time to see and react to things around you, which simply means slowing down. You should drive at a speed that enables you to stop in the distance you can see. Unfortunately, only you can judge the safe speed for the conditions you are in and it is better to be cautious, but if you find yourself often having to brake hard and suddenly as cars in front appear out of the fog, you are driving too fast.

In thick fog, especially on motorways, it is easy to pick up speed without realizing it because you can't see how quickly you are approaching and passing things. So keep glancing at the speedo to make sure it has not crept up. Turning the radio off can help because you can concentrate more easily and you can hear the sounds of the road.

It is also easy to treat the lights of the vehicle in front like a lighthouse and just follow them, but he may be making the same mistakes as you are and there is a risk that you'll just follow him into a lay-by or even his own drive.

Top tip

You must be prepared to vary your speed and don't get lulled into a false sense of security by the fog lifting, especially on fast roads. Fog is often patchy, gathering in hollows, or thinning where conditions allow a little air movement, and at speed you can suddenly find yourself going from light mist into thick fog with no warning. In addition, large vehicles carve a tunnel in the fog, so don't be fooled into overtaking because you think the truck driver is being too cautious: you could find yourself alongside him, blind and on the wrong side of the road. So, don't speed up until you are sure conditions have improved.

High risk fog

People worry most about fog on motorways because of the big news pile-ups we get all too frequently. But it is just as much of a hazard off the major roads. You are far more likely to come in contact with other road users on town and country roads and many pedestrians and cyclists are

(Contd)

not sensible enough to make themselves more visible. You must drive with more caution, treating any object you can't instantly recognize as a potentially suicidal pedestrian. Be particularly careful around schools because children are very difficult to spot among the parked cars and roadside furniture in fog.

In towns fog can be very patchy as buildings provide shelter or channel breeze or warmth into the street. At night, street lighting creates islands in the fog where you can see quite easily, but the shadows in between become far more opaque than they at first appear. In short, take extreme care when driving in a town in fog.

JUNCTIONS

In town or country, take extra care at junctions. Make sure you are aware of what is behind you, so you can make allowances according to how close they are. Signal early if you can and if your junction comes up quicker than expected you are probably better off passing it and turning round than stopping suddenly with someone close behind who may not be able to see the junction. If you are at a stop line, stay on the brakes to give extra warning to anyone approaching from behind and make sure your indicator stays on for the same reason. However, if someone pulls up behind you, come off the brakes to avoid dazzling them.

In thick fog it can help to open your windows when stopped at junctions so you can hear approaching traffic, but remember fog also deadens some sounds. Give yourself time to look around you and, above all, do not linger halfway out or halfway across the junction. A particular danger in fog is turning right across a dual-carriageway: make sure you pull right into the turning lane so your car is completely protected by the central reservation and not overhanging the road, behind or in front, because your lights do not show to drivers approaching from the side.

It is important that you do not do anything unexpected at junctions: do not stop in them, stick to the rules when using roundabouts and do not jump traffic lights because other drivers can't take avoiding action when they can't see you.

Snow

Heavily falling snow has many of the characteristics of fog, so if you haven't read that section, do so now and use lights in the same way. It reduces visibility in the same way and makes bright lights scatter back in the same way, but it also seriously affects the surface you are driving on. However, if you are not used to it, fresh fallen snow can be deceptive because it feels fairly grippy, at least, until you try to stop or turn. Temperature can also affect how slippery fresh snow is. In extremely low temperatures, when the snowflakes are frozen hard, it can offer quite good grip when fresh, so a Canadian used to snow driving at minus 30° C may be taken by surprise when he drives on English snow which is more slippery at only a few degrees below freezing.

The problem is that as soon as your tyre rolls over it, the snow becomes impacted and more like ice. In a straight line this makes little difference, but when you stop or turn, the car may slide or go straight on.

Insight

If you have to get out of your car on a rural road after heavy snow, be cautious about wandering off the carriageway. Snow can hide deep ditches and holes by laying on vegetation and bridging over them or by settling on thin ice. If you fall through, it could be a fatally long time before anyone finds you because they may assume your car is abandoned.

False security

Though four-wheel drive significantly improves the car's traction on poor-grip surfaces, modern systems can create a false sense of security on snow and ice. This is because they have the ability to transfer the drive backwards and forwards according to how much grip the wheels have. So, when the front wheels hit a slippery patch, the torque is instantly moved to the rear until the rear wheels hit the patch. This can rob the driver of the little twitches and lightness of steering feel that warn of a slippery surface, making him think things are better than they are.

Though the 4WD can cope with this in a straight line and on gentle bends, it can't defy the laws of physics, so when you try to stop or turn on an icy patch you have the same problems as anyone else. If the tyres can't grip it really doesn't matter how many wheels are driven.

That isn't to say 4WD is unsafe or a waste of time, far from it. It gives you a greater safety margin in such conditions but you must try not to narrow that margin by driving unwisely.

BE PREPARED

If snow is forecast think carefully about whether your journey is necessary and what route you take. If you must go out, stick to main roads as much as you can because they are always given priority for gritting and clearing and weight of traffic helps keep them clear. It also means that if you do get stuck, help shouldn't be too far away. Certainly, avoid high altitude and exposed routes where the effects of the snowfall will be worse. Never ignore signs saying routes are blocked, even if you are in a 4×4, not least because if you do get stuck, nobody is going to expect you to be there.

It is vital you take clothing suitable for cold weather, including boots in case you need to get out. High-energy food and a hot drink are also wise. Take a shovel and invest in a folding one you can keep in the boot if you regularly need to travel in snow. Something to put under the wheels to give grip may also be useful in freezing conditions: sacking or pieces of carpet are fine.

Finally, let someone know your intended route and your estimate of the time you will arrive, so if you do not turn up they know to call the emergency services.

Insight

If you think nobody would be stupid enough to venture out in heavy snow without preparations, think again. In the worst snowfalls southern England had seen for many years, Kent police were amazed by the stupidity of a man whose car had broken down on a barely passable motorway. In spite of the obviously bad weather, and warnings not to travel being broadcast on national and local radio, he had set out to play squash with only the clothes he was wearing, namely the shorts and tee-shirt he intended to play in. When they found him he was so cold he could hardly speak.

Snow chains and studs

In many places, notably high altitude routes through mountains, the authorities insist cars are fitted either with snow chains or studded winter tyres. Snow chains are sets of chains fitted over the driven wheels' tyres to give extra grip. They are designed to fit certain sizes of wheel and tyre and must be fitted according to the instructions. Also check your car's handbook in case there are restrictions on how chains can be fitted and to which wheels. Failure to follow instructions can lead to serious damage to the car and the risk of people being injured if the chains break up and fly off.

(Contd)

Observe any speed limits suggested in the instructions and avoid driving with snow chains for long periods on tarmac.

Studded tyres, which have metals studs in the tread, tend to be used only by people who live in areas prone to extreme weather. There are always speed limits for studded tyres, which are not designed for high speed use and offer poor grip on hard surfaces.

DRIVING STYLE

In heavy falling snow the same driving considerations as driving in fog apply because your visibility can be severely restricted.

If the snow is building up, you must also drive with sensitivity. Sudden steering movements, braking or changes in throttle can all upset the car's stability and grip. Where snow is drifting, or you have to cross the pile of slush that has grown between the tyre ruts, expect the car to handle differently and lose grip.

Pulling away

Pulling away, even on fresh fallen snow, needs careful consideration. If the snow is deep, it will be easier if you clear some of it away from in front of the wheels so the car is moving a little before having to climb the wedge of snow. Try to pull away in as straight a line as possible because the more you turn the wheel, the harder it becomes for the tyres to grip and in rear- or four-wheel drive vehicles you may just push the turned wheels along without turning the car.

The more slippery it is, the more carefully you must feed the power in. If the wheels spin, ease off to allow the tyres to find some grip: gently moving the steering wheel from side to side may help in a front- or four-wheel drive car. The problem is that you need high torque (pulling power) to start the car moving but too much torque unsticks the tyres.

Some cars can pull away in second gear which reduces the amount of torque transmitted to the wheels so may make pulling away on slippery surfaces easier, though you may need to slip the clutch to stop it stalling. Some automatic gearboxes have a snow button, which makes them start in second gear.

Once on the move, look at the surface before stopping. You will have more problems pulling away on uphill slopes, deep snow or polished icy snow, so try to avoid stopping there.

Be aware of changes in surface. It is easy to continue driving cautiously long after conditions have improved and to drive incautiously into danger when they have deteriorated. Snowfall can be very localized so can leave relatively little on the road in one place and significant amounts just half a mile further on.

In deep snow, try to keep moving and avoid changing gear in the deepest part because as soon as you come off the power, the car will slow and may even stop. Choose a suitable gear to allow you to keep a steady speed through the deepest snow. If your car has an electronic stability programme, turn it off. In normal conditions ESP reacts to the sideways movement of a car drifting out on a bend, so it will do the same when the car slips sideways in the snow and will brake or back off the power when you least need it. It can actually stop you completely in deep snow. (See Chapter 2 for more on ESP.)

In deeply rutted hard snow in a rear- or four-wheel drive car, try to be aware of which way your front wheels are pointing. It is very easy to turn the wheels in the rut so they are pushed along by the rear wheels. While you are in the rut, the car will follow it, but if the front wheels find grip or the rut sides disappear, the car will go in whichever direction the front wheels are pointing. So if you are in a rut, occasionally release your grip on the steering wheel so the steering can self-centre and point the wheels the right way. In front-wheel drive cars, if you turn the wheels in the rut you'll wonder why you are spinning wheels or have stopped. If you are still moving forwards, easing your grip on the wheel may work. If not, open the window and look at which way they are pointing and correct it.

Top tip

Snow is at its most slippery when it falls on ice because it helps lubricate the tyres' slide over the ice. So take care when venturing from a snow-covered gritted road to a side road that may not have seen salt, and when driving into hollows and valley bottoms where the air temperature may be lower.

GETTING STUCK

There are many factors that make the difference between being stuck in snow and getting through, the main ones being depth and condition of the snow itself. It follows that the deeper the snow, the more likely you are to have problems, but, as we said earlier, the temperature also affects how the snow behaves. A few centimetres of snow at temperatures close to freezing may result in a very slippery surface that brings everything sliding to a halt. But many more centimetres of dry, deep frozen snow may be easy to drive over, though it depends how it compacts down: deep soft snow that compresses a lot, like a windblown drift, may leave the car laying on a pillow that lifts the wheels off the ground.

Other factors in getting stuck include:

▶ *the depth and pattern of the tyre tread*
▶ *tyre inflation*
▶ *how you use the throttle*
▶ *the angle of the road*
▶ *how much room for manoeuvre you have.*

Tyre tread

If your tyres are badly worn, don't expect them to grant grip in snow. A deep, blocky tread generally provides the best grip, which is why off-road 'mud and snow' and winter tyres are generally like that. The smoother treads designed for high performance cars may grip well at speed in the wet, but not in snow, so take care. In places where it snows heavily and winter temperatures are very low, drivers often have a set of winter tyres fitted which have a tread pattern suited to snow and are made of a rubber compound that stays relatively soft in low temperatures.

Tyre inflation

Tyres generally grip best if they are inflated to the pressure suggested by the car manufacturer. The only exception to this is that in very deep snow you may get extra grip by lowering the pressure to allow the tread to flex more. However, this should be an emergency procedure only and you should return the tyres to their normal pressures as soon as possible.

Throttle use

A driven wheel loses grip when you try to pass more power through it than the tyre can transmit to the road, which is easy on snow and ice. Therefore, once a wheel has started to spin, there is usually no point in applying more power. In fact, if the wheel spins in deep snow, it digs itself in and may also help polish the icy surface underneath.

In addition, any driven axle has a system of gears called a differential (diff) which allows one wheel to turn faster than the other to make up for the differences in distance travelled by the inside and outside wheels on a turn. So, when a wheel spins, the diff is fooled into behaving as if that wheel needs to turn faster than the other, so all the power goes to that wheel. That means you may only have one wheel in trouble, but the one that could move you is getting no power. In those circumstances you will stay stuck unless your car has a limited slip diff, which only allows a portion of the power to go to the spinning wheel, or an electronic traction control system which will brake the spinning wheel. We'll cover how these help in more detail when we look at getting unstuck.

Always use the throttle smoothly on slippery surfaces. In snow, if you suddenly add or take away power you can make a wheel that was managing to drive you lose grip. This can also seriously affect the car's handling, making it skid (see Chapter 10). So, on snow and ice you must always be gently on and gently off the throttle. Use the brakes very carefully, especially if your car does not have ABS.

Angle of the road
It is obvious that if you need to climb a steep hill in snow and ice, you have a problem. What is not so obvious is that gentle slopes can also cause difficulty. This is particularly so in snow at around freezing point, which is why it can create such difficulties in towns where the temperature is a bit higher than in the colder countryside. Only start climbing a slope if you have plenty of room because if you lose grip you will slide to one side. If you can't get up the slope, try to select reverse to come back down, so you retain control.

If you have to come down a slope, select first at the top and let the car run down with your foot off the throttle. This will allow the engine to slow you down with less risk of locking the wheels and creating a skid. If your car has ABS you may be able to use the brakes to slow you further, but be careful because some ABS systems do not work at very low speeds.

Top tip
If the car starts to slide on a downhill slope, you may be able to regain control by gently applying the throttle. The car is sliding because its forward speed is faster than the wheels' rotational speed so by applying the throttle, especially in a front- or four-wheel drive car you should be able to match the wheels' rotational speed to the forward speed and regain some steering control.

Camber can also cause problems when it is slippery. On a steeply cambered road the car may start to slide down towards the kerb. Easing off the throttle may return grip. Avoid trying to steer back up the slope because this gives the front wheels even less grip. You may get steering control back if you ease the steering towards the direction of the slide. Unfortunately, you generally have little time or space to do much about it.

Room for manoeuvre
You need space to counter the effects of slippery surfaces, so think carefully before entering a restricted area. Only go in if you can drive straight through: so do not enter, say, a narrow bridge until the car in front has got through. In two-way streets, don't try to pass through gaps with someone coming the other way. If you wait for the other driver to pass it means there is only a risk of one car sliding and any resulting impact will be lessened. In addition, if they slide into your stationary car, it's their fault not yours.

GETTING UNSTUCK

It is better not to get stuck in the first place, but even the most skilled snow drivers can have problems, not least because you can't see what is under the snow.

As we said earlier, once the wheels start spinning, there is no point adding extra power. Indeed, easing off the power may be all you need to get moving again. However, traction control systems need power to do their job, so try varying the power and seeing how much helps. The car's first movement with traction control can be very gentle so compare the position of a nearby landmark to, say, the windscreen pillar. On front- and four-wheel drive cars, gently moving the steering wheel from side to side can help the wheels find a little extra grip.

If you're not going anywhere, get out and see why. If you don't, anything you do may make matters worse. You could get stuck because of something trivial, like a single tyre-sized hole so all you have to do is reverse out of it and drive round it. In fact, never forget reverse: if the car went into the drift that way it will almost certainly come out the same way, though you may have to clear snow from round the wheels first.

Often all that stops a car in snow is a wedge building up in front of or behind the wheel and that either needs clearing or the car needs help over it. That is why you can sometimes free a car by 'rocking' it between first gear and reverse: take it as far forward as it will go then, as you let it roll back, select reverse and take it as far back, then repeat the process.

Putting something under the driven wheels to give them grip may get you moving again. It could be something you've brought with you, grit from a roadside bin or vegetation from the hedgerow. In general, your problem is that once something has brought you to a halt, you struggle to get going again, but once you are moving you can keep moving. If you are using something you have carried for the purpose, either tie it to the car with a long piece of string or drive to firm ground before going back to pick it up.

A trick that often helps when the wheels keep spinning is using the brakes. If the handbrake works on the driven wheels, as is the case with rear-wheel drive cars and a few front-wheel drives (like older Saabs and Citroëns) pulling it on a few clicks is enough. Your car handbook may say which wheels it works on. On other cars, gently applying the brakes with your left foot may do the trick. As we said earlier, when a wheel spins, the diff allows it to take all the power but if you partially apply the brakes it can slow the spinning wheel to allow some power to go to the other wheel. However, a few 4×4s, notably older Land Rovers, have a transmission handbrake which works on the drive shaft and should never be applied on the move or while the car is under power because it can seriously damage the transmission. Modern push-button electronic handbrakes can't be partially applied so aren't able to be used in this way.

Top tip

If you own a 4×4 make sure you know how to use its systems. You may have skipped the off-road driving bits in the handbook if you didn't plan to drive off-road, but you need them in these circumstances. In deep snow you should lock at least the centre diff, if it has to be done manually, turn off the stability control and engage the **low ratio gearbox**. If you don't understand any of this, you certainly need to read the handbook because you are going to look very stupid when you get stuck in conditions your car is well able to handle. Knowing how to use these things may not only help you avoid trouble but will mean you can help save others who are in trouble.

Ice

Ice can form on the road long before the air temperature reaches freezing. This is because the ground may be colder than the air, which is usually moving around. In addition, cold air flows into dips and hollows, so while you may have driven many miles without problems, you might find ice in an isolated hollow. This is why cars with ice warning external thermometers start flashing a warning at three or four degrees above freezing.

Other places where ice is more likely to be a hazard are:

▶ *under trees, where they shade the road, and may drip water from their branches*
▶ *on bridges, because there is no earth below them to retain heat*
▶ *under bridges, because they create shade and the road often dips under them*
▶ *anywhere shaded from the sun all day because the ground is never warmed up*
▶ *where water runs off surrounding land across the road, because it washes away any salt*
▶ *at the exit to rough lay-bys because cars trail water out from puddles there.*

Fooling electronics

Sheet ice can stop electronic driving aids, like traction control, working because the electronics detect nothing wrong. As we've explained before, these devices work by sensing differences in wheel rotation speed, but the problem is that if all driven wheels are on ice they can all spin at the same speed. The effect is most obvious with traction control because it may have safely got you over a snow-covered road but you then drive onto a sheet of ice and can hear the wheels spinning, with no action from the electronics.

As soon as you hear this, ease off the throttle. That may be enough to get you moving, if not, try gently moving the steering about, which can create enough difference in wheel rotation speeds to trigger the traction control.

DRIVING STYLE

Many of the considerations given under snow driving apply to ice, except that this hazard is a lot less obvious so if the conditions make ice likely, drive with care. A danger with modern cars is that their heating systems are so good, particularly those with automatic temperature control, that drivers are unaware that the temperature outside has dropped. That is why these cars usually have an outside thermometer to warn the driver. If this says there could be ice, believe it.

Keep your speed down on twisting roads because conditions may change round the next bend. Look out for patches of frost on the verges or iced-over puddles that suggest the temperature is lower locally. Keep the radio turned down, or off, so you can use your ears, too: if you run onto ice, road noise disappears.

On many cars you may feel a significant lightening of the steering on ice because there is no longer resistance on the wheels. Sadly, some strongly-assisted power-steering systems do not faithfully feedback true road feel to the driver so may not give immediate warning. You will only find out what yours is like by trial and error.

If you hit ice, don't panic. The worst things you can do are to suddenly lift off the throttle or to brake. The former can either unstick the wheels or make them suddenly find grip, both situations resulting in unpredictable handling. Braking will cause the wheels to lock up on a car without ABS and even with it, ice can prove more than the electronics can handle. See Chapter 10 on skidding.

Black ice

Black ice forms where water, from rain, dew or ice melting off branches, falls on a road that is colder than the air above it. The result is that the water freezes from below so its surface remains wet, giving it the black appearance of a wet road rather than the pale crystalline look of air-frozen ice.

It is dangerous because it is impossible to detect, especially if the rest of the road is wet, and because the wet surface lubricates it, making it more slippery. Like any other ice it still stops road noise and, in most cars, lightens the steering. Black ice is the best reason for taking care whenever ice may be present.

Rain

Rain is the least scary of bad weather to drive in, but still presents problems. It too reduces visibility and tyre grip, though not to the extent that the previously mentioned weather conditions do.

But with rain you not only have the falling rain reducing vision, you have the water being sprayed back into the air by other vehicles, which often creates far more of a problem.

In the UK, and many European countries, you are required by law to use headlights in rain, and it is wise anywhere. Apart from helping people to see you through the falling rain, it also enables truck drivers, who are relying on rain-spattered mirrors, to see you through the spray their vehicles throw up. Don't forget in town, that lights also help pedestrians see you through rain-covered spectacles or when taking a quicker than usual look down the road because of water blowing in their faces.

WIPERS

Windscreen wipers do not last forever and need replacing every 12 to 18 months. If they are not clearing the glass properly, first check they are clean. Little bits of debris, even dead flies, trapped under the blade edge can cause streaks while an oily blade or screen leaves a patchy film as the wiper sweeps across. Debris can just be wiped off with a finger but oily deposits may need cleaning off with neat windscreen washer fluid or washing up liquid.

But if the blades still fail to clear the glass, or have tears or missing patches, they must be replaced. A blade where the rubber is breaking up will eventually allow metal parts of the wiper to touch the glass, which may scratch it. Cars fail the **MOT** if such damage is in the driver's line of sight.

A smeary windscreen not only stops you seeing potential danger but increases fatigue as your brain tries to cope with interrupted vision.

TYRES

Drivers too often take it for granted that the car can cope with 'a bit of water' yet even in modest rainfall, a tyre has to displace hundreds of litres of water a second to grip the road. It can't do that efficiently if it is worn or incorrectly inflated, so make sure your tyres are in good condition especially after a long hot summer when you may not have noticed the reduction in grip.

The great unwashed

The first rainfall after a long dry spell catches many motorists unawares. It is not that they have forgotten how to drive in the wet but that they have not appreciated how slippery an unwashed road becomes.

If it has rained fairly regularly, all the oil, tyre rubber, tree residue and dust that gathers on a road is washed off. But in a long dry spell this all builds up on the road, though it causes no problems until it gets wet. Ironically, it is usually less of a problem if you get a monumental downpour that quickly washes it away but if you get just enough rain to wet the road it can become very slippery. It is usually worse on junctions and roundabouts because of the volume of traffic and the fact that everything is braking and turning, increasing the vehicular fallout.

So, in the first rain after a long dry period expect the road to be slippery and braking distances to be longer. This is particularly so in desert areas where there can be years between showers and the heat and gritty soils help polish the road surface.

DRIVING STYLE

In gentle rain you need to do little to adapt your driving style, as long as your tyres are in good order and it is not the first rain after a dry spell (see box above). Even so, remember that stopping distances are always longer on a wet road and other road users, like two-wheelers and pedestrians, may not be paying as much attention as usual.

The heavier the rain gets, the more care you must take. Not only does the increasing rain and spray reduce visibility but the effects of the water on the car increase and the risk of deep standing water on the road is multiplied. So you must be aware of the constantly changing conditions and make sure that your driving style adapts with them by slowing down and increasing the distance between you and the vehicles in front.

SPRAY

Spray reduces visibility more than falling rain because the water droplets are smaller so refract the light more. On some roads it is a big problem and may have to be treated like fog but many new road surfaces are designed to reduce spray and some even allow the water to drain through the tarmac, virtually eliminating it. But even on a good road, beware of sudden increases in it as vehicles change surface or hit puddles.

Try to anticipate things that will increase the spray so you can act to ensure you are not temporarily blinded, or surprised, by it blasting across the screen. For example, if you are about to overtake a truck, or see one coming the other way, you know it will throw spray at you so increase your wipers' speed before it does.

STANDING WATER

Water can stand on the road surface as a puddle, as a stream running across the road or as a continuous sheet in heavy rain. The potential effect is always the same: the volume of water can be so great that the tyre can't shift it quickly enough. The result is that a cushion of water forms in front of the tyre, which is felt as resistance, and if it is a puddle it may lurch the car strongly to one side. Try not to react by snatching the steering the other way because that could result in total loss of control, not least because when the puddle 'lets go' the car could lurch the other way. Just try to hold the steering against the pull and ease off the throttle. This can be particularly disconcerting at night when you may not be able to see the water coming.

If you are going fast enough, that cushion can move back under the wheel, lifting it off the road surface. This is called **aquaplaning** and means you no longer have full directional control. You will almost certainly feel the steering go light and if the water affects all four wheels the car may start to wander if it is going in a straight line, or go straight on if it is going round a bend. Ease off the throttle to allow the car to slow down but only brake if your car has ABS or the wheels will lock up. As your speed drops, the grip should come back but this has been your warning that you were going too fast for the conditions, or that your tyres need replacing.

Insight

If you frequently find your car aquaplaning at modest speeds on tyres with plenty of tread, check first that you are using the correct pressures. If you are, you must check with an expert that the tyres you are using are suitable for your climate. Everyone knows rubber gets softer as it gets hotter, so tyre manufacturers must adjust the compound for the prevailing conditions in the country they are intended for. So, a tyre that copes well in a tropical downpour may have a compound that is too hard to be flexible enough when asked to cope with a winter shower in northern Europe. One of the scariest drives I have ever had was on the A1 on a wet November day in a very cheap Asian car fitted with tyres from its homeland – it was aquaplaning at 45mph! For the same reason, be wary about fitting your car with cheap tyres from hot parts of the world, unless you live somewhere warm.

FLOODING

Never venture into floodwater (or a ford) unless you are sure you know how deep it is. If you can't avoid following another vehicle into it, give them plenty of room so you can get round them if they get stuck. On two-way roads avoid going through a flood with something coming the other way because its bow wave could flood your engine.

The water will be more shallow in the centre of the road, because of the camber, but in an ordinary car water that is more than

15 cm (6 in) deep could cause problems. In 4×4s the wading depth could be as much as 50 cm (about 18 in) but at that depth you need special driving techniques (see box opposite).

On petrol engines you are trying to avoid spraying too much water over the ignition and on any engine you want to avoid water being sucked into the air intake.

Top tip

Where petrol engines can cope with a small amount of water being sucked in, diesels can be seriously damaged by it because they compress the fuel and air mixture so much to ignite it and water can't be compressed like gas. That means the piston becomes a hydraulic ram and even substantial components get seriously bent. For that reason, never try to restart a swamped diesel engine but get professional help.

Having decided you want to drive through, select first gear and drive into the water at a steady, low speed. Expect some resistance from the water as you enter. Keep the engine revs up, slipping the clutch if necessary to keep the speed down. By keeping the revs up you ensure enough exhaust pressure to keep water out of the exhaust pipe. If you have to stop with the exhaust under water, keep the revs up to keep the water out, or it may stall and then suck water up the cooling exhaust pipe.

In deep water, putting something over the radiator grille, like a plastic bag, will help reduce the amount of water going into the engine bay. If your car has an electric radiator fan it may be sensible to disconnect it so it can't spray water over the engine, but take care because they can start spinning even with the ignition off.

When you get out of the water, regardless of how deep it was, always check your brakes work. Modern disc brakes are less prone to fading after a dunking, but drum brakes may be rendered totally ineffective by the water in them. Applying the brakes several times, or gently holding them on with your left foot as you drive a short distance, should dry them out.

If the water was muddy or contained a lot of debris, make sure it has not blocked the radiator.

Deep wading

Deep wading in a 4×4 is not to be taken lightly and is best avoided. Your car's handbook should state its maximum wading depth and any special precautions that must be taken, like closing certain vents and drain holes. Many handbooks give advice on wading in their off-road driving sections.

In vehicles with an additional low ratio gearbox it is wise to select it, to allow a low speed with high revs. If you think the bottom may be muddy, consider locking the centre differential if it has to be done manually. If you don't know what this means, you haven't read the handbook and need to learn more about your car before risking deep wading.

Be prepared for considerable resistance when the car enters the water, so enter the water slowly but be ready to increase the power to stop it stalling. As a bow wave builds in front of the car you must maintain a speed that keeps it being pushed ahead of you without breaking over the bonnet. This keeps water clear of the engine bay and area behind it, where axle and gearbox breather pipes are likely to be.

To do this you must be sure the surface you are driving on is fairly even and that you can get through the water in one steady movement. If you have to stop it is essential you keep the revs up because there will be considerable water pressure on the exhaust's tailpipe.

After deep wading it is essential you check the radiator and engine bay are clear of debris.

(Contd)

If you think you may need skills like this, it is sensible to go to an off-road driving school to be shown how to do it safely and properly (see Chapter 13).

Wind

It is mostly side winds that cause problems for drivers and the way they affect different vehicles varies greatly. These days most cars are fairly stable in high winds, though before wind tunnel testing was widespread there were cars with notorious stability problems at speed in blustery conditions. Even so, tall sided, lightweight cars can still be buffeted about and can have a worrying tendency to drift towards large vehicles as they pass in such conditions.

But car drivers must also be aware of how these conditions affect other road users, so they can make allowances. The essential thing to remember is that the faster you go, the more effect a side wind has, in exactly the same way that the faster the car is going the more effect a movement of the steering has.

DANGER AREAS

Wide open spaces are obviously prone to the effects of strong winds, though here the predictability of it reduces the risk. The greater risk is where drivers are suddenly exposed to side winds where they were sheltered before.

Obviously, if you drive out of a cutting onto a bridge, you must expect to encounter side winds but a bridge taking another road over yours also presents a risk because the wind may be deflected along the embankment, catching you as you approach or leave the bridge. For the same reason, roads running along embankments are not always as seriously affected by side winds as one on the flat, because the wind is deflected upwards by the bank. But this means you may encounter unexpected side wind if the road passes from an embankment to flat land.

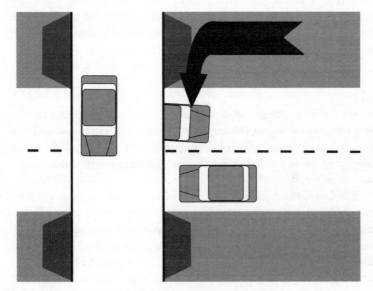

Figure 9.1 Beware of deflected winds when passing under bridges.

Solid objects at the roadside may cause more buffeting in strong winds because they cause turbulence where a gappy barrier, like trees, acts as a windbreak without causing turbulence.

Tall buildings and gaps in walls, including gateways, can channel very strong and sudden side winds across a road.

Look out for the way the trees move and what happens to vehicles ahead of you.

HIGH-SIDED VEHICLES

High-sided trucks and buses can affect you in two ways. If the wind is strong enough they may be pushed sideways, so when overtaking make sure there is plenty of room and try to avoid being stuck alongside them.

In addition they create their own turbulence, but on a windy day, as well as their slipstream, you also have the movement of the wind on top. One effect that catches many drivers by surprise is being drawn towards a high-sided vehicle because the wind passing over the top of it creates turbulence and a low pressure area alongside it. The effect on a motorway can be initial buffeting as you draw alongside, a pull towards the truck and then a push away as you pass it (see Plate 13).

You must be ready for all this movement and not overreact to it. If you throw the wheel one way and then the other you will exacerbate the instability the turbulence causes. Keep a light touch on the wheel and merely hold the car against the movement.

TWO-WHEELERS

Cyclists and motorcyclists represent a danger in strong winds simply because they are more likely to wobble in them, so give them plenty of room.

Heat

Driving on a sunny day can be so carefree but if it gets too hot it can cease to be fun. Though visibility remains generally good, heat shimmer can produce odd optical effects like making a crow walking across the road look like a person. The trouble is you can't always assume it's a crow.

Heat can be fatiguing, especially in cars without air conditioning, and may bring on other problems like hayfever. So, carry water with you and if you have allergies, keep medication with you but be aware of its side effects. If you feel you are getting too hot, find somewhere cool to take a break.

In heavy traffic, keep an eye on the car's temperature gauge for overheating. If the engine temperature rises it may need nothing more than a stop with the bonnet raised, unless you are low on coolant.

In very hot weather the tar on the road may start melting. This doesn't usually cause problems for car drivers beyond messy paintwork but keep your speed down because it can be slippery. Look out for motorcyclists for whom these conditions can be tricky and they need room to avoid the wettest patches.

Insight

An open-topped car may not save you from the worst hot weather can bring. I have known people to get serious sunburn and sunstroke riding around in open cars in hot weather simply because the pleasant cooling breeze wafting over you helps disguise the effects of the sun on your skin. You can also become dehydrated without realizing how much water you have lost because you don't get sweaty with the breeze quickly drying the moisture from your skin. So, take the precautions anyone sensible takes in the sun by wearing suntan lotion and a hat and drinking plenty of water. If it gets too hot, admit defeat and raise the roof.

10 THINGS TO REMEMBER

1 *Before setting off in bad weather ask yourself if the journey is really necessary.*

2 *Be prepared: take suitable clothing, equipment and food and drink.*

3 *In frosty weather, de-ice windows properly before setting out.*

4 *Use lights in rain and poor visibility to help others see you.*

5 *Only use foglamps in fog or falling snow with visibility below 100 metres.*

6 *Make sure you know how your ventilation system's demister works so you do not create your personal 'fog'.*

7 *In fog drive at a speed that means you can stop in the distance you can see and check your speed frequently.*

8 *If your wheels start spinning on snow or ice, ease off the throttle: more power won't help.*

9 *On ice, road noise disappears, so listen and do not suddenly brake if you hit ice.*

10 *If the steering suddenly goes light in rain, the car is aquaplaning so slow down gently.*

10

....

Skidding

In this chapter you will learn:
- *what a skid is*
- *what causes a skid*
- *how to avoid skidding.*

A lot of people after an accident will tell you 'the car went into a skid' as if the car did it of its own accord through no fault of the driver's. In truth, it is drivers who cause skidding though there are occasions when it may not be their fault, for example, because they can't have known or seen something was spilled on the road.

A skid happens when the rotational speed of the wheel doesn't match the directional speed of the car, because it is going too fast, too slow or in the wrong direction. In other words, the driver has failed to recognize the road conditions and is using the throttle, brakes or steering incorrectly.

Cars' handling has become much more benign. In general, cars are far more predictable in extremis than they used to be and electronics are increasingly used to protect drivers from their own mistakes. But none of this can defy physics. It raises the safety margins, but in the end it all comes down to how much grip the tyres have: once they lose grip on the road there is nothing for the electronics, 4WD or even a skilled driver to work with. So don't assume that because your car has ABS and sophisticated traction and stability controls it absolves you from using common sense and driving in a manner that suits the conditions. Indeed, there is real danger that when a car with very high handling limits does let go, you will be going so fast that your accident will be far worse than it would have been in a car of lesser ability.

Terms explained

There are two terms often used to describe car handling and skidding that it might be useful to explain: understeer and oversteer. Understeer is when the car runs wide on a bend as the front wheels lose grip. In the worst cases it feels as if the car is going straight on instead of turning the corner. Oversteer is when the back loses grip and swings round, turning the car into the bend as if the driver was steering too much.

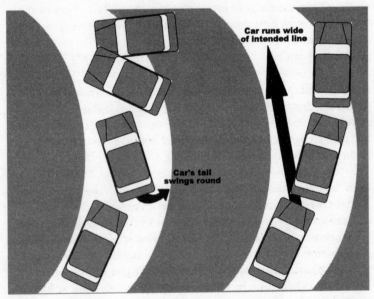

Figure 10.1 Oversteer (left), sees tail swing round; understeer (right), sees car run wide.

Skid pans

There is a lot to be said for skid pan training, which is part of learning to drive in some northern European countries. It enables you to learn what skids feel like, what causes them and how to counter them in a safe environment with an instructor who can tell you what to do and pick up on your mistakes. They can also demonstrate the veracity of driving theories: you can tell a driver that once the wheels lock up under braking you have no directional control, but seeing how you have just slid across the pan in a straight line with the steering fully turned brings it home.

However, don't let such a course lull you into a false sense of security. You will be better equipped for an emergency but skids on skid pans happen at relatively low speeds with plenty of room to react to them, and you know they're coming, which is very different to one at 60 mph on a two-way road.

Insight

Skid pans often reveal odd things about drivers' perception of danger. It was once pointed out to me that, like many other drivers, I was driving better on the side of the pan where the safety barrier was a long way off than on the side where it was closer. Though the surface conditions, turn and speed were the same on both sides, drivers felt there was more 'danger' on the side with less space, so they drove differently. It emphasized a point skid pan instructors make which is that if you are looking at what you are trying to avoid, instead of where you want to go, you are more likely to hit it!

Causes

A driver creates a skid through the inappropriately excessive or harsh use of four things:

▶ *speed*
▶ *throttle*
▶ *brakes*
▶ *steering.*

SPEED

Speed is always the overlying cause of a skid. If your speed was appropriate to the conditions you would probably have got away with turning hard into a bend or modest braking.

But this doesn't mean keeping to the speed limit, it means driving at a speed appropriate for the road conditions. In bad weather, or on a narrow, twisting road, this could be well below the speed limit.

The higher your speed the more carefully you must use brakes and steering. Throw the steering over or brake while taking a bend at 30 mph and you may get away with it. Do the same on an autobahn at 130 mph and you'll have a fraction of a second to realize how stupid you were before you hit the crash barrier.

How can you tell if speed is appropriate? You are probably going too fast for the road conditions if:

▶ *the car feels unstable*
▶ *things seem to be coming up on you faster than expected*
▶ *electronic traction or stability control devices are activated*
▶ *you often have to brake harder than expected*
▶ *the steering needs correction on bends*
▶ *the wheels lock or ABS is activated on modest braking.*

THROTTLE

Misusing the throttle isn't the same as misusing speed: you can be
going slowly and still misuse the throttle in a way that will cause or
exacerbate a skid.

If you accelerate hard, you throw the car's weight back and lighten
the load on the front wheels. That reduces the front wheels' grip,
lightening the steering on any car, and increases the risk of the
front wheels spinning on a front-wheel drive car. On a rear-wheel
drive car you risk the power making the back wheels spin which,
in some, can even drive the back sideways on a straight while, at
the same time, you have lightened the load on the steering and so
reduced your ability to steer to counter this.

Suddenly coming off the throttle has the same effect as braking,
throwing the car's weight forwards, lightening the load on
the rear wheels and increasing it on the front. That can totally
change the car's cornering stance, making the nose tuck in and
the tail come round. Indeed, on some cars you get what is called
'lift-off oversteer': this is where the car starts to understeer so the
driver quickly lifts off the throttle, throwing the weight forward
which gives the front more grip and the back less grip, so the
car switches into oversteer. Some cars treated like this, notably
rear-engined sports cars, can snap immediately from understeer
to oversteer, leaving the driver little opportunity to stop that
turning into a spin.

So, in an emergency, for example, if cornering starts going wrong, resist the temptation to lift your foot straight off the throttle. Try to do it smoothly and retain some power. This also means the car still has power to drive it through any steering changes you make, rather than relying on its momentum to do it.

BRAKING

When you brake, you feel yourself thrown forwards and must understand that the same is happening to the car's weight. This in turn lightens the load on the rear wheels, increasing the likelihood of their losing grip.

Most cars on the road today at least have a load sensing valve, or electronics, in the back brakes to stop them locking the wheels in these circumstances but if rear wheels do lock up, the back tries to overtake the front. But this change in stance can also ask a lot of the front wheels and once tyres lose grip, the wheels can be locked by the brakes: when they stop rotating, they slide. You then have a situation where, effectively, tyres are no longer in contact with the road and when this happens to the front tyres they can no longer steer the car.

If you do not have ABS and carry on pressing the brake pedal, you can twiddle the steering as much as you like and the car will just carry straight on, whether you are trying to go round a corner or avoid a child. Unfortunately, the automatic reaction in these circumstances is to keep pressing the brake harder and that is the worst thing you can do.

Round the bend

As we've said, braking throws weight forward, increasing the load on the front and reducing the load on the back, but so does cornering so combining the two is not a good idea. This is why you should always try to drive so that you finish braking before you turn into the bend and remember that if you must brake in the bend it will almost certainly upset the car's balance and change its stance. You must remember, too, that suddenly lifting off the throttle has exactly the same weight-transferring effect.

Without ABS there is also an increased risk of locking a wheel or two.

Avoiding brakelock

Brakes are at their most efficient just before the wheels lock up: go beyond that and the car may actually start going faster. We'll deal with cars fitted with ABS next, but without it, it is up to the driver to react properly. First, whenever you brake, especially in an emergency, be prepared to stop doing it.

This is against your natural reaction. If the car is going somewhere you don't want it to, you want to stop it. The fact is, you won't if you carry on braking because the brakes are no longer effective and you have no steering. Ease off the brakes, or come off altogether, and the wheels should start rotating again, giving you back control.

Cadence braking

If brakes are at their most efficient just before the wheels lock but you lose control when they do lock, why not take them to that point, then release them and try again? That is what cadence braking tries to do.

In music a cadence is falling rhythm like the succession of chords closing a musical piece and it is that that you are trying to achieve with your foot on the brake pedal. Done well, you should start with hard, quick pulses of braking, slowing and extending them as the speed drops. In truth, if all you succeed in doing is banging the brakes on and releasing them in quick succession it will be better than just standing on the pedal. This is a skill best learned on a skid pan.

Done properly, it should maintain braking efficiency and allow you some steering control to go round obstacles.

ABS

Electronic anti-brakelock systems were initially expensive extras on luxury cars. For example, in the mid 1980s ABS on a BMW 325i cost ten per cent of the car's list price. As systems became cheaper they began to become standard equipment and today all new cars in the EU, and many other places in the world, must have it.

It does the same as cadence braking but far more efficiently and far quicker than any human driver could do it and it does it with individual wheels. Its wheel rotation sensors are so sensitive that they are even used on some cars to provide low tyre pressure warning: they can detect a wheel is rotating faster because lower pressure has reduced the circumference. The electronics take this information and analyse it at high speed, releasing pressure to the brake on an individual wheel if it starts to lock up. That means it can react to one wheel being on a more slippery surface than the others, like on ice, which a driver cannot do. So, ABS not only retains braking efficiency and steering control but also optimizes the car's stability under braking on variable grip surfaces.

However, it can't defy physics: if you are going too fast for the tyres to grip as you turn the steering even without braking, ABS isn't going to save you.

Using ABS

In a car with ABS you can safely just stand on the brake pedal to stop the car. Unfortunately, many drivers ease off the brake when they feel the characteristic pedal pulse and noise of the system working, though some cars now come with emergency brake assistance (EBA) electronics which help counter this by keeping the pressure on. The pulsing is deliberately engineered in so drivers know the system is working and to act as a warning that if it trips in under normal braking, you were going too fast for the conditions.

If you are new to a car with ABS, find somewhere safe, like an empty wet road, and experience the effect before you need to use it in anger. It will come on even more easily on a muddy road or wet grass.

ABS alone does not stop you any quicker than efficient braking without it but it vastly increases your chances of staying in control. Early research with it showed that it significantly improved all drivers' chances of avoiding trouble but when drivers were taught how it enabled them to steer while braking heavily, their accident avoidance increased further. It is the fact that it opens up that option and, to an extent, removes that risk when braking in corners that makes ABS a life-saver.

Insight

Though ABS does not stop a solo car quicker, research has shown that in a towcar it can shorten emergency braking distances by up to a half. This seems to be because ABS improves the braking stability of the car even though it is being pushed by the weight of the trailer. I've experienced it on a test track, braking from 50 mph with a highly unstable trailer yet the car kept the outfit in a straight line and under control. However, it wrote off all four trailer tyres because the wheels locked and the tread was shaved off in a cloud of smoke.

The psychology of avoidance

The sad thing about skidding is that no matter how well someone is taught to do it in controlled conditions, reflexes and panic take over in an emergency, no matter how skilled the driver, because you may only have fractions of a second to react.

Your cadence braking or ABS may be perfect but in an emergency we tend to steer in the direction we are looking. Unfortunately, if you are trying to avoid something, you are almost certainly looking at it.

(Contd)

If you try to condition yourself to always look where you need to go, you are more likely in an emergency to do that and steer away from the child or into the bend.

So, a child steps out in front of you. You are never going to stop in time, but the ABS is working to slow you down while retaining control. If you stare at the child, you won't see the gap to his right that you could be aiming for. On skid pans they often demonstrate this by telling you to brake as if a bollard in front of you was a child. When you've hit it once and go for another attempt the instructor will suddenly point to something away from the bollard saying 'look over there' and most drivers miraculously avoid the 'child'.

Similarly, if you go into a bend looking towards your exit, even if it means looking through a side window, you are more likely to steer that way if anything goes wrong.

STEERING

As you turn into a bend the car's weight is transferred forward and to one side, so again you are taking weight off some wheels and putting it on others. In addition, as soon as you turn a wheel you present its tread to the road at an angle to its direction of travel, until the car turns, while centrifugal force is also building up. Because of all this it is important that steering movements be made smoothly so as to ease the car into a turn and not upset its balance.

Be aware of how the car is responding to steering movements because this can be the first warning of trouble ahead. Any sudden lightness or need to turn on more lock than expected suggests a deterioration in surface or that you are going too fast for the conditions.

Once the car has started skidding, steering action must remain smooth, though quick, because suddenly snatching the wheel over may make matters worse. Remember, too, that if the front wheels have come unstuck the wheels offer little resistance to steering movement so it is very easy to turn the wheel more than you need to. If the grip then comes back, the car may turn unexpectedly sharply.

Get to know your car's steering. Some cars offer excellent feedback but others don't. If you can feel every change in road surface and know straight away if it is losing grip, it can be trusted but if it feels no different when it hits deep water or ice, treat its feedback with caution and take care in bad conditions.

Correcting a skid

Often all you need to do to stop a skid at modest speeds is to take away the cause. Reducing the power, coming off the brakes or backing off the steering may be all that is required to give the tyres back their grip.

As speed increases, or the road conditions get worse, or you simply don't react quickly enough, further remedial action may be required.

OVERSTEER

Just about everyone must know the old 'steer into a skid' saying. When it comes to the classic rear-wheel slide, oversteer, you won't do anything else but the problem is that that may be all you do.

The psychology is simple: you are looking where you want to go, so when the back swings right you will steer right simply because it turns the car back in the direction you are looking. The trouble is that when the rear comes back into line, you are still looking where you want to go so have no incentive to turn the steering back. That is why cars often 'fishtail' after oversteering, as the driver repeatedly corrects it, or it leaves the road some way after the bend on the opposite side to where the skid first pointed it towards.

This type of skid is also made much worse by braking or suddenly lifting off all the power, because those actions further lighten the load on the rear wheels. Ease up on the power, but not completely because you still need some to drive it through what you will do next, then steer towards the direction the rear is going. But as the rear responds and turns back into line, you must return the steering back to the direction of travel, being careful not to turn it too far the other way.

In fact, it is possible to use this technique, called opposite lock, to balance the car in this tail out stance, which is what rally drivers often do to exit a bend quickly. But even they would not recommend it on the road.

UNDERSTEER

When the front wheels lose grip first, the car understeers, drifting out on a corner. Quite often all that is needed to counter it is to ease off the throttle, but beware of suddenly lifting off because, as we said earlier, this suddenly transfers the weight forwards, improving the front wheels' grip while lightening the load on the rear. Most modern front-wheel drive cars' handling remains benign if you do this in most circumstances, but even then you must be prepared for a sudden change in the car's stance, perhaps even snapping into oversteer. Racing drivers often deliberately tap the brakes when a car is understeering to put it into oversteer, but their skills and reactions are well above average and they have had the opportunity to practise where they know nobody is coming the other way.

If reducing power fails to do the trick, you again need to steer into the skid, though this is not as intuitive as with understeer. Most people's reaction to understeer is 'I don't want to go that way', so they turn the steering harder in the direction they do want to go which not only makes matters worse, but if the front wheels regain grip as speed is lost, they are now turned strongly towards the edge of the road. This is one reason why after, say, a tight left-hand bend you see the hole in the hedge on the left where you might have expected that cars failing to make the turn would have gone straight on to the right.

If the car is running out to the right with the wheels turned to the left it follows that the wheels' rotational speed and direction doesn't match that of the car. So, by turning the wheels to the right, even momentarily, you help match the two and should regain some control. But, as with oversteer, immediately you have regained control you must turn the wheels back the way you want to go. The technique is to turn the wheel right for a few seconds, and then back left in a quick but smooth movement. In a strong slide you may need to do this repeatedly to kill the sideways movement and you may need more road space than you've got.

ELECTRONIC STABILITY PROGRAMMES

Electronic stability programmes (ESP) go under many names and initials and may be called dynamic stability control, electronic stability control, electronic traction and stability control, vehicle stability assist or whatever a car company's marketing department thinks sounds good (the words 'programme' and 'control' seem interchangeable). But whatever it is called its job is to help control understeer.

It uses the ABS sensors and braking control as well as other movement sensors and when it detects that the car is drifting sideways it initially applies the brakes to whatever wheels need it to kill the drift. If this isn't enough, or the driver hasn't eased off the throttle, it will then reduce the engine's power.

In the initial stages of ESP's reaction, the driver would be totally unaware it has come in, which could be dangerous because he would not adjust his driving style to recognize he was overdoing it or that conditions had changed. For that reason, cars fitted with it always have a warning light, which is usually amber and either an exclamation mark in a triangle or, more commonly, a skidding car symbol. This may flash up quickly, therefore it pays to know where it lives on the binnacle so you recognize the light even if you don't see the symbol. Once ESP cuts engine power it is entirely obvious that it is working but that doesn't stop those who haven't read their handbooks complaining of 'loss of power' on bends.

It is remarkably effective and so significantly raises the safety margin. Latest research suggests that if all cars had ESP it would reduce accidents by about 30 per cent. But like everything it can't work miracles and if you have gone into a bend so fast that the tyres no longer have grip, or on ice, this device may still not be able to save you and you'll probably be going too fast to save yourself. So if ESP trips in, take it as a final warning to slow down.

Doing nothing

Doing nothing isn't an option if your car is skidding. For example, if the back starts coming round and you react properly, it will be nothing more than a twitch of the tail but if you leave it, the car will go out of control and may spin or roll.

SPINNING

If a car spins, don't fight the steering to try to stop it. When it is facing along the road, release your grip on the steering wheel and let the steering's self-centering bring it back into line. The steering wheel will spin very quickly and you'll need to stop it with the palms of your hands, not by trying to grasp it, or the spokes will rap your fingers.

ROLLING

Rolling is a particular danger with tall vehicles, like 4×4s, when they get sideways on to the direction of travel or if they are cornered too hard. If the vehicle is starting to tip over, try to turn the steering in the direction it is falling. This may be enough to tip it back onto all four wheels, but be ready to steer back the way you need to go.

If you can't stop the roll, push yourself back in the seat to get maximum protection and support from it. Your hands will be thrown up, but try to bring them back down towards the wheel, especially if the car has a glass sunroof, which is likely to shatter.

LEAVING THE ROAD

Rally drivers often say that if the car leaves the road the first thing you should do is let go of the steering wheel. There is wisdom in this, at least in rural areas. If the car is ploughing across a field, there is little you can do with the steering and there is a great risk of 'kickback' where the shock of the wheels hitting things kicks back through the steering system to the steering wheel. If you habitually hold the wheel with your thumbs inside the rim, kickback can make the spokes break your thumbs. Then, if the car slows enough to grant steering again, you'll be in no condition to use it.

If you leave the road in a rural area, take care when getting out of the car and going back to the road. In the dark it will be very difficult to see ditches, rivers and ponds and it is entirely possible that the car has flown over one.

In urban areas if you leave the road the chances are that you'll still be on a hard surface so may be able to regain some control. However, kickback from hitting a kerb can be severe. You may also be leaving the road into a pedestrian area and your first priority must be to avoid them. Your car will protect you from impacts with objects so the people around you are far more vulnerable than you are. Most street furniture these days is designed to collapse on impact in a way that stops it overriding a car's safety features, so using a lamppost to stop the car is probably the lesser evil than running out of control among pedestrians.

10 THINGS TO REMEMBER

1 Cars do not skid on their own, drivers cause skids.

2 Oversteer is the car's back coming round, understeer is the car drifting out on a bend.

3 Speed is the underlying cause of a skid.

4 Do not ignore warning signs, like a car feeling unstable or the electronic driving aids kicking in.

5 Use throttle, brakes and steering smoothly, especially on wet or muddy roads.

6 If a car starts to slide, do not suddenly lift off the throttle or brake hard.

7 If your car does not have ABS, learn cadence braking.

8 If your car has ABS, keep the pressure on the pedal when it pulses.

9 Steer into skids, but remember to stop steering when the car comes back into line.

10 In an emergency look at where you want to go, not what you are trying to avoid.

11

Breakdowns and accidents

In this chapter you will learn:
- *how to cope with breakdowns and accidents*
- *how to get help*
- *how to help yourself.*

Breakdowns and accidents are something every driver will experience, no matter how careful or well prepared they are. If you go prepared for the worse, you'll be able to cope better when it happens, and help others in worse trouble.

You can help avoid breakdowns by getting to know your car and by carrying out the basic regular checks outlined in Chapter 5. If you need to know more about maintaining your car, and getting it repaired after a breakdown or accident, see *Car Buying and Ownership* in this series, which also contains basic faultfinding information.

If your car isn't under warranty breakdown cover, join a breakdown organization. Basic breakdown cover is cheap and even the most expensive and comprehensive packages are still likely to be cheaper than the police duty garage's fee for recovery from a UK motorway. Breakdown cover is also not only cheaper than a garage call-out but you know who to call no matter what time of day or where you are.

It should be noted that the legal requirements set out here for what
you must do at the scene of a breakdown or accident are for the
UK and they vary greatly from state to state, so you must check
what is required of you locally.

Essential equipment

At least have:

▶ *a high visibility vest**
▶ *a torch*
▶ *a jack and* **wheel brace** *(except on cars with no spare wheel)*
▶ *a screwdriver.*

Preferably have:

▶ *a small set of spanners*
▶ *pliers*
▶ *insulating tape and fuses*
▶ *a warning triangle**
▶ *a first aid kit**
▶ *a fire extinguisher**
▶ *spare bulbs**
▶ *waterproofs*
▶ *gloves.*

*Compulsory items in some countries.

WHEEL-CHANGING KIT

If you car has a spare wheel, make sure it has a working jack and wheel brace and that you know where it all lives. Some are awkwardly stowed but do not be tempted to just leave them lying in the back, especially on cars without a separate boot. Tools are substantial lumps of metal that can do a lot of damage just crashing about as you hit bumps and take corners, but in an accident they become lethal missiles smashing into anyone and anything in their path.

If you are not very strong, try undoing the wheel nuts with the car's brace and if you can't exert enough force, buy a wheel brace with an extending handle or find something you can use as an extension to the car brace's handle.

Insight

While you are checking the car's tyre-changing kit, check the handbook to see if it has a removable towing eye and make sure it is with the tools if it needs one. To give cars a tidier appearance, many manufacturers have done away with fixed loops to attach tow ropes to and replaced them with ones that screw in, usually into a hole in the bumper with a removable cover. Unfortunately, these often do not get passed on with secondhand cars. As a 4×4 owner living in the country, I sometimes get asked to pull foolish drivers out of the mud or snow and if they do not have this towing loop you can't help them. They must call a breakdown organization or garage who either have replacement loops or alternative ways of recovering the car.

TOOLS

It's also wise to add a few other tools to the basics supplied with the car because it is daft to be stuck for the sake of a loose screw. You only need a basic kit small enough to be kept in a large pencil case. Buy either a double-ended screwdriver, which has a single blade that has a flat head at one end and crosshead at the other, or a multi-bladed set. Add a small set of spanners and an adjustable one that can tackle nut sizes not catered for in the set or to be used when you need to hold a bolt steady while doing up the nut. A pair of pliers, insulating tape and a small knife are also useful. Another solution is a multi-tool device that has many of these tools folding into a single handle.

Most cars now have provision in the fuse box to keep one of each type of fuse used, but if yours hasn't, keep some spares in a small plastic box (a 35 mm film canister is ideal).

PERSONAL SAFETY

A few cars now come with high visibility reflective vests in their toolkits because in many countries these are a legal requirement if you get out of a car at the scene of an accident. They are also a very sensible thing to carry for emergency situations and are very cheap life-savers if you buy them from places like builders' merchants. Posh cars also often include a pair of heavy cotton gloves in the toolkit, which fastidious or sensitive-skinned drivers might want to copy. Alternatively, keep moist wipes in the car.

TRIANGLES

Some, mostly German, cars come with a warning triangle, which is compulsory in some countries to warn other drivers of an obstruction. They are a wise thing to carry and should be set up about 50 metres behind the car and further back if you are round a bend. The trouble with triangles is that you can always hold it in front of you as you walk away from the car, drawing drivers' attention to the fact you are there, but you have to walk back hoping they take notice of the triangle by the road. That is one reason why *The Highway Code* no longer recommends their use on motorways, though anything placed even close behind your car to draw attention to the fact it has stopped is a good idea.

LIGHT

All this is wasted if you can't see what you're doing on a dark country road, so keep a torch in the car but put it in the glove box, or somewhere else in the cabin, so you can find it before getting out of the car to help you seek out tools. Use alkaline or lithium ion batteries because these don't run down when they're not used, unlike rechargeables.

COLD AND WET

If you don't want to carry a coat in the car, at least keep a compact emergency waterproof with the tools. Outdoor clothing shops stock basic waterproofs that fold up into a small pack. In cold weather take appropriate clothing even on short trips because a car quickly gets cold once the engine stops. If you are driving in extreme weather, or through a remote area, it is sensible to carry snacks because your body can't keep warm without fuel. If you regularly drive in remote, cold areas consider keeping at least one foil 'space blanket' in the car, which can be bought cheaply in outdoor pursuit shops. In hot weather, take a bottle of water. Women wearing shoes unsuitable for walking should keep a more sensible pair in the car in case they have to walk to get help: mobile phones don't work everywhere.

What to do at a breakdown

The most important thing when something goes wrong in a car is not to make the situation worse. You want to minimize damage to the car without increasing the risk to you, your passengers and other road users. That means not ignoring the early signs of something going wrong, like a warning light, odd noises or the car behaving strangely, but not panicking and overreacting so you do something others don't expect. So don't suddenly swerve towards the side of the road or stop on a blind bend to change a wheel.

Driving to a safe place might wreck the tyre, but getting hit by a truck does a lot more damage.

There is a temptation if something catastrophic happens, like the engine suddenly cutting out, to hit the hazard warning lights. Only do this if you are sure it will not confuse people and you do not need to indicate your intention to pull across the road. Even if the engine cuts out, you still have some forward momentum to carry you to reasonable safety, as long as you depress the clutch or slip an automatic into neutral. But you usually get enough warning of something going wrong to pull over.

Hard shoulders

Motorways and many dual-carriageways have hard shoulders for emergency use. As soon as you stop on the hard shoulder, use your hazard warning lights and remember it is a dangerous place because of the risk of other drivers following you onto the shoulder, not realizing you have stopped. There are said to be more fatal accidents on the hard shoulder than on the live carriageways. If you can, get out of the car on the passenger side, away from the traffic.

Even if you know it is something you can deal with yourself, let the authorities know you are there. On motorways and some major A-roads there are marker posts which bear a number and a sign showing the direction to the nearest emergency phone (see Plate 14). Even if you have a mobile phone, it is better to use these free phones because they show the police or Highways Agency control room where you are. It is common for people to think they are on, say, the M1 when they are on the M6.

Before you go to the phone, check you have all the things you need.

▶ *Write down the number of the nearest marker post because that gives a unique location on the motorway.*

▶ *Find your breakdown organization membership number.*
▶ *Check you know your car make, model and registration number.*

Give the controller your details, the nature of the problem and say if you have special needs, like a disability, children or animals in the car or are a woman travelling alone. They will call your breakdown organization. Listen to any safety advice the controller gives and don't hang up until they tell you to in case they do not have all the necessary information.

SAFETY

If you must work on the traffic side of the car, think carefully about how close you will be to the moving traffic. Even a glancing blow from a car at motorway speeds could be fatal. If it looks unsafe, ask the motorway control for help or call your breakdown organization who have the advantage of a large truck with flashing lights or the option of towing you off the motorway.

Top tip

Because of the risk of drivers colliding with the car on the hard shoulder, it is best for everyone to get out and wait on the verge, well away from the road. If there is a barrier, get the other side of it. Never sit on a barrier with your legs on the traffic side of it because if anything hits you, your legs will be crushed against the barrier. If you are working on the car and have passengers, get them to watch the traffic while you work so they can raise the alarm if anything endangers you.

REJOINING THE ROAD

When rejoining the carriageway afterwards, match your speed to the traffic's by accelerating along the hard shoulder, with your right indicator on. Check your mirrors, not just looking at the inside lane, but the next one over in case anyone is moving over in spite of you indicating your intention to move out.

Ordinary roads

On ordinary roads, use your hazards and get off the road if you can but take care if you pull off the tarmac not to pull onto soft ground or into hidden obstacles or ditches, especially at night.

If you are in an unsafe place, like on a bend, think carefully about whether it is better to risk further damage by driving on to a safer location.

Top tip

It may be sensible to ask a passenger to go down the road and wave down anyone approaching the scene too fast, or at least to keep an eye on the traffic as you work on the car.

CALLING FOR HELP

Away from the main roads you have no alternative but to use a mobile to call for help, but first, gather information. If you are in a town, find out what street you are on. If you are out of town, try to remember the last village or town you went through. Some mobile phone traffic information services start with phrases like 'You are on the A11 near Thetford...' and if your phone has an internet connection it may give access to a mapping website that recognizes where you are.

As on the motorway, you need your breakdown organization membership number, car make, model and registration number but you also need the breakdown organization's phone number, which you should programme into your phone and have written down in case of problems with the phone.

Personal security

Apart from the dangers from other traffic, being stranded at the roadside leaves you vulnerable in other ways, though the majority of people who stop are likely to be doing nothing more sinister than offering help.

If you are or feel vulnerable, make sure the motorway controller or your breakdown organization know. If waiting by the car, leave the passenger door ajar so you can jump in and lock it if necessary. Talk to people through a partially open window until you are sure they are genuine and don't accept lifts from strangers unless you absolutely have to. If you do, make a note, perhaps on your mobile phone, of the car's registration number.

Breakdown organizations sometimes use contract garages instead of their patrols. These people should know who you are and have details of the incident. If they can't provide proof that the organization sent them, call your breakdown service provider and check. It could be a garage trying to trick you into letting them work on the car to surprise you with a bill later, claiming you asked them to do it, or even someone with more dangerous intentions.

Changing a wheel

A puncture is the most likely 'breakdown', not least because it is something that afflicts all cars regardless of how new or well-maintained they are.

> ⚠ **Warning!**
>
> To change a wheel you must be on firm, fairly level ground or the jack may slip at the wrong moment.

The wheel-changing mistake most people make is to start jacking it up first, so let's start at the beginning.

1 *If you don't know where the car's* **jacking points** *are, check the handbook. These are areas of the body that have been shaped or reinforced to take the jack and the stresses of lifting the car.*

2 *Now, apply the handbrake and put a manual gearbox in gear or an automatic in 'park' to eliminate the risk of it rolling.*

Top tip
Using the gearbox to help hold it steady is especially important when lifting one of the wheels on which the handbrake works, which is usually at the back (although a few front-wheel drive cars have handbrakes on the front, notably older Saabs and Citroëns).

3 *Get the tools and spare wheel out and if your car has alloy wheels with locking wheel nuts, you'll need the key if it is not kept with the wheel brace.*

4 *Remove the wheel trim, if there is one. There may be a special hook tool for this in the toolkit. With locking wheel nuts there is often a chromed cap that is removed with a tool that usually looks like a plastic socket spanner.*

5 *Now use the wheel brace to loosen all the nuts so they are finger tight. By doing this before you jack the car up, you can exert force without fear of rocking the car off the jack or having the wheel turn instead of the nut. Wheel nuts usually undo anticlockwise.*

6 *Now jack the car up, making sure that the jack isn't slipping as the car's weight is taken up.*

Top tip
Raise the wheel more than is needed to remove the flat tyre because the inflated one is taller.

7 *Completely remove the wheel nuts, putting them somewhere safe and clean, like onto the tool pouch or an upturned wheel trim.*

8 *Lift the wheel off, remembering it will be dirty and heavy, especially if it is a steel wheel.*

Sticking wheels

A wheel can get stuck to the hub by corrosion. Sometimes it is enough to lever it with the wheel brace, though don't lever against the shiny brake disc or you may scar the disc badly enough to need replacing. Also remember that alloy wheels are softer than the steel brace so can be damaged by it.

If leverage isn't possible or doesn't work, try putting the wheel nuts back on so they are not quite touching the wheel, then lower it back to the ground. Often the car's weight is enough to loosen it. If not you can try rocking it, but if this fails you need help from your breakdown organization.

9 *Lift the spare wheel onto the hub aligning the holes in the wheel with the threaded studs or holes in the hub. Hold the wheel against the hub with your hand or foot and put the nuts on finger tight.*

10 *Lower the wheel to the ground and fully tighten the nuts in diagonal pairs to evenly pull the wheel onto the hub. Do not apply excessive force or you may damage the threads or even stretch the studs that the nuts screw onto.*

Top tip

Most people finish off by going once round the nuts in order, checking their tightness because a nut can feel tight until its diagonally opposite number pulls the wheel on flat. You should recheck the nuts for tightness after about 30 miles.

11 *Replace any wheel trims, then properly stow tools and the wheel you removed. If you have a pressure gauge, check the tyre's pressure or do it at a garage soon afterwards, unless you have checked it recently.*

Figure 11.1 Tighten wheel nuts in diagonal pairs to pull the wheel evenly onto the hub.

Alternative spares

Some cars are supplied with a space-saver spare, temporary repair kit or runflat tyres.

SPACE-SAVERS

If your car has a space-saver spare tyre, it has a speed limit, usually of 50 mph, which is often displayed as a sticker on the wheel and is certainly in the handbook, along with any mileage limit (see Plate 15). Note that the wheel stickers often show the limit as kilometres per hour (kph). It is illegal to exceed the limit and the wheels are now painted a bright colour so the police can see you have a space-saver in use.

REPAIR KITS

Temporary repair kits are either a canister of sealant mixed with compressed air to repair and reinflate in one go or, more commonly now, a sealant and an electric tyre pump. Follow the instructions for their use in the handbook and get the tyre properly repaired as soon as possible.

Insight

Though repair kits cope with most punctures, a friend of mine was stuck beside a motorway after a piece of metal on the road took a large chunk out of a tyre that the sealant simply could not fill. So don't expect miracles: if the tyre has a large hole or a long cut, especially in a side wall, do not waste your repair fluid on trying to fix it but call your breakdown organization.

RUNFLATS

Runflat tyres also have a speed and distance limit, given in the handbook. Though you can carry on driving it is sensible, when safe, to check it to make sure the tyre isn't so severely damaged there is a risk of it breaking up and that it doesn't have any large objects stuck in it that might come flying out or damage the wheel rim. These tyres can run while deflated because they fit to a rim designed to stop them rolling off and their side walls are reinforced and lubricated to stand up to rotating while being squashed.

The wrong fuel

Thousands of motorists a year put the wrong fuel into their cars. These days it is usually diesel car drivers filling with petrol, because diesel fuel nozzles are larger than those for unleaded petrol, but if you have an old non-catalyst petrol car it is possible to fill it with diesel because it has a larger filler pipe.

If you know you've done it, don't try to start the car because it will mean having to clean the entire fuel system instead of just the tank and may do serious damage. A petrol car won't run for long with diesel in the system, anyway.

DIESEL DANGER

The most serious damage you can do is run a modern diesel with any amount of petrol in the system. It was said to be safe to run old diesels with a small amount of petrol contaminating the fuel, though you had to be sure it was a small amount. Modern direct injection and common rail diesels have fuel systems powered by high speed electronic pumps that run at extremely high pressures (20,000 to 30,000 psi) and they need the lubricating properties of the diesel oil to do it. Petrol dilutes the oil, robbing it of its lubricating qualities.

So, if you run a modern diesel on petrol-contaminated fuel you will almost certainly need a new pump and, probably, new injectors which is a hefty repair bill that your insurers will refuse to cover unless the service station made a mistake.

If you make the mistake, call your breakdown organization or a garage to get the car towed in so the system can be cleaned.

A touch of glass

The days of windscreens that shattered into a lace of glass cubes are passing, thankfully, though side windows still do it.

There are two main types of glass used in cars, toughened and laminated. Toughened can take a lot of knocks but when it breaks, stress patterns in the glass make it break into small cubes, which, though sharp, are not as dangerous as shards would be. Laminated glass is two layers of glass, the inner one of which may also be toughened, sandwiching a plastic membrane which spreads stress and holds the glass together if it is broken.

LAMINATED GLASS

It has long been a requirement for new cars to have laminated windscreens because they are safer. It is less likely that anything hitting the screen will come into the car and if an unbelted occupant is thrown into the screen it usually bends enough to absorb some of the impact but keeps them in the car. A few cars are now fitted with laminated side windows, or offered with it as an option, because of its anti-theft and sound-deadening properties, but most still have toughened glass in windows other than the windscreen. Laminated glass chips or cracks, rather than shattering, and small chips may be repairable, but a cracked laminated screen must be replaced because the crack will grow and the bonded-in screen is an integral part of the car's stress-sharing structure.

TOUGHENED GLASS

If a toughened glass windscreen goes it has an area in front of the driver that breaks into larger pieces so you can still see through well enough to get to safety. With any toughened glass pane there is a chance that a second impact will make it burst into the car, so don't be tempted to drive with it in place. However, don't try punching it out, as suggested in films, because you can seriously injure yourself. If you need to remove the glass, do so wearing gloves or with hands wrapped in cloth.

Top tip

If a toughened glass window breaks it covers you in tiny splinters of glass, so don't brush your clothes with your bare hands. Close your eyes if you have to pull clothes over your head because the material is full of splinters that might harm them. You might even have to throw clothes away, especially knitted garments, because the glass splinters won't wash out. As soon as you can, brush or comb your hair, with your eyes closed, and wash it thoroughly.

Driving windowless

If you lose a windscreen and need to drive the car you must keep your speed down or the air pressure inside the car may pop out other windows. If the rear screen goes, drive with a front window open to prevent exhaust fumes being sucked back into the car.

Mechanical breakdown

⚠ Warning!

If mechanical breakdown involves the steering, brakes, clutch or gearbox giving up, there is little you can do at the roadside except call for help. It is very dangerous to carry on driving with faults to the braking or steering systems.

RUNNING ON EMPTY

If the engine misbehaves, you may be able to do something. If it gently runs out of power, perhaps stuttering as it does so, it is likely to be a fuel problem.

Check the fuel gauge but even if that registers fuel, think about when you last filled up because if the car seems to have been unusually economical you may have a faulty gauge. If you are in a quiet place, try taking off the fuel filler cap and rocking the car to see if you can hear fuel sloshing about. If you can't, you have probably run out.

If you decide to get more, rather than calling out the breakdown organization, make sure you get it in a canister designed to carry that type of fuel, which should come with a flexible nozzle so you can pour it into the tank without spillage. It is illegal to transport petrol in any other type of container because it is explosively flammable and as it warms up gives off vapour which can burst inadequate containers.

ENGINE ELECTRICS

If an engine suddenly stops, it is likely to be an electrical problem. Before you call for help, just check connections. With the ignition off, give **sparkplug** leads a push and follow them through to make sure connectors at the other end are on. On older cars with a conventional **distributor** instead of a modern electronic ignition, a common fault is that a thin lead running to the distributor, called the low tension lead, comes undone or breaks. The distributor is the bit all the leads go to, like a plastic octopus.

Insight

Before probing around under the bonnet, make sure you have no loose clothing, including dangling ties and scarves and remove any jewellery. There are lots of moving belts under the bonnet and, even if the engine is off, the radiator fan can switch itself on without warning: you do not want your tie getting wound round those things. Jewellery, especially necklaces and loose bracelets, can also get caught up with the added risk that they conduct electricity.

SPLASH!

If a sudden stop happens after hitting water, you may have splashed water over the ignition leads and if they are old the insulation has invisible cracks allowing the water to short them out. With the ignition off, try drying all the leads, connections and distributor cap with a cloth or tissues and see if the car will restart. However, if this happens with a diesel, don't try to restart it because diesels don't have an ignition to get wet, so if it has stopped you have almost certainly forced water into the engine air intake. Starting it could cause serious damage as the engine tries to compress water instead of gas. You need professional help.

ELECTRICAL FAILURES

If electrical items fail with the engine still running, check the fuses. With lights, a single one going out is probably bulb failure but if more than one goes out it could be the fuse, though a fuse usually works the front and rear sidelights on one side rather than both fronts or both backs.

A headlight with bulb failure usually works on beam but not dip, or vice versa, and combined brake/tail lights work as one but not the other. However, if both functions fail, check the fuse before replacing the bulb.

Top tip

If all the lights go out, check that the earth strap is still connected: it is either a cable or a braided metal strap from the battery's negative connection to the body.

CHANGING FUSES

The handbook tells you where the fuses are and which fuses work what, which may also be printed or moulded into the fuse box lid. There may be more than one fusebox.

Fuses sometimes blow because of a very temporary problem and sometimes seem to go just because they're old, but if they repeatedly blow, there is a fault that should be investigated professionally. Modern fuses are easy to check because they have a hole in the plastic through which you can see if the fuse strip is still intact. Most fuse boxes have a little pair of tweezers for removing and replacing fuses.

The fuses are colour-coded and numbered according to amperage. You must replace a fuse with one of the same amperage because a lower amperage will blow straight away and a higher one does not protect the wiring. If it has a 10 amp fuse it's because the wiring is designed for a 10 amp fuse – fitting a 20 or 30 amp fuse means the power could exceed the wires' capacity which is a fire risk.

If you do not have a fuse of the right amperage for something vital in the car, look at what else fuses of that amperage run. You can do without interior lights so that you can run the indicators or sacrifice the heated rear screen for the wipers.

Battery problems

The most common reason for calling out a breakdown organization is a battery problem. Admittedly, this is often down to driver error, such as leaving the lights on.

If you suspect a battery problem, always start by making sure the cables are securely connected and undamaged.

If the lights won't come on, the battery is either faulty or totally flat. In either case you'll need your breakdown organization's help because a new battery will have to be found if it is faulty or if it is that flat it may need more of a kick than a jump-start from another car.

If you have regular battery problems, make sure there is nothing staying on, like a faulty boot light, then get the battery and charging system professionally checked.

⚠ **Warning!**

Batteries are dangerous. The power is direct current so if your body or tools make a connection between live and neutral terminals (which includes the car's bodywork) the current holds you instead of jolting you away like the alternating current in your house would. That is always painful and can cause serious burns. It can damage the car, too. Never try to jump-start a damaged battery or it might burst, spraying acid.

Modern cars have many electronic systems that won't take kindly to a power surge so it is vital to check the car's handbook in case there are any precautions you must take before jump-starting. Indeed, if your handbook's advice differs from that given here, follow its instructions because the manufacturer must have a good reason for it and if you cause damage by doing anything else it isn't covered by the warranty.

You must use jump-leads specifically designed for the job and that are in good condition with no damage to the insulation, because if they make contact with something that they shouldn't, including your hands, they could do serious damage. When buying jump-leads look for the **DIN** approval number 72 553 which shows they are of a safe standard.

JUMP-STARTING

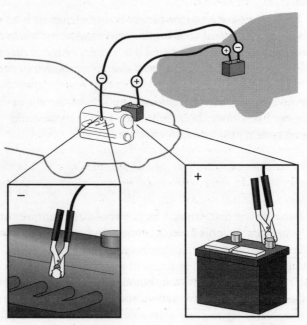

Figure 11.2 The jump-start cables both go to the good battery but the negative one is clipped to bare metal on the dead car.

Both batteries must be of the same voltage: you can't start a 12-volt car with a 24-volt lorry, for example. Some large diesel engines, like those in off-roaders, may need a more substantial boost of power than small car batteries can manage even though both are 12-volt. We will assume both cars have a negative earth, which means a cable from the battery's negative terminal goes direct to the car's body. Vehicles with a positive earth tend to be classic cars.

1 *The cars need to be close together but must not touch. Take care when opening doors during jump-starting that they do not touch the other car.*
2 *Check all electrical systems are switched off, though if you are on or near the road you should leave the donor car's hazard lights going.*
3 *With both ignitions off, connect the red jump-lead to the positive terminal on the flat battery then connect the other end to the positive terminal on the donor battery.*
4 *Connect the black cable to the negative terminal on the donor battery. The other end is not connected to the flat battery but to that car's engine or bodywork away from the battery, to reduce the risk of a short circuit. It is best to attach it to bare metal, like the engine block. In many modern cars the front wings are plastic so will not do the job.*
5 *Check you have connected the terminals like-with-like and that the cables are clear of the engine fan and the exhaust manifold.*

6 *Start the donor car and bring it to a fast idle, then try starting the car with the flat battery. Do not run its starter for more*

than 15 seconds at a time and if the jump-leads become hot, stop to allow them to cool.

Top tip

If the car with the flat battery still won't start you may have another problem. Most likely, you need a new battery because the lead plates inside have collapsed so you no longer have a connection running through it.

When you remove the cables, do it in the reverse order, disconnecting the black lead first then the red. This reduces the risk of sparking by disconnecting the earth first.

Modern methods

With some cars the handbook may advise running the donor car with the batteries connected for 15 minutes to charge the flat battery, then disconnecting everything before starting the car with the flat battery. This is to protect the car's electronics.

Accidents

Fortunately, the majority of accidents are damage only, but even one where only the cars get hurt can be traumatic, particularly as modern cars protect occupants so well that they can still be very severe impacts.

OUT OF THE FRYING PAN

If you are involved in an accident keep your temper and don't panic. Whatever you do, don't leap out of the car to confront the other driver – assess the situation first. You could easily leap into the path of another vehicle whose driver is too busy gawping at the accident to notice you. So, check passengers are all right and see what is happening on the road around you.

It is only in films that all crashed cars immediately explode into flames. In real life that is extremely rare and even then the car must be so severely damaged that fuel tank protection and fuel shut-off systems have been wrecked. Diesel cars are safer still because the fuel needs to get so hot to ignite.

However, it is still unwise to smoke after an accident and, especially if you smell petrol, you should walk away from the wreckage before using a mobile phone. The signal from a mobile can cause sparks off metalwork in certain circumstances, which is why you are not allowed to use them in filling stations.

Legal requirements

There are few, if any, countries in which you are not legally obliged to stop after an accident no matter how minor. In the UK you must give your name and address and that of the vehicle's owner to anyone having reasonable grounds to ask for it.

NON-INJURY ACCIDENTS

If it is a damage-only accident and you don't give your name and address to the owner of the damaged property at the time, you must report it to the police within 24 hours. This does not just apply if you damage another car, but if you damage anything, including fences, road signs and telegraph poles as well as most domesticated animals.

INJURY ACCIDENTS

If anyone is hurt, you must report the accident to the police within 24 hours, regardless of whether you exchanged details at the scene, and produce your insurance certificate within seven days. If you don't have the certificate or your driving licence for administrative reasons, tell the police within seven days so they can give you an extension until it arrives.

GETTING HELP

Some people think the police must be called to all accidents and that vehicles can't be moved until they have arrived. This is not so in the UK and failure to move vehicles only holds everyone else up, though you should not move vehicles with injured people in them. If a damage-only accident blocks the road, or part of it, because the cars are so severely damaged they can't be moved, you may have to call the police to safely direct traffic and help arrange recovery. Some insurers and breakdown organizations have accident helplines where they can arrange recovery of a badly damaged car as well as giving you advice on what to do.

At the scene

> ### ⚠ Warning!
>
> No matter how badly damaged the car is, or whose fault it is, the first priority must be to any casualties and to ensuring road safety at the scene. Always ensure you do not become a casualty while helping others or just by being there. Ensure nobody else is going to crash into your crash, getting someone to direct the traffic if necessary, and always keep an eye on oncoming vehicles yourself.

CASUALTIES

We can't go into roadside first aid in detail here. At least read a book like the Red Cross approved *Five-Minute First Aid for Travel* published by Hodder Education or, better still, take a first aid course. If there are casualties call for expert help by dialling the emergency services before you try to do anything else and if you ask someone else to make the call, tell them to let you know when it has been made successfully so you can be sure it has been done. Unless you are a trained first aider you should stick to ensuring people can breathe and are in as little danger as possible.

Top tip
When checking casualties, start with the unconscious and quiet ones – if they can scream they can breathe.

Do not move serious casualties unless they are in danger. Be particularly careful where neck and back injuries are suspected because moving someone with damage to the vertebrae could turn them from a casualty with a treatable injury into a paraplegic for the rest of their life. Neck injuries are a very common in motorcyclists and horse-riders but also to car occupants, as a result of whiplash when a car has been struck from behind. Helmets and safety hats should never be removed from casualties because of the risk of worsening head and neck injuries.

Bleeding can be slowed down by applying pressure, taking care not to move broken bones or push debris into the wound. If someone has an object stuck in them, do not try to extract it because pulling it out may do further damage, perhaps to a blood vessel or vital organ it missed on the way in.

RECORDING THE SCENE

When casualties have been taken care of, or in non-injury accidents, take a note and, if you can, photos, of the positions of the vehicles and move them out of the road if possible.

Swap details with the other drivers, asking to see their driving licence or other identification to confirm who they are. In addition to the information you are legally required to give, it also makes sense to give them a phone number and your insurer's name and address, with your insurance policy number. Keep a note of these things in the car.

Also make sure you get the registration numbers, makes, models and colours of the other cars involved as well as details of what damage you can see, so nobody can claim for a different car or damage you didn't do.

Note down:

- ▶ *the time of the accident*
- ▶ *your speed when it happened*
- ▶ *the weather and road conditions (was it wet, dry, icy or covered in loose chippings?)*
- ▶ *what lights vehicles were showing, including your own*
- ▶ *the name of the road and the names of roads at any nearby junctions (you may have to check this on a map later if name signs are not visible)*
- ▶ *speed limit signs especially if it is different to the national limit for the road (like 50 mph on a rural dual-carriageway where the limit is normally 70 mph).*

Make a sketch map of the scene showing the positions of the cars, witnesses, road markings and signs.

Top tip
Some insurers include a pamphlet with their paperwork to help you record details at the scene, so keep that in the car, too.

LIABILITY

Do not admit liability. That means you do not say it was your fault even if it was and do not say things like 'I'm sorry, I didn't see you'. There are two reasons for this. First, you are probably not a legal expert and even if you were, you would not be in a state to thoroughly assess the situation. Second, your insurance policy expressly forbids you to admit liability – that's what you pay your insurer to sort out. If anyone pressurizes you, simply point out that all insurance policies have this clause and if anyone involved in the accident breaks that condition it could make it harder to get payments sorted out. This is not strictly true because the insurers would probably pay for repairs and other compensation, then argue over who was really to blame and who's going to foot the bill, so take note if anyone else admits liability.

WITNESSES

If there are any witnesses, for either side, take their names and addresses and a note of where they were when they saw what happened. If anyone is reluctant to get involved, point out that next time they could be the person in your situation and that the most onerous thing they are likely to have to do is fill in a short form saying what they have seen. If someone refuses, especially in an injury accident, take their car number so they can be traced if things get difficult or if the police want to get them to a court or inquest.

Leaving the scene

Before driving off, assess the condition of your car.

- ▶ *Is it safe and legal?*
- ▶ *Is it leaking anything?*
- ▶ *Do the lights work?*
- ▶ *Are the tyres damaged?*
- ▶ *Do the doors close properly?*
- ▶ *Is there any broken glass that needs removing?*
- ▶ *Does it still have number plates?*

AT THE WHEEL

When you start driving, does it feel right? Apply the brakes to check they work at low speed before going any faster. If you have any doubts about these things, arrange recovery.

If you are comprehensively insured, recovery will be covered by the insurer, though the policy may insist you arrange it through their accident helpline. If you only have third party cover, you may be able to get it back off the other driver's policy, if they are to blame (see *Teach Yourself Car Buying and Ownership*).

Any car in which the airbags have gone off is likely to be too badly damaged to drive because the bags only go off in severe impacts. If you drive off and have another accident when something fails, you will be entirely to blame and the car may not be able to give you full crash protection.

ARE YOU ALRIGHT?

Remember, you are shaken up, so drive cautiously and always stop and look carefully in both directions at junctions – when you are under such stress your brain does not react quickly enough to register moving objects if your head is also moving as you look for them.

Don't drive if you feel odd, especially if you have hit your head and don't be surprised if about 15 minutes after the accident you suddenly feel dreadful, even shaking or crying. This is the effect of coming down from the adrenaline rush the accident provoked and you must at least stop until you feel better. The best thing is to either get someone to collect you, go home on public transport or book into a hotel. After a serious accident you may also stiffen up, but go to a doctor if you have serious problems moving or any strange sensations.

10 THINGS TO REMEMBER

1 Carry the essential equipment listed in this chapter.

2 Make sure you know where your car's jack and toolkit are kept and that everything is present.

3 Use hazard warning lights as soon as you stop on the hard shoulder.

4 Remember that the hard shoulder is a dangerous place.

5 It is better to use motorway emergency phones than a mobile because they automatically show controllers where you are.

6 Only jack a car up on firm ground, with the handbrake on and the gearbox in gear or 'park'.

7 Loosen the wheel nuts before you jack the car up.

8 After an accident, assess the situation before getting out of the car.

9 Ensure casualties are safe before doing anything else and do not move them unless vital for their safety.

10 Keep calm and make sure you collect and give all the information you are required to by law and for insurance purposes.

12

Driving abroad

In this chapter you will learn:
- *how to prepare for driving abroad*
- *how to get accustomed to different roads*
- *about driving on the 'wrong' side.*

One of the great pleasures that confident motoring opens up is the chance to explore other countries with greater freedom than organized travel or public transport can offer. But whether you plan a short trip to a neighbouring country or a drive across a continent or two, a little forward-planning can save a lot of grief.

In Europe we are lucky because the countries of the EU recognize each other's driving licences and insurance while making it easy to cross borders with your car and luggage. Indeed, on mainland Europe you are often unaware of crossing borders, especially on minor roads. But if you plan to go further afield you must research what documentation you need both as a driver and to 'import' your car and belongings. Motoring organizations, tourist bodies and embassies can help you here and it is worth searching the internet for 'blogs' by people who have been there for tips and in case reality on the ground is different from what the administration says should happen. Border crossings outside Europe may take hours with officials expecting bribes or trying to get fees for unnecessary 'insurance' or documents.

Note that if the car is registered to anyone other than you, perhaps to a leasing company or your employer, you must have a letter from them giving you permission to take it abroad, even if you are only travelling between EU countries.

It also pays to research speed limits, any odd local signs including warning phrases, local parking laws, any unusual rules of the road and whether you are required by law to carry things in the car like fire extinguishers, warning triangles and first aid kits.

Insurance

Always check the territorial limits of your insurance cover. European insurance must at least give third party cover in all member states but remember that in an accident this only covers damage to other people's vehicles (the third party after you and the insurer) and does not repair or replace yours. Most policies demand that you notify them if you plan to drive abroad and some may demand an extra fee to issue a '**green card**' which is a document showing you have cover abroad.

If you are going outside the territorial limits of your cover you will have to make special arrangements with an insurer and in some parts of the world may even have to take out cover locally.

Check green cards and policies are valid for long enough for you to complete your trip with some time in hand in case you are delayed.

Top tip

In most countries you are required to carry original documents. Avoid leaving these in unattended cars and always make photocopies so you can keep one with you (separately from the originals) and leave one at home in case of emergencies. Keep documents where you can get at them, but not somewhere obvious like the glove box. Many travellers keep them under seats or with the spare wheel.

BREAKDOWN COVER

Many motoring organizations and insurers offer breakdown and recovery packages for trips abroad, especially in Europe. These have three advantages:

- ▶ *If you break down you call an English-speaking control centre who send a local garage contracted to them.*
- ▶ *Recovery and repairs will not eat into your travel budget.*
- ▶ *If you and your car need to be brought home, they will arrange and pay for it.*

If you go further afield try to arrange repatriation cover for the car or at least have an emergency budget for it.

Fuel

In developed countries fuel shouldn't be a problem not least because modern cars' fuel systems can adjust themselves to changes in grade, up to a point. In less-developed countries, check on the availability of the fuel for your car. If the fuel there is of a lower grade than your car handbook specifies, check with the car manufacturer to see if modifications are needed.

In undeveloped countries where fuel may be supplied from drums, take a funnel with a fine mesh filter as dirt could clog the fuel system. If you are stuck without a means of filtering you may be able to do it with lint free cloth or chamois leather in a funnel.

If you plan to carry spare fuel in the car, check the local regulations. Many countries have rules about what sort of containers and quantities are allowed and in some it is totally forbidden to carry petrol except in the petrol tank.

In a filling station where someone serves you, never assume they know what fuel your car needs. So, take care not to pull up in front of the wrong pump and always state what fuel you want, or point to the pump.

Language

Don't assume there will always be someone who speaks English and even if you speak the language of the country you are in, carry a phrase book that gives car terms.

In any country it pays to find out the local words for:

▶ *fuel filling station*
▶ *garage (for repairs)*
▶ *petrol*
▶ *diesel*
▶ *unleaded*
▶ *fill it up*
▶ *oil*
▶ *water*
▶ *my car has broken down/run out of fuel/has a puncture.*

The wrong side

The thing that scares most people about driving abroad is driving on what is, for them, the wrong side of the road. Whether it is an English driver going to America or an American visiting England, the problems are the same.

It goes beyond just making sure you avoid head-on crashes because being on the wrong side of the road totally changes your view of the road. You see bends from a viewpoint you are not used to, at junctions the cars closest to you are approaching from a different side and you turn across traffic when turning left instead of right, or vice versa. This is why you get a feeling of things not being quite right until you have driven for some time.

DANGER AREAS

You are at greatest risk of making a mistake if anything takes you away from driving on the correct side of the road, not least because it may put you onto the side you feel more comfortable using.

These high-risk times include returning to two-way streets after:

- *one-way streets*
- *single track roads*
- *car parks, or*
- *when leaving premises (especially on the opposite side from your direction or travel).*

Take extra care at these times and warn passengers to be on their guard to warn you if you get it wrong. If you can, avoid using filling stations and car parks that are not on your side of the road. Remember, too, that the rules of the road usually apply in car parks.

Be particularly careful returning to the road after an overnight stay, because you've had time to relax and may be starting to feel more confident. As confidence builds there is always the risk that you stop thinking about it.

EXITS

Take care when leaving premises or side roads that you don't look the wrong way. This is a particular danger if you are not turning across the traffic, as when turning right in a country where they drive on the right.

If you are used to driving on the left, you are used to the traffic closest to you, and on what will be your side of the road when you join it, approaching from the right. That means when turning left onto a wide road you may get away with only looking to your right (though this is unwise in case someone is overtaking). The trouble is that abroad there is a risk of turning right while, through force of habit, looking right so not seeing close traffic approaching from the left.

You must also beware of this when walking in a foreign country because you tend to walk across junctions while looking the wrong way. When driving in tourist areas look out for your compatriots making the same mistake.

OVERTAKING

If you are driving a car with the steering wheel on the wrong side for the country, overtaking needs much more care.

Your view of the road is much more restricted and even on a dual-carriageway you must be careful because you are judging the speed and distance of overtaking cars in a mirror that is much further away than you are used to.

If you keep back from the vehicle in front you'll be surprised how good a view you often get down its kerb side if you move to that side. But in most overtaking you will have to rely on a passenger to tell you when the road ahead is clear. It is certainly unwise to use a passenger who can't drive as a spotter, because they don't know what they are looking for, and it is better if the passenger has some idea of how the car performs.

Top tip

Agree phrases between you so there is no confusion. 'Yes' and 'no' are clear, but 'not yet' could be misheard as 'now, yes' while 'go' could be heard as 'no' and vice versa. It is also safer to say 'after the red car' rather than 'after the Renault' in case of misidentification. If advice is rescinded, the co-driver must repeat it loudly, so they say: 'Yes... NO, NO!'

JOINING MOTORWAYS

When you join a motorway or dual-carriageway your view from the sliproad of traffic on that road is far more restricted if your car's steering wheel is on the 'wrong' side. If you are driving alone, take great care and remember that even if you look back over your shoulder, the car's rear pillar seriously obstructs your view.

If you are driving with a passenger, ask them to glance back down the road to make sure nobody is in your blind spot.

You will also need their help at staggered junctions on ordinary roads, though there you may be able to angle the car so that you can see.

Foreign familiarity

If you are used to driving on the left and have driven abroad before, be careful if you visit a country where they drive on the left (there are many more than most people believe).

The problem is that you have conditioned yourself to think that when you are abroad you drive on the right, but if you are, say, an English driver in Japan you are somewhere that is totally foreign to you so driving on the left seems wrong.

As it feels wrong, you may give in to that feeling and find yourself turning into a road on the wrong side.

Similarly, if you are used to driving on the right and your first visit abroad is to a left driving country, take care if you visit a right drive country. An American whose first driving abroad experience is in England runs a real risk of driving on the left in France because he associates driving abroad with driving on the left.

Acclimatizing

Even in countries that drive on the side you are used to, you must give yourself time to get used to different road layouts, sights, signs, road hazards and local habits.

It takes time to get used to where they put signs, how junction layouts work and even how much grip the road surfaces offer. Then there are national traits to take account of: British drivers tend to be more polite and safety conscious than most but sloppy on motorway lane discipline; Germans can generally be relied on to stay in the right lane and though motorways often have no speed limit, where a limit is applied it is rigorously observed; Italians can be quite competitive while disregarding speed limits; the French often overtake much closer to bends than is sensible while their police seem to allow locals more leeway than foreigners; Scandinavians are well educated on safety matters and can display amazing car control in poor conditions but they do not suffer foolish drivers gladly; and finally, drivers in Arab countries and the Indian subcontinent seem to have great faith in God or fate to keep them alive no matter what risks they take.

So, give yourself time to get used to all these differences and don't expect people to do the things they would do at home. Equally, try not to do anything that would surprise them. It might seem normal to you to stop at a pedestrian crossing to let an old lady across, but the Frenchman behind won't expect you to do it.

Hire cars

Hiring a car at least puts you in a vehicle suitable for local roads but add getting used to an unfamiliar vehicle to acclimatizing to local conditions and nobody can see you are a foreigner so they don't know to make allowances. Insist that the hire company let you take over the car somewhere where you can safely familiarize yourself with the controls and adjust the mirrors. If they can't, pull over as soon as you can to sort yourself out.

You must find:

- ▶ *how to adjust mirrors and seats*
- ▶ *the horn*
- ▶ *the lights*
- ▶ *the indicators*
- ▶ *the headlamp flasher*
- ▶ *the parking brake, if it's not the obvious lever*
- ▶ *how to engage reverse*
- ▶ *the childproof door locks (to activate if you have children and turn off if you don't)*
- ▶ *how to use any automatic door locking systems.*

Insight

Some of these things may sound unimportant, but you do not want to find out that the horn isn't where you thought it was when someone is about to step into the road in front of you and even in a sunny holiday destination you may still need lights in daytime. For example, lights are a legal requirement when entering a tunnel in many countries. Nobody wants to start a holiday with a fine for something as simple as that.

WHEEL DIFFICULTIES

Don't be surprised in a car with the steering wheel on the opposite side to what you are used to if it takes a while to get the interior mirror adjusted and for the driving position to feel right. It will take time to get used to everything being on the wrong side and even then you still grab the door pocket instead of the gear lever or parking brake if you try to do it in a hurry.

Drive with caution at first because you are not used to judging distances from this side of the car. Ask passengers to warn you if you get too close to anything, though their flinching is usually a good indicator.

Though you are now on the correct side of the car for the road, so overtaking is easier, remember that your view of the road is different so bends will feel unfamiliar and you may find judging speed and distance hard at first.

Back home

If you visit a country that drives on the other side of the road you are most likely to drive on the wrong side when you come home. Many a driver has proudly boasted how they didn't once make the mistake abroad only to leave the airport car park on the wrong side. So be careful not to do it yourself and look out for others doing it. This is because you have been aware of the danger abroad where the different location has been a constant reminder, but when you get home, you stop thinking about it.

Though you usually only make this mistake in the first few miles, if you have been away a long time you may have relapses later, especially while boring passengers with what a great time you had.

Insight

I must confess, I have driven on the wrong side more often at home, after trips abroad, than I have in foreign countries. I have also more than once been with highly experienced international drivers who have gradually wandered to the wrong side of a, fortunately, quiet country road while describing their latest trip. I am told this is a particular problem for people who have lived abroad for any time and one friend returning from a posting abroad said he irritably flashed his lights at an oncoming driver before realizing who was on the wrong side.

10 THINGS TO REMEMBER

1 Check out the documentation and insurance you need for your destination well in advance.

2 Check availability of suitable fuel in undeveloped countries.

3 Be prepared for non-EU border crossing to take time.

4 Learn basic motoring phrases.

5 When driving on what is to you the 'wrong' side, be careful if returning to a two-way road after using one-way streets, single track roads or car parks.

6 Avoid using filling stations and car parks on the opposite side of the road.

7 Take care to look both ways at junctions because the traffic closest to you is approaching from the opposite side to that which you are used to.

8 Give yourself time to acclimatize to different driving conditions and local habits, even in a country that drives on the same side as yours.

9 If you hire a car, take time to familiarize yourself with important controls before setting off, even if it is a model you drive at home.

10 When you get home, take care to drive on the correct side of the road.

13

Training

In this chapter you will learn:
- *how to get further tuition*
- *how to find out how well you drive*
- *what specialist training is available.*

Unfortunately, though the UK, like most countries, has in recent
years significantly updated and extended its driving test, a lot of
basic driver training is still aimed at getting you through that test
and little more. A conscientious driving instructor will try to pass
on the things you need to know in addition to the test syllabus
but the instructor can't cover everything. In addition, provisional
licence holders are not allowed on motorways and it is entirely
possible for someone to get through their test without ever having
driven at night.

Many instructors offer an 'after the test' lesson where they do
things like taking you on a motorway and it is well worth doing
this. Many new drivers benefit from having a lesson like this in their
own car so the instructor can point out differences between it and
the car they learned on. But driving instructors should not be seen
as people who only teach learners: they are trained teachers who
have to keep up with motoring regulations and can pass on their
knowledge to anyone. So if you think you have a driving problem
or need to learn more about some aspect of driving, why not give
your old driving instructor a call even if you passed your test some
time ago?

The organizations in this chapter are in the UK but they have equivalents in all developed countries.

Keeping up

As we said at the beginning of the book, *The Highway Code* is the basis of all driver training in the UK and is regularly updated. Sadly, most drivers see it only as something learners read which is why, for example, if you see rear fog lamps being misused it is usually by an older driver who passed before advice on their proper use was included in the *Code*.

You cannot expect to keep up with changes to vehicles, the road system and the law if you do not occasionally reread *The Highway Code*, at least whenever a new edition comes out. A new edition is always well publicized, unlike most changes in driving laws, and as ignorance is no defence in law, a court will take a dim view if it is something that has been in the *Code* for years.

In addition, with the internet it is now easy to check on legal and safety issues on websites belonging to organizations mentioned in this chapter, motoring groups or the British Government's websites at www.directgov.gov.uk and www.thinkroadsafety.gov.uk. Most developed countries have an equivalent of *The Highway Code* and their highway authorities have information websites.

Pass Plus

It is a sad fact that you are more likely to have an accident in your first two years of driving than in the rest of your driving career and one in five drivers has an accident in the first year. It was with that in mind that the UK's **Driving Standards Agency** set up **Pass Plus** to try to boost new drivers' understanding of motoring's risks.

There is no further test at the end of the course but you are assessed continually through it and will need at least six hours tuition. The cost varies according to where you live and the instructor, though some councils support tuition costs. The course modules cover driving in town, all-weather, out of town, at night and on dual-carriageways and motorways.

At the time of writing, 18 insurance companies have agreed to give discounts to drivers who reach the pass standard. In most cases they give straight discounts (usually 10 per cent) but some treat you as if you have one year no claims bonus. The latter is particularly good value because if you do not make a claim, the benefit is passed on to subsequent years so the saving can be considerably more than the cost of lessons. (Insurance no claims bonuses build up year on year so if you get, say, a 10 per cent saving in the first year and make no claims, you'll get 20 per cent next year.)

Many driving instructors automatically give pupils who pass the test details of Pass Plus but you can find out more at www.passplus.org.uk or by calling 0115 936 6504.

Teaching others

The days are long gone when you could pass your driving test after a few 'lessons' from parents because the test has become much more sophisticated with theory sections, including hazard perception, and a high standard expected in the practical test. Indeed, in some countries you must have professional tuition by law.

There is nothing wrong with taking a learner out between lessons to add to their experience, but only do it if you

(Contd)

have patience (and courage) or you may do more harm than good by damaging their confidence. It is also vital that you do not contradict the instructor and that the learner knows to ignore anything you say that does contradict them: driving instructors teach according to standards laid down by testing authorities, they know what examiners are looking for and they know the mistakes learners are likely to make. For example, an experienced driver may safely enter a roundabout without stopping but a learner may not have the skill or experience to assess the situation quickly enough, so is best advised to stop.

Before taking this on, consider these points:

▶ *Does your insurance cover them? Check with your insurer because if it doesn't, you both commit offences.*
▶ *Can you legally accompany them? In the UK you must have held, and still hold, a licence for the class of vehicle for three years and be over 21. You are legally in control of the car so you must also be under the drink-drive limit and must not use a hand-held mobile phone.*
▶ *Have they learned basic car control from a professional? Your car does not have dual controls so you can't intervene if they get it wrong.*
▶ *Is your car suitable? It's a bad idea to put a learner in something large or powerful, or a difficult to drive classic car.*
▶ *Are you prepared to accept they may get it wrong and damage your car?*

IAM

The Institute of Advanced Motorists is probably Britain's best known driving 'further education' organization and has a sister organization in the Republic of Ireland. It is best known for its advanced driving test but in 2007 introduced a cheap Drive Check for people who are interested in safe driving but feel they are not ready to take the test. It is conducted by your local IAM Group and takes about an hour including a drive of about 40 minutes, after which you get a written feedback form saying what you need to brush up on and if you are good enough to take an advanced test.

If you want to take the IAM test they do a Skill for Life package that includes the IAM book *How to be an Advanced Driver*, an initial assessment and test preparation with your local group and the test entry fee.

Several insurance companies give discounts to IAM members and there are other benefits, like cheaper breakdown cover.

The IAM is at www.iam.org.uk or on 020 8996 9600 while the Irish Advanced Motorists shares the IAM website but can also be contacted on 056 7771778. This website also has links to safer driving sites in many other countries, including the USA and Australia, as well as a list of UK skid pans.

RoSPA

The Royal Society for the Prevention of Accidents' Advanced Drivers and Riders programme takes its driver testing a step further than the IAM. It grades passes as gold, silver and bronze and demands that you must have a free retest every three years to ensure you maintain a high standard.

It strongly advises getting free tuition from its local members' groups because most drivers who do not either get a low pass grade or fail. Its test is based on *The Highway Code* and the government Stationery Office publication *Roadcraft – The Essential Police Drivers' Handbook*.

You will find contacts for local members' groups on their website at www.roada.org.uk or can call for further information on 0121 248 2127.

Specialist training

There are many organizations that offer specialist driver training in everything from circuit driving to towing trailers. Though some of these courses may not directly improve your road driving, anything that increases your understanding of how a car behaves has got to be good for your driving ability. To find courses local to you look on the internet, in your telephone directory and in specialist magazines.

SKID PAN SESSIONS

This is probably the most worthwhile additional training you can take because it has a direct bearing on your safety. It will help you understand why skids occur and show you what they feel like and how to respond to them. However, do not let it lull you into a false sense of security because skids on skid pans are expected and happen at relatively low speeds.

OFF-ROAD

A few off-roader manufacturers have offered free all-terrain driving to customers and found a hardcore of owners whose attitude is 'I'll never need to do that'. They're the ones who will look stupid stuck in the snow or on a slippery roadside verge in their 4×4 because they don't know how to use its systems.

Even if you don't plan to drive off-road, this tuition will help you understand why the vehicle is built like it is, how to correctly use its systems so avoid breaking them, what its limitations are and what your responsibilities are if you venture off-road.

If you do plan to go exploring, a course covering conditions you are likely to meet is essential. Off-road driving is not to be taken lightly because you can get into a lot of trouble at very low speeds and if you do, there is unlikely to be anyone passing by to help you. Inept off-road driving also causes much more environmental damage than a properly driven vehicle.

RACE AND RALLY SCHOOLS

Track driving pushes the car and driver to limits nobody sensible would try on the road where trucks and less skilled road users may be coming the other way. However, it teaches you the skills of car control in an exciting and repeatable way and the techniques involved in cornering a car on a dry track at 70 mph are the same as those on a slippery road at 40 mph. Track tuition is often combined with skid pan sessions so you can hone skills at lower speeds before trying it out on the track.

TOWING

Even if your licence allows you to tow trailers of any size, it is sensible to get some tuition before doing so, especially for larger trailers (which includes caravans). As well as considerations like suitable weights for the towcar and trailer, loading the trailer and pre-trip checks, there are essential skills to learn like hitching up, reversing and safe cornering.

Because some drivers must take a towing test to tow certain sizes of trailer (see box on page 292) there are now many driving schools and lorry training centres offering tuition. If you need to take a towing test, training is essential.

Towing the line

In Europe you must take a towing test to tow trailers (including caravans) of certain sizes. In the UK the B+E test, as it is officially known after the licence categories for a car (B) and trailer (E), applies to anyone who passed their driving test after 1 January 1997. Unless otherwise stated, the weights mentioned below are maximum authorized mass (MAM) which is also known as gross or maximum laden weight, and is laid down by the manufacturer.

If you passed your driving test before January 1997 you can tow trailers up to 3.5 tonnes as long as the combined weight is below the maximum for your licence (normally 8.25 tonnes). Those who passed after January 1997 may drive a car of up to 3.5 tonnes with a 750 kg trailer or a heavier trailer with a lighter car providing their combined weight is no more than 3.5 tonnes and that the trailer's MAM is less than the car's unladen weight. Note that it is not the trailer's actual weight that matters but its legal maximum.

If the trailer falls outside those limits you must take the towing test, though you can drive such an outfit if you show L-plates and are accompanied by someone over 21 who has held the relevant licence category for three years (including a pre-1997 driver). Trailers likely to fall into the B+E category include large caravans and all double horse trailers.

You cannot tow anything on a provisional licence. If you plan to tow abroad, check local regulations because some countries have different weight limits and restrictions on driver age and experience.

Taking it further

For contacts for training organizations please see Chapter 13.

Breakdown organizations

(The following phone numbers are for membership enquiries. The websites contain a lot of helpful motoring information, including route planners.)

Automobile Association (AA) www.theaa.co.uk 0800 0852721
Britannia Rescue www.britanniarescue.com 0800 591563
Green Flag www.greenflag.co.uk 0845 246 2766
Royal Automobile Club (RAC) www.rac.co.uk 0800 096 0731

Government bodies

All the UK Government motoring authorities have a presence at www.directgov.gov.uk in the website's motoring section. This includes the facilities to download most forms, renew car tax, check all kinds of information and fees and book a driving test. In addition these organizations have their own websites, but many 'consumer' links just take you back to Directgov, which is also available on digital television.

Insight

I'll apologize in advance if any of the web addresses or phone numbers below are out of date. Unfortunately, Government agencies seem to change these more frequently than most organizations, making it difficult to keep up with them.

Driver and Vehicle Licensing Agency (DVLA), responsible for all licensing and registration matters, www.dft.gov.uk/dvla. Driver enquiries 0300 7906801. Vehicle enquiries 0300 7906802.

Vehicle Operator Services Agency (VOSA), responsible for MOTs and construction and use matters, www.dft.gov.uk/vosa. The local office is in the phone book. Headquarters: 0300 1239000.

To check the validity of an MOT certificate go to www.motinfo.gov.uk.

Driving Standards Agency (DSA), responsible for driving tests and driver training, www.dsa.gov.uk. Local offices in the phone book.

Highways Agency, responsible for maintaining main roads and for safety on motorways. Provides the control rooms that answer roadside emergency phones, www.highways.gov.uk. Headquarters: 08457 504030 with regional offices in phone book. Traffic information via website or 08700 660115.

Department for Transport's 'Think!' road safety campaign for general road safety information including downloadable pamphlets including one on child safety seats: www.dft.gov.uk/think.

Mapping websites

www.transportdirect.info: UK government funded site that provides information for all forms of transport and includes a road route planner.

www.streetmap.co.uk: finds addresses in the UK including by postcode.

www.ordnancesurvey.co.uk: considerable information about mapping in the UK.

www.multimap.com: same as Streetmap but with access to sites for other countries.

www.trafficmaster.co.uk: traffic information services and devices.

Google Earth mapping software can be downloaded free at http://earth.google.com/download-earth.html.

(Also see the AA and RAC websites listed above.)

Further reading

Henderson, J. *Car Buying and Ownership*, 2010, Hodder Education

Henderson, J. *Photographic Guide to Preparing for the Towing Test*, 2003, J. A. Allen

Institute of Advanced Motorists *How to be an Advanced Driver*, 2004, Motorbooks International

Government Stationery Office publications (also available through bookshops):

Home Office *Roadcraft: The Police Drivers' Handbook*, 1997, The Stationery Office

Department for Transport Environment and the Regions *The Highway Code*, 2005, The Stationery Office

DSA *Driving – the Essential Skills*, 2001, The Stationery Office

Glossary

2WD Two-wheel drive

4WD Four-wheel drive

4×4 Four-by-four a military acronym for 4WD (four wheels, four driven) now often used to describe off-road vehicles or sports utility vehicles (SUV) (see below)

ABS Anti-lock brake system Electronic system that stops the wheels locking under heavy braking and so prevents skidding

Acceleration lane The short extra lane feeding into a main road to allow you to accelerate

Active cruise control (ACC) Radar cruise control (see below) that not only maintains a steady speed but keeps a safe distance from cars in front

Adaptive or active automatic gearboxes Boxes that 'learn' from the way the car is being driven and adapt the way they shift to suit

Adverse camber Where the camber (see below) of the road tips the car in the wrong direction for the bend

Airbags Safety devices that inflate, using a pyrotechnic gas generator, to protect occupants in a crash. They are commonly in the steering wheel, passenger-side fascia, over the windows and in the seat sides but are sometimes in the steering column to protect drivers' knees and in the backs of the front seats to protect rear occupants.

Alternator The car's generator

Aquaplaning When a cushion of water builds up under a tyre, lifting it from the road

Belisha beacons Orange flashing globes on poles used to mark 'zebra' pedestrian crossings, named after a British transport minister

Bluetooth A wireless connection system used to link mobile phones to hands-free devices

Camber The curve in a road surface sloping from its centre down to the edge to aid drainage

Child safety locks Manually or electronically activated locks that stop rear seat passengers opening the doors from the inside

Clutch A friction-plate system that engages and disengages the engine and transmission (see below) so that the driver can change gear

Countdown markers Signs that count down the distance to an exit at 100-metre intervals

Cruise control An electronic device that keeps the car at a steady speed (see also Active cruise control and Speed limiters)

CVT Continuously variable transmission – a type of automatic gearbox using belts and pulleys instead of gears

Daylight driving lights Lights that come on with the ignition for use in daylight

Deceleration lane The short extra lane leading into a sliproad to allow you to slow down on leaving a motorway

Differential (diff) A system of gears that allows one driven wheel (see below) to turn faster than the other when cornering. All cars have at least one but full-time 4WD requires one in each axle and one in the middle.

DIN German standards body

Distributor A mechanical device that 'distributes' the power to each sparkplug (see below) in turn, now replaced by electronic control

Driven wheels The wheels turned by the engine

Driving Standards Agency (DSA) British government agency responsible for driver training and testing

Driver and Vehicle Licensing Agency (DVLA) British government agency responsible for driving licences and registering vehicles

Dynamic stability control Another name for electronic stability programme (see below)

Electronic stability programme or control (ESP) Electronic driving aid that helps stop the car drifting out on a bend (often combined with traction control to prevent wheel spin)

Emergency Brake Assist (EBA) Electronics linked to ABS (see above) to boost brake pressure and keep it on during emergency braking

Glowplug A device that warms diesel engine cylinders prior to starting

GPS Acronym for Geo Positioning Satellites, the geo-stationary satellites used by satellite navigation systems (see below) to pinpoint the car's position

Green card A colloquial term for an insurance document (traditionally on green paper) that shows the car is fully insured abroad

Hazard warning lights A system that flashes all the indicators at once for emergency use

Head restraints The correct name for what are often called head rests; they restrain backward movement of the head in a crash, preventing whiplash injuries (see below)

High level brake light A central brake light positioned higher than the ordinary brake lights – compulsory on new cars in Europe

Highway Code (The) The government road advice booklet on which British driver training is based

Highways Agency British government agency responsible for the maintenance and safety of main roads and motorways

Hill start assist An electronic device that holds the brakes on for a short time to aid hill starts

Immobilizer A device that prevents the engine starting usually by interrogating a chip in the key and often linked to an alarm

Inertia reel seatbelts Seatbelts which roll in and out of a reel that locks on sudden movement. They adjust automatically to fit the occupant (see also Static seatbelts).

Isofix The modern, safer, universal fitting system for child safety seats established by the International Standards Organization

Jacking points Reinforced points on the car's body able to take the weight of jacking it up.

Kickdown A system on automatic gearboxes that makes them change down a gear or two when the throttle pedal is pushed down hard for overtaking

Kph Kilometres per hour (1 kph = 0.621 mph)

lb ft or pounds feet Imperial abbreviation for the measurement of torque (see below)

Low profile tyres Tyres on which the side walls are low in relation to the width of the tread. High performance cars' tyres may take this to extremes.

Low ratio gearbox Off-roaders designed for true all-terrain work offer high and low settings in their transfer gearbox (see below). This effectively doubles the number of ratios available in the main gearbox providing a gear for every circumstance. Sometimes called a 'dual range transmission'.

MOT Britain's roadworthiness test, still known by the initials of the Ministry of Transport which has long been replaced by the Department of Transport. All cars over three years old must have an annual MOT test.

Mph Miles per hour (1 mph = 1.609 kph)

Multipurpose vehicle (MPV) A multi-seat car with a versatile 'one-box' body. Originally applied only to large seven-seat vehicles like the Renault Espace and Chrysler Voyager, but now applied to more compact vehicles of similar shape which may only seat five.

Newton metres (Nm) A metric measurement of torque (see below) (1 Nm = 5.163 lb ft)

PAS Power assisted steering

Pass Plus A British scheme of further education for new drivers. Taking it may reduce insurance costs.

RDS Acronym for Radio Data System, which transmits coded information alongside a radio station's broadcast so the car radio can show the station name and keep track of that station as its frequencies change over a journey

Revs or rpm Revolutions per minute, the measurement of engine rotational speed

Satellite navigation or sat nav A system that combines digital mapping with signals from geo-positioning satellites to provide directions

'See-you-home' lights Headlights that stay on for a set time after the ignition is turned off to light you to your house door

Sequential gear shift Correct name for the manual touch-change on modern automatic gearboxes that allows you to move up and down the gears in sequence by tapping the gear lever or buttons/paddles on the steering wheel. Sometimes called a Tiptronic gearbox.

Sparkplug The device which ignites the fuel/air mixture in a petrol car (sometimes called a sparking plug)

Speed limiter A device that allows the driver to set a speed limit above which the car will not go

Static seatbelts Old style seatbelts which have three fixed mounting points so must be manually adjusted to fit (see also Inertia real seatbelts)

Tiptronic The first sequential shift (see above) developed by Porsche

Torque Twisting power In cars it is often called pulling power and gives an engine driving flexibility

Torque converter An oil-filled device that takes the place of a clutch in an automatic transmission (see above)

Traction control An electronic system that prevents wheel spin. Often uses the ABS (see above) sensors and is usually allied to ESP (see above)

Traffic Message Channel (TMC) A traffic information signal transmitted alongside a radio station's broadcast, which is used by sat nav systems (see above) to avoid jams or is displayed as a text message on some car radios

Trailing throttle When the driver lifts off the throttle pedal and allows the car to continue under its own momentum. Not good practice when cornering.

Transmission Everything that transmits the drive from the engine to the wheels, including the clutch, gearbox, drive shafts and differentials

Wheel brace A long handled spanner for undoing wheel nuts. Called a 'tire iron' in America.

Whiplash Potentially serious injuries to the neck caused by the head being whipped backwards (see Head restraint)

Index

standing water, 220–1
windscreen wipers, 218
RDS radios, 73–4
rear seatbelts, 55, 60
rear-wheel drive, 33
reverse parking, 122–4
reversing sensors, 125
right turns, 102–6, 114
    at crossroads, 104–5
    positioning, 103–4
    refuges, 105–6
roadworks on motorways, 143–5
roof racks, 61
RoSPA (Royal Society for the Prevention
of Accidents) programme, 289–90
roundabouts, 88, 106–11
    approaches, 107–8
    on dual-carriages, 147
    exiting, 110–11
    mini-roundabouts, 111
    observation, 109–10
    signals, 108–9
route planning *see* journey planning
rural roads, 157–81, 157–82
    animals, 160, 165–7, 173
    bad weather, 205
    bends, 167–71
    cattle grids, 174
    changing conditions, 157–8, 160,
      161
    cyclists, 190
    hills, 177–9
    holidaymakers, 159
    humps and dips, 160–1
    junctions, 171–2
    loose surfaced, 175–6
    night driving, 161, 180–1
    observation, 160–2
    overtaking, 162–5
    pedestrians on, 184
    single track roads, 173–4
    skidding and leaving the road,
      243
    speed, 158–9, 165

safe parking, 118–19
safety equipment, 53–60
    airbags, 56–7, 272
    and breakdowns, 248
    child locks, 59–60
    child seats, 57–9
    seatbelts, 53–5
safety switches, 29–30, 80
satellite navigation, 11, 14–15, 68, 70–3

identifying current location, 72
points of interest (POI) links, 149
sensible use of, 72–3
and speed limits, 91
updates, 73
school-run parents, 93
schools, driving past, 93, 185, 204
seat adjustment, 46–50
seatbelts, 53–5, 60
security
    and breakdowns, 252–3
    car keys, 44, 126
    de-icing cars, 197
    locking systems, 43–4, 125–6
    parking, 119
    service area car parks, 149
    valuables in the car, 126–7
security devices, 42–4, 125–6
service areas on motorways, 148–9
setting out, 77–83
    fuel, 80–2
    looking around you, 82
    pulling out, 82, 83–4
    regular checks before, 77–8, 80
    signalling, 82
    in snowy conditions, 208–9
    starting the car, 79–80
side roads, 147, 172, 210
signals
    changing lanes, 140–1
    junctions, 101–2, 103
    roundabouts, 108–9
    rural roads, 164
    setting off, 83
    sliproads, 133
single track roads, 173–4
skidding, 229–44
    causes of, 232–9
    correcting a skid, 239–42
    and electronic driving aids, 229–30
    leaving the road, 243
    psychology of avoidance, 237–8
    rolling, 242–3
    skid pans, 231, 290
    spinning, 242
    understeer and oversteer, 230,
      239–41
sliproads, 131–4
snow, 205–15
    de-icing windows, 197
    driving style, 208–10
    and four-wheel drives, 206,
      209–10, 214–15
    getting stuck, 210–13